My Heart's Best Wishes for You

McGILL-QUEEN'S STUDIES IN THE HISTORY OF RELIGION
Volumes in this series have been supported by the Jackman Foundation of Toronto.

My Heart's Best Wishes for You

A BIOGRAPHY OF ARCHBISHOP JOHN WALSH

JOHN P. COMISKEY

McGill-Queen's University Press
Montreal & Kingston · London · Ithaca

© McGill-Queen's University Press 2012
ISBN 978-0-7735-4013-2

Legal deposit third quarter 2012
Bibliothèque nationale du Québec

Printed in Canada on acid-free paper that is 100% ancient
forest free (100% post-consumer recycled), processed
chlorine free

McGill-Queen's University Press acknowledges the support
of the Canada Council for the Arts for our publishing
program. We also acknowledge the financial support of the
Government of Canada through the Canada Book Fund for
our publishing activities.

Library and Archives Canada Cataloguing in Publication

Comiskey, John P., 1956–
My heart's best wishes for you : a biography of Archbishop
John Walsh / John P. Comiskey.

Includes bibliographical references and index.
ISBN 978-0-7735-4013-2

1. Walsh, John, 1830–1898.   2. Catholic Church – Ontario –
London – Bishops – Biography.   3. Catholic Church –
Ontario – Toronto – Bishops – Biography.   4. Catholic
Church – Canada – History – 19th century.   5. Bishops –
Canada – Biography.   I. Title.

BX4705.W294C64 2012   282.092   C2012-901431-1

Set in 9.5/12.5 Baskerville 10 Pro with Poetica Ornaments
Book design & typesetting by Garet Markvoort, zijn digital

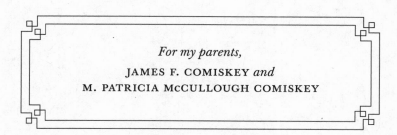

For my parents,
JAMES F. COMISKEY *and*
M. PATRICIA McCULLOUGH COMISKEY

CONTENTS

ACKNOWLEDGMENTS

THIS WORK WOULD NOT HAVE BEEN POSSIBLE WITHOUT THE assistance of many people, and a debt of gratitude is owed therefore to all who supported me with their kindness, concern, generosity, and prayers. Since this present work builds on my doctoral dissertation, I renew my gratitude for all who made my studies in Rome a possibility, and who guided and assisted me in that initial work. Indeed I am indebted to numerous people, not all of whom can be mentioned or credited here. I begin, though, by thanking His Excellency, Bishop John Sherlock, emeritus bishop of London, and Father Patrick Fuerth, former rector of St Peter's Seminary, London, who launched me on the path of further studies. I thank my family and friends from home and Rome who sustained me with their interest and encouragement. For the dissertation, a number of historians and archivists from across Ontario and Quebec, from France to the United States to Rome, gave much assistance and counsel, and I thank them all, but I mention especially Joan Lenardon, London; Rolland Litalien, PSS, Rome and Montreal; Matteo Sanfilippo and Giovanni Pizzorusso, Rome; Marc Lerman, Toronto; and Sister Teresita Kennedy, CSJ, former assistant archivist of London diocese. Their timely assistance, dedication, and labour in various archives made my work easier. Thanks is also due to Michael Power, of Welland, who not only shared research material with me, but offered support, counsel, and encouragement throughout the preparation of my dissertation, and of the present work.

Many others have assisted in bringing this work to completion. I want to acknowledge again the many archivists across the country who answered questions and gave clarifications where needed. Special thanks go to Debra Majer, assistant archivist of the diocese of London, and to Frances Theilade and Rita Ulrich, at the A.P. Mahoney Library at St Peter's Seminary, London. Historian and writer Daniel Brock, of London, provided numerous bits of information, especially obscure names and economic data to illustrate the value of the nineteenth-century dollar. Meteorologist Jay Campbell, London, provided historical weather data for key dates in Walsh's life. Fr Richard Charrette ensured that I had made the best translations of the correspondence written in French.

I have also enjoyed support both personally and intellectually from Joseph B. Gavin, SJ, of Montreal, my former thesis advisor in Rome. He was a constant source of stimulus and assistance while I was writing the thesis, from the earliest to the final stage. During the course of my time in Rome we became friends, and we have kept contact throughout the intervening years, with Dr Gavin all the while encouraging me – dare I say, goading me? – to write the complete life of John Walsh for publication. He, therefore, willingly guided me in the transformation of the thesis into a biography, when a sabbatical presented me with the time for further research and writing. Dr Gavin's interest in this project has been a great boon, and it was a real pleasure to work closely with him once again. Our friendship even survived! I owe him much more than this brief acknowledgment can convey.

A copy editor is a key person in bringing a work such as this to completion. I am grateful for the work of Grace Seybold, who has helped me to keep on track while telling this story.

Finally, while I have had great collaborators in this project, I take full responsibility for any mistakes that appear in the text.

John P. Comiskey
London, Ontario
Solemnity of Sts Peter and Paul, 2011
126th anniversary of the dedication of St Peter's Cathedral

FOREWORD

AN OBSERVER IN THE 1840S IN MOONCOIN, IRELAND, OR DURING the 1850s in Montreal, might have thought him a young Irishman like any other, who desired to become a Catholic priest and then to serve on the mission in British North America. Many a young man in Ireland or Montreal dreamed of being a missionary priest, after all, ministering in the parishes and mission stations scattered throughout the vast hinterland of pre-confederation Canada. Indeed, John Walsh was one such young man. To that end, he immigrated to Montreal in 1852 to take up studies at Le Grand Séminaire and, after his ordination to the priesthood in Toronto in 1854, to serve the Irish immigrants in the New World, alongside the several priests who earlier had emigrated from Ireland during the terrible 1840s. He seemed most likely destined for no other role.

During those early years of John Walsh's ministry in the diocese of Toronto, there were other young priests, Irish and French-Canadian, who might have seemed more apt for promotion within clerical ranks, perhaps even more suitable to become bishops than John Walsh ever was. Without "connections" in the United Canadas, and not being a member of La compagnie des prêtres de Saint-Sulpice in Montreal (the influential ecclesiastics among the Canadian bishops before 1867), the lofty office of a bishop seemed out of reach for him. He was recognized, of course, as an intelligent young man, spiritually sound and congenial, yet he seemed like someone who was fitted to serve well as a parish priest for his life's work.

Yet, that was not to be his story. However John Walsh may have been judged in his earlier and youthful days as a seminarian and young priest, he was by far unlike the many other Irish and French-Canadian men who passed through Montreal's seminary. Not only was he highly intelligent, theologically sound, and well versed in the Scriptures and Church law, he was also a hard worker, generous to a fault, good-humoured, unpretentious and astute, and totally given to serving others. Indeed, it did not take the perceptive John Lynch, coadjutor bishop of Toronto, long to become aware of John Walsh's abilities and amiable personality. The bishop judged the young priest wisely when he first promoted him in 1860 to be the rector of Saint Michael's Cathedral and then, two years later, to become the vicar general of the diocese of Toronto at the early age of thirty-two. That was the beginning, and John Walsh never looked back. Within five years he was promoted to the see of London (then called Sandwich) where he would remain until his translation to the prestigious archbishopric of Toronto in 1889.

His is a story that has needed telling ever since his death in Toronto during the summer of 1898. It is this story that Dr John P. Comiskey gives us, the story of a remarkable man who, surprisingly enough, seemed not to seek honours or promotions for himself, and was more surprised than anyone when he received them. As Dr Comiskey so rightly observes in this volume: "John Walsh was neither born great nor had greatness thrust on him, but had to work his way out of obscurity in Ireland, and later in Montreal and Toronto as a young priest, by his own talents and deeply rooted desire to serve fully the Catholic faith he so greatly loved." His extraordinary combination of humanity, evangelism, wit, polished manners, oratory, and theological and political skills made John Walsh one of the more noted and likeable Church figures in nineteenth-century Canada. This is the man Dr Comiskey brings to life for us in this biography. It is indeed a life worth the telling.

Jos. B. Gavin, SJ
Montreal, Quebec
24 June 2011
Saint-Jean-Baptiste Day

PREFACE

THIS WORK IS A BIOGRAPHY OF JOHN WALSH, WHO WAS THE SE-
cond bishop of London from 1867 to 1889, and who afterwards was promoted to be the fourth bishop – and second archbishop – of Toronto
from 1889 to 1898. It is an expansion of my doctoral dissertation presented at the Gregorian University in Rome. In my previous work, I
focused on the early life of both Walsh and the diocese of London, to
give the context of the situation he inherited from his troubled predecessor, Bishop Pierre-Adolphe Pinsoneault. Pinsoneault was forced
to resign so that Walsh could come in and repair what had gone wrong,
and rebuild the Catholic Church in southwestern Ontario. Much of
that historical background on London has been expunged so that this
book can more properly present Walsh's life and work.

A biography is usually presented chronologically. However, I am
presenting Walsh's life following a thematic development but with an
overarching chronology. It reflects best, I believe, the many facets of
the man who became a bishop at the time of Canada's Confederation,
and who, by the strength of his personality and talents, became a major
player on the ecclesiastical and public stages of the growing Catholic
Church in a developing new country. It begins with his early life and
the situation in London left by his predecessor, but it quickly moves to
his own episcopate in London, the truly defining years of his life.

There, as he grew into the office and role of a bishop in nineteenth-
century Ontario, I present how his life was lived and how his episcopal
ministry mirrored the challenges of all bishops to be the chief priest
or sanctifier, the chief teacher, and the chief administrator in their dioceses. It continues with the final decade of his life, as archbishop of
Toronto. This means that at times the narrative moves chronologically,
at other times historically backwards and forwards as I present various themes in the tableau of his life.

A few points for clarity for the reader: First, London in Ontario will simply be "London," whereas London in England, whenever referred to, will always include "England." As well, all dollar figures appear as they do in the original sources. To understand the values of those figures from the last half of the nineteenth century, one can take the value given and multiply it by 21 to find an approximate value in current dollars. Values change from time and place, so this is only a rough guideline. It should be noted, as well, especially when considering gifts of money presented or monies raised for a building, that there was a relatively small number of Catholics at the time who made incredible sacrifices of the resources they had.

Stained Glass Window from St Peter's Cathedral, London –
photo by Mark Adkinson (DLA)

Bishop François-Armand-Marie le Comte de Charbonnel
(ARCAT PH992.03/01)

facing page, above
Bishop Pierre-Adolphe Pinsoneault, c. 1856 (DLA)

facing page, below
Bishop Pinsoneault's Palace, Sandwich, c. 1860
(Windsor Community Museum, P5547)

Archbishop John Lynch, CM –
photo by J.H. Lemaitre & Co. (ARCAT PH04-03)

Bishop Walsh (ARCAT PH05-07)

above
Bishop Walsh with the Clergy of London, c. 1870 (DLA)

below
The Bishop's Palace, 1874 – photo by O'Connor & Lancaster (DLA)

RT. REV. JOHN WALSH, D. D.

BISHOP OF LONDON.

Presented with the "Catholic Record," London, Ontario.

EDY BROS. PHOTO.

Bishop Walsh – from the *Catholic Record* –
photo by Edy Brothers, London (DLA)

Bishop Walsh – photo by Frank Cooper, London (ARCAT PH05-01)

facing page, above
The original St Peter's Cathedral with palace in background, c. 1875 (DLA)

facing page, below
The Fathers and Theologians of the First Provincial Council of Toronto, 1875
(ARCAT PH992.04/10)

Monsignor Jean-Marie Bruyère (DLA)

New St Peter's Cathedral 1885 – *London Free Press* photo

Coat of Arms of Archbishop Walsh – artwork by Philip Aziz (DLA)

*Per pale, dexter Argent a representation of the Immaculate Conception proper
standing upon a crescent Argent issuant from clouds of the last, sinister Azure a lion
rampant Or debruised by a fess per pale Argent and Azure edged Argent.*

The shield carries a representation of the Walsh family on the right,
signified by the lion and the blue colour, with the bar. The diocese of
London is represented on the left, with a figure of the Blessed Virgin,
recalling the dedication of the diocese to the Blessed Virgin under
the title of the Immaculate Conception.

The heraldic hat, with ten tassels on each side, and metropolitan cross,
signify the shield is that of an archbishop. John Walsh used this
coat of arms while bishop of London and archbishop of Toronto,
with the variation in hat and cross signifying the difference.

Archbishop Walsh with Monsignor Merry Del Val, 1897
(ARCAT PH05-13)

Archbishop Walsh (ARCAT PH05-06)

My Heart's Best Wishes for You

The work of the Church ... is God's work – carried out often through very inadequate human agencies. And this is for Us a ground of confidence and consolation, in accepting the responsible position which the Church assigns Us. Paul may plant, Apollo water, but it is God who gives the increase.

BISHOP JOHN WALSH
FIRST PASTORAL LETTER
11 NOVEMBER 1867

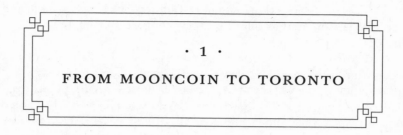

· 1 ·

FROM MOONCOIN TO TORONTO

The bishop is ... the legislator and ruler of the Church in his diocese; he is
the judge of faith and the executor of canon law, the father of his priests,
the pastor of the faithful, the chief preacher of God's holy word
and the guide of souls.

BISHOP JOHN WALSH, 1 MAY 1889

JOHN WALSH HAD BEGUN THE DAY WITH A SENSE OF EXCITEMENT
and anticipation. It was a typical early November day, with sunny skies
but cool temperatures, as the winds swept away the last leaves from
the trees. The archbishop was the special guest that day at a concert at
the Loretto Abbey, with songs, recitations, and words of congratulations from the students. Now, standing at his episcopal throne, on the
raised dais with its requisite canopy, he was able to survey the crowds.
St Michael's Cathedral brimmed with excitement, and already the
aroma of incense filled the sanctuary as the music of one of Haydn's
Masses, performed by a full orchestra with an organ and an eighty-
voice choir, floated down from the loft. Despite the crowds, the archbishop was able to see clearly the faces of family and friends gathered
there; many of them he had known for twenty-five years.[1]

Present to celebrate the Golden Jubilee of the foundation of the
archdiocese and Walsh's own Silver Jubilee of consecration (it being
the exact date of his anniversary) were half a dozen bishops from
across Canada – Montreal, Ottawa, Kingston, Hamilton, Peterborough, London – and one from Rochester, New York. Priests were also
there in great numbers, from Toronto, Hamilton, and London, and
other places. The lay people, by far the greatest number of those gathered, included such dignitaries as the lieutenant governor, members of
Parliament and of the Ontario Legislature, and the mayor of Toronto,
along with prominent citizens of Toronto and London, and a host of
others. The celebrant of the Mass was the bishop of Hamilton. Yet

aside from the grandeur of the building, the beauty of the music, and the sheer size of the enthusiastic crowd, in reality all came to see and hear one person, and to offer him their congratulations, best wishes, and prayers.

In his turn, Walsh preached the sermon, based on the parable of the mustard seed from Matthew's gospel (13:31–2). From his own deep appreciation of the history of the Catholic Church, giving a brief over-view from the time of the apostles to the Church in Canada, he turned his thoughts to the Golden Jubilee of the archdiocese: "Here again we find the law of growth and expansion which characterized the Church in all the ages of its history, marking its life and mission in this sec-tion of Ontario. It is the grain of mustard seed planted by the early Catholic settlers, and watered with their sweat and tears, and carefully nurtured by holy Bishops and zealous Bishops and priests, growing up into a mighty tree, overshadowing the whole land."

He went on to praise his episcopal predecessors for their work in nurturing the faith, and also gave credit for the growth of the diocese to those who had passed on, the priests, Religious, and the generous faithful: "They bore the burden of the day and the heat; they sowed in tears that we might reap in joy." Then in closing, using his typical eloquent language, he charged his listeners to carry on that legacy:

> It is for us to take up their work and carry it on with zeal, self-sacrifice, and generosity during our day. The cause of the Church is the greatest, the most sublime cause in the world. It is the cause of God's truth, the cause of Christ's work on earth, the cause of human happiness here and hereafter, it is the cause of immortal souls made in the image of God and redeemed by the sufferings and death of Jesus Christ. It is the cause of all the best and highest interests of humanity. It is the noblest cause that can enlist our greatest love and best energies.[2]

The tributes that followed were further testimony to the affection and esteem of all those present for their archbishop, John Walsh. Indeed, the fourth bishop and second archbishop of Toronto had come a long way from his home in Mooncoin, County Kilkenny, Ireland!

John Walsh was born 23 May 1830.[3] His parents were James Walsh and Ellen McDonald, and he had four sisters and two brothers: Mary, Richard, Margaret, William, and two named Anastasia, the elder of these dying months before the younger was born. All seven were born between the years 1820 and 1838.[4] A variant spelling of the family name renders it "Wallis." The name is pronounced in some localities as "Welsh," which may attest to the family's place of origin, Wales. The name may instead have a Norman origin, with some claiming that the first members of the family came to Ireland in the invasion of 1171, accompanying the Earl of Pembroke, known as Strongbow.[5]

Throughout the English Protestant Reformation until the reform of the Penal Laws in 1829, one year before John Walsh's birth, the practice of the Catholic faith was restricted, and several Walshes died as martyrs, including a bishop of Meath and an archbishop of Cashel. Others offered their services to the armies of England's enemies, France and Austria: "The branch which remained at home ... lived for generations in a condition of comfort and independence which the better class of farmers enjoy. Such homes in Ireland have been shrines of simplicity, paternal authority and filial affection. Their greatest wealth has lain in their energy; their coronet is their faith; their crest is their patriotism."[6]

While this flowery language of an earlier century was meant to edify the reader and convey a certain perspective of the Irish Catholic faith, nevertheless it does indicate the type of home in which John Walsh was likely raised. It is not surprising that his family maintained a strong Catholic faith, sowing the seeds of a priestly vocation in him. Walsh's early education took place at the Chapel Street school in Mooncoin, and then at the Franciscan friary in Carrick, where he studied science and the classics. It was there that he decided to study for the priesthood. To that purpose, and to prepare for the possibility of ordination, he entered St John's College at Waterford as a seminarian for the diocese of Ossory, where he then pursued studies in philosophy and theology.[7]

While at St John's, Walsh proved an excellent student, standing first in his class in philosophical studies. During this time, he grew interested in becoming a missionary as well as a priest. He was not alone: "From [the homes of the Irish Catholic faithful] have gone forth to all quarters of the globe earnest, devoted priests, who might have won distinction at home had they not chosen devotion in exile."[8] A local history of Mooncoin parish, however, indicates that Walsh had an altercation with the president of St John's College after being caught playing a game of hurling, contrary to the college rules. The writer of that unpublished history stated: "John parted company with the College and then with Ireland in 1852."[9] Be that as it may, the far-off foreign missions of British North America had an appeal for him, no doubt influenced by the large number of Catholics who had emigrated there in the 1820s, 1830s, and 1840s. So with the approbation of Edward Walsh, the bishop of Ossory, and the acceptance of the bishop of Toronto, Armand-François-Marie le Comte de Charbonnel, PSS, John Walsh set sail for Canada in April 1852 at the age of twenty-two years.[10] Why Walsh chose Canada is not certain. One biographer has suggested that Walsh may have been influenced by Archbishop William Walsh of Halifax, who had earlier been a student at St John's College.[11] Another biographer included the names of two theological students who accompanied Walsh to Canada on that voyage, namely John Synnott and James Hobin, both of whom became priests of the diocese of Toronto.[12] These names are also included in an earlier work which refers to "several other ecclesiastics of Irish birth" who studied with Walsh in Ireland.[13] Certainly, the comforting support of like-minded friends would have been a great influence on Walsh's choice of Canada.

It should be kept in mind that, at the time, the bishop of Toronto was continuously searching for priests who could speak the languages of the various members of his flock, especially English, Irish, and Scottish.[14] Therefore, it would not be surprising for Bishop de Charbonnel to have made overtures in those countries for priests. Possibly he did so during his trips to Rome, such as the one he made for his consecration in 1850, when he might well have visited those countries' seminaries in Rome. Requesting priests for the missions would also have been the work of the Congregation for the Propagation of the Faith, which had responsibility for the mission lands, including all of North America at that time.[15] In all likelihood, Walsh "answered a plea" for priests in the missions, and so made his way to the shores of British North America.[16]

In the autumn of 1852, Walsh commenced studies at Le Grand Séminaire in Montreal. He impressed his professors there, as he had done at St John's College: "His industry and talent, his exemplary conduct, his strict observance of the rule won the approbation of his superiors, and justified hopes concerning his future which have since been realized." The possible grades given at that time at Le Grand Séminaire were *optime, bene, sufficienter,* or *mediocriter.* At the end of his first year, 1852–53, he received *bene.* In the year 1853–54, he did better; Walsh was one of four students out of thirty who received *optime,* which was exceptional.[17] According to the custom of the day, he received the tonsure on Saturday, 21 May 1853, from Bishop Joseph LaRocque, then coadjutor bishop of Montreal, and minor orders (lector, porter, exorcist, and acolyte) on 17 December of the same year from the bishop of Montreal, Ignace Bourget.[18]

The years from 1851 to 1854 were a devastating time in British North America, when a cholera epidemic swept the colony, claiming thousands of victims and killing over five thousand people.[19] Walsh contracted the disease in the summer of 1854, while on his way to Toronto from Montreal at the close of the school year for his first visit to his adopted diocese. He was stricken to the point that no hope was held for his recovery. In time, however, he did regain his health, but this illness would affect him throughout his entire adult life, causing him to occasionally suffer from fevers. Since the seminary in Montreal was closed for a time due to the epidemic, he did not return there that fall, as earlier planned, but took up residence in Toronto.[20]

After a matter of months, Walsh received major orders. These began with the sub-diaconate, conferred by de Charbonnel, 22 October 1854, in his private chapel. One week later, 29 October, he was ordained a deacon. Ordination to the priesthood followed three days later, on 1 November, the feast of All Saints, in a ceremony at St Michael's Cathedral. Walsh was twenty-four years old, and had been in his adopted country for little more than two years.

His first ministerial assignment was to serve as a "saddle-bag" priest in whatever parishes in the diocese happened to be vacant, which were "in those days only too numerous. To these scattered districts he went, catechising the young, preparing children for first communion, bearing spiritual consolation to the dying, sowing the seeds of eternal life in the hearts of all."[21] This work continued with his first parochial appointment, the Brock mission on Lake Simcoe, some 125 kilometres north of Toronto. His residence, however, was in Oshawa, on the shore of Lake Ontario, some sixty kilometres south of Lake Simcoe and thirty kilometres east of Toronto. He was the first resident pastor of the parish, which included the townships of Brock, Reach, Uxbridge, Scott, Georgina, North Gwillimbury, Thorah, and Mara. There, for the most part, he was "far removed from any clerical society, in the midst of a rural population whose time and energy were taken up with the gigantic task of clearing farms, with no railroad accommodation and with worse than indifferent roads."[22] He was required to cover 1,700 square kilometres either on horseback or on foot. Perhaps he may have had a wagon or a small carriage, not unusual at that time.

One of Walsh's characteristics, which would bear much fruit in future years, was his insatiable appetite for reading and learning. A student by nature, he found that this period of solitary living lent itself to his pursuit of knowledge. It allowed him time for the study of theology, which was, for him, easy and pleasant. "Endowed with a clear judgment, possessing an extraordinary memory and a rich imagination, he [had] all the qualifications which form an earnest and successful student. It was therefore a pleasure, as well as an obligation imposed by his surroundings, for him to have time which he might employ to such advantage for himself and his future."[23]

What is significant is that he did more than merely read theological works. He also began writing articles and letters which he submitted to the *Toronto Mirror,* the only weekly paper published especially for Catholics at the time, which had the largest circulation of its kind in Toronto. He used the pseudonym "Ossory," the name of his ancestral diocese in Ireland. Since it would not have been prudent for a priest to publish articles in a mainly Protestant city, the pseudonym gave him liberty to express his personal views without endangering his reputation.

As well, he oversaw the construction of a church during that period: St Anthony the Hermit, at Virginia in Georgina Township, on the southern shore of Lake Simcoe.[24] After two years in the Brock mission, due to the onerousness of parochial duties and the travelling involved, as well as his recent bout of cholera, he was forced to return to Toronto for a period of convalescence lasting several months.[25]

Walsh's large mission was not the only place where the population was growing. Following the steady increase in the number of Catholics in the southwestern part of the diocese of Toronto by the 1850s, it became increasingly clear that some kind of division of the diocese had to take place. Bishop de Charbonnel was very aware of this, and of the need for a leader of vision and strong character in this vast and disparate pioneer region which he found increasingly difficult to administer. Shortly after becoming bishop of Toronto in 1850, he had expressed his concern at being overwhelmed and unable to carry out his work effectively. In fact, he twice offered Pope Pius IX his resignation, which was politely refused. Failing in that, the bishop had two choices: to have a coadjutor bishop appointed to assist him, or as a last resort, to seek the severance of the diocese and the creation of three smaller dioceses.[26]

With the support of the archbishop of Quebec, Pierre-Flavien Turgeon, and his suffragan bishops, de Charbonnel requested the latter option. In consequence, in June 1854, shortly before Walsh was ordained to the priesthood, the bishops of the ecclesiastical province of Quebec petitioned the pope to erect two new dioceses, with Hamilton and London as the seats. The main reasons for this petition were, they wrote, "the extraordinary and continual increase [in population] in this part of the Province; the majority and great power of the Protestants; the need for priests, churches, schools, instruction, worship, discipline, and temperance in drink; and wherefore the solution of all these needs which are urgent in all parts of the diocese."[27]

This threat of Protestant proselytization was a growing concern for the hierarchy, as was their apprehension about the need for "discipline and temperance," especially among the many Irish immigrants who, it was said, suffered a weakness for liquor.[28] Many others viewed the erection of new dioceses favourably, such as the Jesuit missionary Pierre Point, SJ, vicar general and dean of Sandwich.[29] The Jesuits had been working in that region since the 1700s. Point also recognized the need to stave off the spread of Protestantism.[30]

In 1856, Pius IX issued the apostolic briefs which formally erected the dioceses of London and Hamilton on 21 and 29 February respectively. John Farrell, a missionary of the diocese of Kingston, was appointed bishop of Hamilton, and Pierre-Adolphe Pinsoneault of Montreal was appointed bishop of London in other briefs that followed on 29 February.[31] De Charbonnel was relieved of a great deal of responsibility, but the decision to name Pinsoneault bishop would have unforeseen consequences for the diocese of London and for John Walsh in later years.

After his recovery, Walsh was appointed in April 1857 to remain in Toronto, and for the next ten years worked at various assignments in that city, beginning with the pastorate of St Mary's parish in the growing western district. At the same time, he took on chaplaincy duties for a convent of Sisters of the Institute of the Blessed Virgin Mary, who were commonly known as the Sisters of Loretto. Walsh was their spiritual director at their Bond Street convent, which included a boarding school, a day school, a novitiate, and the Sisters' motherhouse. He was instrumental in obtaining for them the property which would later become Loretto Abbey on Wellesley Street, Toronto.[32]

In June 1858, he was given charge of the parish of St Paul in central Toronto, which had been established in 1822, and which had quickly become one of the city's principal parishes. There he inherited a difficult situation, where his talent for conciliation became evident. He was succeeding a priest, Thomas Fitzhenry, who had been abruptly dismissed by de Charbonnel because of a personal disagreement over a matter of administration. Fitzhenry had been very popular in the parish, and his dismissal was not readily accepted by the parishioners. Despite their reluctance to have a replacement, however, Walsh was able to maintain unity in the parish by the magnetism of his personality, and in the end, he won the enduring respect of the formerly disgruntled parishioners.[33] Near the same time, in 1859, de Charbonnel was successful in naming a coadjutor bishop, John Joseph Lynch, CM, who succeeded him the following year.[34] It was not surprising, therefore, that Lynch, several months after his nomination and consecration, named Walsh rector of St Michael's Cathedral in March 1860.

There Walsh immediately found himself in the centre of the never-ending hostilities between Protestant – and notably Orange – Ontario and Catholic Ontario. The battles were intense, highly inflammatory at times, and seemingly without solution. The Protestant groups leading the fight against Catholic rights in Ontario, noted for their outright prejudices and anti-Catholicism, were well known to Walsh even as a young priest. Indeed, this antagonism plagued the religious life of Ontario throughout the nineteenth century.[35]

Anti-Catholicism was everywhere in Ontario. Most of the first settlers after the French, being mainly Scottish and Irish Protestants, brought with them an unfailing assurance that Catholicism was a superstitious and foreign – and, therefore, highly disreputable – religion, if it could even be called such. Members of the Orange Order, in particular, had imported their anti-Catholic animosities from Ireland, where for centuries there had been no distinction between religion and politics: a Protestant was a loyal British citizen; a Catholic was not. Meantime, too, ever firm in their faith and in the belief that all Protestants had fallen dangerously away from true religion, Catholics were equally eager to convert the world to their beliefs. There were few compromises on either side.[36] The resulting enmity was endemic in the cultural, social, and political life of Ontario. It may have been expressed in many hues, but nevertheless it ran the full range of the spectrum from violence on one end to simple ignorance on the other. Protestant pulpits thundered with denunciations of Catholics, while the press in Ontario, all robustly Protestant, carried on a vitriolic anti-Catholic campaign which often led to violence or near-violence. That was especially true on the "Glorious Twelfth" (of July), the Orangemen's day. Attacks of various sorts were directed against Catholics as a group; personal attacks took the form of discrimination in matters of employment and general advancement in society.[37]

Against that troublesome and at times unseemly backdrop, Walsh, as the new rector of the cathedral, played a major role. It required on his part a force of personality, of course, but his natural talent as a conciliator and a bridge-builder, and his innate desire always to seek Christian harmony and peace, remained at the fore. In September 1860, the Prince of Wales, the future King Edward VII, was making an official visit to Canada and to the United States of America. The Toronto Lodge of the Orange Order, noted for its public antagonism against Catholics, was planning to participate in the parade organized to greet the prince in order to stage an anti-Catholic demonstration. In preparation for the parade, members of the Lodge had constructed a series of arches festooned with the emblems of the Orange Order, under which the prince was to pass on his way from Union Station. This meant, however, that all in the parade would also have to pass under the arches.

The same controversy was raging at the same time in Kingston, the first stop planned for the prince in Upper Canada. Henry Pelham-Clinton, the Duke of Newcastle (the prince's advisor and travelling secretary), informed those responsible for the visit that the prince would not be able to appear near arches of the Orange Lodge. The Lodge and its insignia were outlawed in England, he explained, and the prince could not compromise himself by being associated with them. Some members of the Lodge in Kingston agreed. Many, however, including John A. Macdonald, a minister in the colonial government and representative for that riding, believed that since Canadian law did not forbid the insignia, the prince should respect the sovereign laws of his future colony. The ship on which the prince and his entourage were travelling sat in Kingston Harbour for twenty-two hours while the debate raged. On the morning of 5 September, the prince's ship steamed away from Kingston to the next port-of-call up the lake, without his ever setting foot in the city.[38]

Meantime in Toronto, the city's Catholics, unaware of the events in Kingston but insulted nonetheless by the idea that they would have to pass under the arches, attended a meeting called by Walsh to discuss the impending crisis. During that meeting, he called for calm and peaceful behaviour, and urged that everyone throughout the city should avoid any confrontation or violence. He gave a most stirring speech, in which he spoke at length about the controversy, and emphasized how strongly Catholics desired to participate in the welcome being offered to the prince. In effect, his concern was to demonstrate that Catholics were loyal by principle and not by caprice because the Catholic Church taught loyalty to lawfully constituted authority. He wanted all to know that Catholics were equal members of Canadian society.[39]

At the same time, Walsh called for calm in order to avoid a brutal clash between militant Catholics and Orangemen. "Orangeism," he said, "which was born in the defeat of our fathers, which, springing into existence in order to commemorate that defeat, and which raised its throne on the wreck of our common liberties, that institution should not be planted on our virgin soil to perpetuate the hatred and discord that cursed our native land."[40] Walsh was also proud to inform the meeting that several influential Protestants of the city were equally opposed to the actions of the Lodge. In fact, due to the impudence of the Orange Order against other citizens, the majority of Protestants denounced the demonstrations as an insult to themselves as well as to the Catholic population. They considered the prince's visit an occasion on which all citizens should be united under the Crown.

Those at the meeting also decided to present their case to Pelham-Clinton, himself a Catholic, unaware of his already-expressed sympathy on this question. This presentation, like Walsh's speech, expressed the loyalty of the Catholics toward the British Crown along with their fervent desire to participate in the official welcome. They pointed out that they might be prevented from participating, because their self-respect would not allow them to pass under the offensively decorated arches. Thanks to Walsh's efforts to resolve the crisis, and to the co-operation of Catholics and Protestants, conciliation won the day. As in Kingston, the Prince of Wales refused to publicly recognize the Orange Order, and all the arches but one were dismantled. Even this last arch was stripped of the Order's symbols and slogans which were so offensive to Catholics, the prince, and others. In the end, the Lodge members did not even march in the parade. "The prince's visit turned into a humiliating defeat for Orange fanaticism and a victory for Irish Catholic moderation."[41]

Walsh's efforts to find a solution to the strident antagonism between Catholics and Protestants, so that harmony might prevail, was characteristic of his relations with anyone who might disagree with him. He believed not only that Catholics had rights too, but also that all individuals had rights in any society, no matter their religious beliefs. Those rights, however, could never be in opposition to the common good.

Four years later, another incident demonstrated the Orangemen's enmity against Catholics. Walsh wrote to Lynch, who was away from Toronto for holidays, to apprise him of the "Orange unrest" that was then rampant in the city. According to rumour circulating, one of the Orange Lodges was preparing to burn an effigy of Daniel O'Connell, the noted Irish Catholic nationalist. Some of the Irish Catholics, or Hibernians as Walsh sometimes referred to them, were determined to arm themselves and prevent the burning by force. Walsh lamented that Toronto was no longer "the home of quiet and peace of mind," and that Lynch had better stay away for his own good health, so necessary for the people of his diocese.

To attempt to ease the situation and prevent bloodshed, Walsh called a meeting with the Catholics of the city. It was decided that they should send a representation to the mayor, as chief magistrate, to request that he intervene in order to avoid a Protestant demonstration and a breach of the peace. It was also decided that the priests in the city should call in the leaders of the Irish Catholic group, to advise them to remain at home on the night of the scheduled Orange demonstration. The mayor, himself an Orangeman and quite unsympathetic to Catholics, responded that he knew nothing of the burning – which was highly unlikely – but that as chief magistrate, he would do his best to prevent it.

> We called upon the leading Hibernians and used every argument we could think of to dissuade them from making any demonstration whatsoever on that night, but all our arguments were lost upon them; for go they would and go they did, armed to the teeth with guns and pikes. Fortunately no collision took place between the hostile parties as the Orangemen failed to carry out their part of the programme. The Hibernians however were seen in hostile array. The cries of an intended popish massacre were raised and hence the most fearful excitement prevails.[42]

Walsh's peaceful efforts were successful. Moderate Protestants convinced the more extreme amongst them to cease and desist. Several of the leading troublemakers were arrested, and had to appear in court. Though nothing much came of the anti-Catholic manifestation, and the incident was short-lived, it had a long-term effect: "This excitement," Walsh noted, "like many others will blow past but before doing so it is likely to do a great deal of harm."[43]

Peace at any price was not Walsh's desire. On one hand, he sought ways to ease tension and keep peace, yet on the other, he had no hesitation about speaking his mind publicly, even on unpopular matters; he would not compromise the truth. It was clear to many, therefore, that the victories for the Catholics of Toronto were not to be laid at the feet of Prince Edward alone in the first case, nor of the mayor in the second; as much as anyone else, Walsh, with his talent as a conciliator, was responsible for having prevented riots or violent outbreaks of some sort. His oratorical skills were noted in this whole affair as well. His gift for public speaking had already been evident in his sermons from the time he was a young priest. Indeed, to many, it seemed he did all things well: "Full of the spirit of his holy vocation, Father Walsh applied himself to all his manifold duties with energy and constancy. Loretto Convent found in him a devoted chaplain, the schools a self-sacrificing champion, and the parish a father and friend. But amidst all he still found time to give himself to study and the careful preparation of sermons, which soon earned for him a well deserved reputation as a pulpit orator."[44]

Walsh's rhetorical abilities were not limited to the pulpit, to theological subjects, or to special meetings. His skills were evident to the general population in the many public lectures that he was called upon to deliver. "He was a superb rhetorician in the classical sense and [was] no less enthusiastic about his strictly secular speeches. He gave many lectures concerning the history of Ireland's political struggles to audiences largely composed of 'exiles' like himself."[45]

These special skills were manifested on any number of occasions when he was invited to preach, such as during a memorial Mass in 1865 for the recently deceased Nicholas Cardinal Wiseman, archbishop of Westminster, and at the blessing of a new bell for St Michael's Cathedral in 1866. All the while, despite the many demands for speaking engagements – too many for him to fulfil – Walsh continued to write and contribute to the public press.[46]

During the decade that Walsh served in the parishes within the city of Toronto (St Mary's, St Paul's, and St Michael's), the new diocese of London was spiralling into grave difficulties under its first bishop, Pinsoneault, who – it became quite apparent – was in the wrong place at the wrong time. He had been born into a prosperous and influential family on 23 November 1815 in Lower Canada, southwest of Montreal. He studied at Le Petit Séminaire of Montreal from 1824 to 1836, at which time he became an aspirant for the Society of St Sulpice. He then studied at their seminary in Paris until 1840, and officially entered the Society in 1839. On 19 December 1840, he was ordained a priest near Paris, but was later incardinated in the diocese of Montreal, where he worked until he was nominated bishop of London.[47] He was consecrated bishop on 18 May 1856, Trinity Sunday, by de Charbonnel at the cathedral church in Montreal.[48]

From his earliest days as bishop until his resignation, Pinsoneault's problems were exacerbated by his endemic mistrust of people and their mistrust of him, by his inability to administer the temporal affairs of the diocese, and by his disastrous policies regarding personnel, priests, and Religious. Even before arriving in the diocese he stumbled; while preparing to take over the church in London, St Lawrence, that would become his cathedral, he renamed it St Peter, stamping his own name on the diocesan church.[49] Unfortunately, this provoked French–Irish nationalist conflict, something which he encouraged, however unwittingly, and which in the end would lead him to leave London for more friendly terrain.[50]

This resentment was aggravated because of a completely different matter with the dean, Thaddeus Kirwan, pastor of the church in London, since Pinsoneault signalled his intention to displace Kirwan so he himself could take charge of what would become his cathedral church. Not only was Kirwan a beloved pastor, but many had hoped he would be their new bishop. Hence, when trouble arose between Kirwan and the bishop, it seemed to have another meaning: that is, that somehow the new bishop did not like his Irish co-religionists. Kirwan made the mistake of refusing to move, which gained some support among the parishioners. In response, not only did Pinsoneault foolishly refuse to enter London until Kirwan had left the cathedral, but, in a rage, he also blamed de Charbonnel for not moving Kirwan out of the London parish in a timely fashion, and threatened to place the whole parish under interdict.[51]

Another immediate effect was that Pinsoneault also displaced the Sisters of Loretto who occupied the London parish house. He simply notified them of his arrival and of their expected departure. They left London to take up residence in Guelph, in the diocese of Hamilton. Afterwards, when he invited two French-speaking congregations to replace the Sisters, it further enhanced the perception that the bishop was prejudiced against the Irish. De Charbonnel warned him, but Pinsoneault failed to heed the advice, fearing he would give the impression of being weak.[52] He was soon denounced in a campaign of letters and articles which appeared in the *London Prototype*. Some of the people of London, however, came to his defence.[53]

Within less than a year of his installation in London, Pinsoneault made plans to move his episcopal seat to the predominantly French-speaking parish of the Assumption in Sandwich. In order to receive a papal rescript for such a move, he had to have the support of his fellow bishops, to whom he appealed in January 1858, asking for their counsel.[54] The majority of bishops were opposed.

Leading the opposition was Jean-Charles Prince, bishop of Saint-Hyacinthe, who, on 4 February 1858, wrote a formal memorial to Pinsoneault to highlight his disagreement and addressed each of the motives given in Pinsoneault's January letter. Prince focused on the needs of the poor and small Catholic population of London, drawing comparisons with St Peter, St Francis de Sales, and Cardinal Wiseman: "The most beautiful passage of Cardinal Wiseman's manifest was the one in which he boasted as having, as his legacy in the opulent city of London [England], the poorest and humblest section of Westminster. London [Canada] must be the reflection of London [England]."[55]

Insisting that a bishop is "master in his own diocese," Pinsoneault refused to be convinced by his fellow bishops, and, on his own, formally requested the Holy See to grant a rescript for the change. Soon afterwards, he travelled to Rome to support his petition in person, and remained away for over seven months.[56]

The rescript, issued 2 February 1859, changed the seat and the name of the diocese to Sandwich. (The change of name would bring its own problems.) The Catholic reaction within the diocese was swift. They felt deceived by the secrecy and enraged at his duplicity, since Pinsoneault had announced that he was going to France and made no mention of Rome. Immediately a committee in London formed which petitioned the Holy See and sent a copy of their petition to Turgeon, the archbishop of Quebec, requesting his intervention. Pinsoneault's neighbouring bishop, Farrell of Hamilton, wanted the move postponed, fearing that the Jesuits would be lost to the diocese since Pinsoneault intended to take over Assumption Church, which they staffed, for his new cathedral.[57]

From all appearances, Pinsoneault was paranoid, convinced that his episcopal colleagues were conspiring against him, and "his autocratic conception of the role of the episcopacy in a frontier diocese eventually mitigated against any advantages that might have resulted from the move to Sandwich."[58] Even the French-speaking people there soon tired of their bishop, who "hid himself in his house, rarely assisted in the church, and scolded too much when he preached."[59] When the bishop finally took up residence at Sandwich in September 1859, the Jesuits, as expected, were forced to vacate the presbytery.

Further difficulties soon awaited the bishop. From its foundation, the diocese had a large debt of $10,000, due to the cost of building new churches. That was not unusual in the nineteenth century, due to the rapid population expansion.[60] As well, from the very beginning of his time in Sandwich, Pinsoneault complained about the presbytery's location and its unworthiness as a fitting residence for a bishop. Already having added to the debt by his move, he further burdened the diocese when he built for himself a palace in the style of a seventeenth-century French château, which he deemed would be a more suitable accommodation, and hired a staff he considered worthy of his episcopal rank.

The palace became a nightmare. The cost, estimated to be $30,000, was an extreme sum given the poverty of most Catholics in that pioneer rural area. It only further burdened the financial situation of the diocese and decreased Pinsoneault's reputation. To make matters worse, the roof leaked, which forced people to use umbrellas indoors when it rained. The poor heating system caused the pipes and wash basins to freeze in the winter, and let people see their breath hovering over their heads.[61] Furthermore, in order to make the grounds more to his liking, the bishop declared that the cemetery was too close to his residence. He therefore had the graves opened, the bodies exhumed, and the remains buried again in a new cemetery elsewhere. The relatives of the deceased were furious. When Pinsoneault enhanced the entranceway of the palace with rows of chestnut trees lining the driveway and three arched gateways, people felt that he had gone too far. It only further stoked their anger when they realized that they had to share the cost of what quickly came to be known as "Pinsoneault's Folly."[62]

Perhaps due more to bad fortune than to maladministration, a further difficulty arose for him in the delivery of the mails. Many letters addressed to the bishop of Sandwich – especially from Propaganda Fide – ended up in the Sandwich Islands (now called the Hawai'ian Islands) in the South Pacific, or in the town of Sandwich in County Kent, England. His numerous pleas to the secretary of Propaganda Fide, begging him to write "Canada" on the envelope, failed to rectify the situation. Sometimes months would pass before certain letters made their way into Pinsoneault's hands.[63]

To all his mounting costs, he added another which in the mind of many Catholics shortly became one more "folly." When he moved to Sandwich, he was geographically close to over half the priests and to the majority of Catholics. Within only a few years, this had changed, however, and transportation throughout his diocese had become a major concern. Travel was fatiguing on the poorly maintained roads, while the steamship routes were not helpful because of irregular service, and railway service was minimal. Pastoral visits, thus, were difficult to plan under such circumstances.[64] Pinsoneault came up with a solution: his own personal episcopal barge for use on the lakes and rivers. This barge would have sleeping and dining quarters and a chapel complete with a marble altar. He believed (perhaps rightly) that the vessel would allow him easier access to a greater portion of Catholics, and (probably wrongly) that it would enhance his prestige since people would line the banks of the rivers and channels to see him as he passed. Unfortunately, before any of that could happen, the barge sank at its launching in the Detroit River. With it sank $1,500 and, moreover, the reputation of the bishop of Sandwich.[65]

Several financial transactions went awry. In one, the bishop had endorsed notes for a firm of brokers which failed, and was then held responsible for a part of the debts. In another, he had purchased a cemetery in London without obtaining proper deeds, and was forced to pay twice for the same property. Thus, within a matter of a few short years, he "found himself utterly swamped with debt." His financial record is best summed up thus: "In an older and better established diocese, Bishop Pinsoneault might have proven a more successful prelate. In this diocese quite the reverse was the case, for he never seemed to realize that his was but a poor struggling missionary district. In his endeavour to play the part of an old French Seigneur, he overlooked the fact that his resources were exceedingly limited and that the greatest frugality and economy were necessary in order to build up churches, schools and institutions."[66]

However serious his financial problems were, underlying them were his parishioners' loss of confidence in and respect for him, and, even more seriously, his poor relationships with his priests and Religious. The Sisters of Loretto would not return to work in the diocese until the next bishop's episcopate, while the Jesuits would leave permanently. Their departures, as well as the bishop's grandiose ideas of how educational systems should operate, seriously hampered the development of education during the remainder of his years there.[67] He tried and failed to attract the Basilian Fathers to replace the Jesuits, and although he did bring in a community of Benedictine monks from Latrobe, Pennsylvania, to run Assumption School in Sandwich, they stayed there only two years. They continued to maintain a parish until 1865, at which time they left the diocese completely, unable to tolerate the bishop's "difficult behaviour." One further attempt to save the school also ended in failure like all the others.[68]

Pinsoneault's "self-delusion and authoritarianism," coupled with his lack of awareness of the dignity and value of the Religious congregations involved in the college, continued in other ways. They were most notable when he exercised his authority over women Religious, especially those who still remained under the jurisdiction of Montreal's bishop. Among these were the Sisters of Charity of Providence, a French-speaking congregation, whom Pinsoneault quarrelled with and eventually expelled; the Ladies (formerly Madams) of the Sacred Heart, to whom he gave responsibility for the school in London vacated by the Sisters of Charity; and the Grey Nuns, to whom he gave a new residence and school, which in turn forced the Sisters of St Joseph to leave the diocese, where they had been serving since 1853.[69]

It was his removal of some of the Grey Nuns to Amherstburg without the approval of Mother Deschamps, their superior in Montreal, that brought matters to a head. She took strong exception to his acting without consulting her about the move, and even more, when he tried to convince the small community to disengage itself from the motherhouse in Montreal. Armed with a letter from Ignace Bourget, the bishop of Montreal, the superior made her way to Sandwich. On 4 December 1861, under cover of darkness, she presented herself unannounced at the convent. After reading Bourget's letter to the Sisters, she led them to her waiting boat. Later that evening she did the same at the Amherstburg convent. Then, undeterred, she returned the next day to clear out the two convents, and to confront the angry bishop. With the Sisters' departure to Montreal, Catholic education and the influence of women Religious suffered seriously in the diocese. Pinsoneault nonetheless successfully attracted two other teaching Religious congregations, the Ursuline Sisters and the Holy Names Sisters, who would remain active in education for years to come.[70] Pinsoneault's problems caused considerable concern among his fellow bishops.[71] The final crisis came in October 1864 when, seriously alarmed at the damaging reports from Sandwich, Charles-François Baillargeon, the new archbishop of Quebec, wrote Propaganda Fide begging it to intervene. Soon additional complaints were sent by various Religious congregations, members of the laity, and other Canadian bishops. For Baillargeon, and eventually for Propaganda Fide, the time was right to make a radical change in episcopal leadership.[72]

The chorus of opposition had won out: the decision by Rome to remove Pinsoneault was made in the summer of 1865. Bourget of Montreal was delegated to ask for his resignation, which, Pinsoneault was told, could be offered for reasons of health and would be accepted without question. Stubbornly, Pinsoneault was unmoved. At that point, Bourget had to admonish him that failure to resign would lead to canonical procedures against him. It would still take another year before Pinsoneault finally resigned.[73]

Meanwhile in Toronto, in September 1861, John Walsh had resigned as rector of the cathedral to return to being pastor of St Mary's. That would be his last assignment as a pastor in the diocese. The move had been triggered once again by his poor health, expended on behalf of his parishioners and in care for the Irish immigrants.[74] Oddly enough, while there, he was given greater administrative responsibilities none-theless: "Partly because [Lynch's] health was often poor, but also because the work load became progressively greater, Lynch was not reluctant to delegate authority." He judged well the talent of his priests and increasingly relied upon a select group, including Walsh, to assist him in his episcopal responsibilities and to carry out his plans.[75] So it was that on Easter Sunday, 20 April 1862, the bishop named Walsh vicar general of the diocese at the early age of thirty-two. Furthermore, the following year, in May 1863, Walsh was appointed to accompany Lynch as his official theologian to the third Provincial Council of Que-bec. Even more importantly, a year later, Lynch delegated Walsh to deliver his *ad limina* report to the Holy See; this was Walsh's first visit to Rome.[76] Perhaps Lynch was grooming his young colleague for the episcopacy.

It is important to note that within a decade, while still a relatively young man, Walsh had already won the respect, affection, and admira-tion of the Catholics in Toronto, which were demonstrated prior to his departure for Europe by gifts and addresses presented to him. Among the gifts was a gold watch from the parishioners of the cathedral. It bore the warm inscription: "A token of affectionate esteem to the Very Rev. J. Walsh, V.G., from his friends in St. Michael's parish, Toronto." As if that were not enough, they also gave him a gold cross to present to his mother on their behalf. It was "very massive and beautifully wrought with wreaths of shamrocks, bearing on the reverse side the following engraving: 'A souvenir sent from Toronto, C[anada].W[est]., to the mother of the Very Rev. J. Walsh, V.G., from his admiring friends.'" The parishioners of St Mary's, where he had served with much acclaim for over six years, in their turn presented him with a parting gift of money and delivered a heartfelt address expressing their esteem and affection.[77]

Once in Rome, besides conferring with the officials of Propaganda Fide, Walsh was received in a private audience by Pius IX. Afterwards, and having toured parts of Europe, he visited the land of his birth, his first return there in twelve years. The warm welcome given him, a native son who had done so well in his new homeland, who had been accorded such honour and prestige there, and who had just visited the pope, was mixed, however, with sadness. His father had died the year earlier, and his brother William shortly before that. In a letter to Lynch from Ireland, Walsh poignantly expressed his feelings: "I sadly miss the well remembered faces of my poor father and brother who sleep in their fresh graves in the neighbouring graveyard."[78] He remained in Ireland a few months before setting out once again for Canada. He would not return for another eighteen years.

Within two years after Walsh's visit to Europe, the diocese of Sandwich became *sede vacante* on 18 December 1866 with the resignation of Pinsoneault, its first bishop.[79] Careful thought had to be given to the matter of a successor due to the grave problems that weighed heavily on the diocese. Throughout the troubles of Pinsoneault's episcopate, the bishops of Canada had carefully considered whom they might recommend to Propaganda Fide to replace him. As well, there were any number of individuals among the priests and laity of the diocese also speculating on who should be appointed.[80]

As was the custom with vacant dioceses under the jurisdiction of Propaganda Fide, the bishops of Canada presented a *terna* (a list of three names) to that Congregation. It was signed on 18 January 1867 by Baillargeon, the administrator of Quebec, along with the bishops of Toronto, Montreal, Hamilton, Kingston, and Saint-Hyacinthe. The name of John Walsh, who was by this time forty-five years of age, was placed at the top of the list of possible candidates for Sandwich as *dignissimus,* the most worthy. The second choice, *dignior*, worthier, was the pastor of Brockville in the diocese of Kingston, John O'Brien, approximately thirty-four years old. Rémi Ouellet, a thirty-five-year-old professor of theology at the Collège de Saint-Hyacinthe, was their third choice, or *dignus,* worthy. Three months later, the candidates were discussed in the General Congregation of 8 April, and Walsh was chosen. Pius IX gave his approval on 14 April. The brief of nomination was issued 4 June 1867.[81]

This choice came as no surprise to those who knew Walsh, because of his many successes in his priestly assignments, his proven administrative abilities, and the confidence shown in him by the bishop of Toronto, as revealed in this assessment of his character at that time: "Father Walsh enjoyed the reputation among the clergy of being a sound and deeply-read theologian, well versed in the sacred scriptures and canon law, an eloquent and flowery speaker, and *au courant* in general literature. His amiable character, polished manners, and great force and decision of character, won him general esteem."[82]

The news of his nomination reached him by early autumn, and preparations began in earnest for his consecration and installation.[83] Following the announcement, he received many letters of congratulation, including one from Edward John Horan, bishop of Kingston. Walsh wrote in turn to thank Horan, but hinted at the difficulties he faced: "I thank you most sincerely for your very kind favour of the 27th inst[ant]. I strongly suspect Your Lordship has had a large share in involving me in my present difficulties and embarrassment, and it requires a great exercise of charity to forgive you for it. The burden of the Episcopate is in itself heavy enough but when that burden is increased by the difficulties special to the diocese of Sandwich it becomes too heavy for my poor shoulders."[84]

The next week, on 16 October, Walsh wrote to Bourget of Montreal, informing him that he had accepted the nomination. He again expressed his sense of unworthiness: "I feel very truly how unworthy I am of the sacred office of the Episcopate but my confidence is in God who hath chosen the weak things of the world and the things that are not, that he might confound the things that are." Walsh announced the date of his consecration would be 10 November, asked Bourget to be an assisting prelate for the consecration, and begged his prayers and blessings.[85] Two days later, Charles LaRocque of Saint-Hyacinthe offered words of encouragement in his letter of congratulations: "You are young and full of all the gifts to carry out, with dignity, the work and the functions to which you are called."[86] He assured Walsh that he would be present for the consecration. Having been one of the nominators, the bishop of Saint-Hyacinthe was surely satisfied that his candidate had been chosen.

That same day, 18 October, Jean-Marie Bruyère, the administrator of Sandwich diocese since Pinsoneault's resignation, announced the name of the new bishop in a circular letter to the diocesan clergy and faithful. He stressed how this "illustrious clergyman" was, in every respect, "qualified for this high office, and well deserving the esteem and confidence of the Clergy and People of this Diocese." He went on to point out that the abilities, zeal, and prudence of the new bishop, seen in all that he had done, were "a sure guarantee of what can be expected from him in the high office to which he has lately been elevated." He encouraged the clergy and people to extend a hearty welcome and to offer prayers for their new bishop.[87]

The task of repairing and rebuilding the diocese had now to begin. To a very large degree, because of his ineptitude, Pinsoneault can hardly be considered the founding bishop of the diocese of London. That title should more deservedly go to its second bishop, John Walsh.

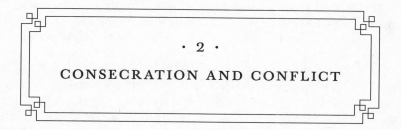

· 2 ·

CONSECRATION AND CONFLICT

A long unbroken chain of Pontiffs stretches away into the venerable past,
uniting Pius IX, appointing Bishops and commissioning them to go and
teach, with our Divine Lord sending St. Peter and the other Apostles
to go and teach the world.

BISHOP JOHN WALSH, 11 NOVEMBER 1867

THE FIRST DAYS AND MONTHS OF ANY ADMINISTRATION USUALLY indicate the kind of leadership that people can expect from it. Given the precarious situation of the diocese at the time of Pinsoneault's resignation, it was all the more critical that Walsh take charge and address the problems that frustrated the growth of religion and the development of the diocese in the Great Lakes peninsula.

The nomination, consecration, and installation of a bishop are moments for a diocese to celebrate. That was especially true for the people of Sandwich in 1867. In a ceremony on 10 November 1867, the "extraordinary grandeur" of which "indicated not only the great progress the Catholic Church had made in Ontario since the beginning of the nineteenth century ... [but] was also an augury of the rather dramatic career presently to befall [him]," Walsh was consecrated bishop of Sandwich at St Michael's Cathedral in Toronto.[1]

It was a very pleasant November day that was mostly sunny, with temperatures hovering at eleven degrees centigrade. Almost the entire Canadian hierarchy was present for the occasion, indicating the high regard in which they held Walsh.

> The morning of Sunday, the 10th inst[ant], which was so anxiously looked forward to, broke brightly and auspiciously. The ceremony was announced to commence at nine o'clock; but long before that hour the streets around the Cathedral and Episcopal Palace were astir, and crowds of persons [had] begun to pour in

from every quarter of the city. The church itself was not opened –
after the last of the early morning masses – till near nine o'clock,
when, notwithstanding that admission was obtained by ticket,
and the length of the ceremony, it soon became completely
thronged.[2]

The *Canadian Freeman* listed all those who formed the procession,
which was led by servers and the band from the Christian Brothers'
school. There were nearly fifty priests, including the vicars general
of many of the Canadian dioceses and several leaders of educational
institutions, and nine bishops accompanying the bishop-elect.[3]

> The procession proceeded slowly, singing appropriate psalms
> ... to the main entrance of the Cathedral. The sight was an
> extremely grand and interesting one. The number of priests in
> cassock and surplice, in rich vestments and copes, the Deacons
> and sub-Deacons of honour of the Mass in their splendid dalmat-
> ics, the Bishops magnificent in the deep purple of their robes,
> their costly mitres and croziers, formed a positively brilliant
> scene. As the procession entered the Cathedral, the choir, with
> organ and orchestral accompaniment, sang with grand effect the
> *Gloria* from Mozart's Twelfth Mass ... Wreaths of evergreens in
> graceful festoons entwined the pillars, and a beautifully formed
> arch, suspended from the lofty roof, spanned the whole width of
> the sanctuary. The numerous faldstools, with their rich crimson
> covering, prepared for the Bishops, added greatly to the general
> effect and appearance of the holy place.[4]

The consecrator was Charles-François Baillargeon, archbishop of
Quebec, assisted by co-consecrators Bourget of Montreal and Lynch
of Toronto, Walsh's long-standing friend and confidant.[5] The preacher
for the occasion was Patrick Dowd, SS, a prominent Sulpician priest
from Montreal and another personal friend, who spoke of the new
bishop having to sever his ties with his home and friends.[6] Dowd emphasized also Walsh's spirit of sacrifice that enabled him to accept the
"onerous dignity for which he had been chosen": "Content to labor
for you [in Toronto] to the end of his career, desiring no other earthly
reward than that which he possessed in your love and confidence, he
was happy and at peace. But at the call of duty he sacrificed all ...
He knew that the true pastor should not only live, but should also be
prepared to die, for the salvation of souls. You see him there to-day,

before the altar of God, prepared to consummate that last sacrifice of pastoral charity."[7] Such a display of persons, vesture, and decorations, a religious spectacle rarely seen in Protestant Toronto, undoubtedly impressed many.

The festivities continued as the new bishop made his way from Toronto by train on the Grand Trunk Railroad to his new episcopal see of Sandwich, accompanied by Baillargeon, Horan, and Farrell, along with an entourage of priests from the dioceses of Sandwich, Hamilton, Toronto, Saint-Hyacinthe, and Detroit who three days before had attended his consecration. While *en route* to Sandwich, they stopped in London, where they were met at the station by a large, enthusiastic, and multi-denominational crowd. The crowd accompanied the bishops and priests to St Peter's church where an official welcome was given by Augustine Kelly, OP, the pastor of St Peter's; Peter Crinnon, dean of Stratford; and Francis Smith, the mayor of London.[8] Crinnon's address on behalf of the priests began with a hearty welcome and a promise of prayers. He underscored the problems that Walsh was facing, yet more importantly, he enthusiastically emphasised the happiness of the clergy on hearing of Walsh's appointment:

> We know how much the welfare of a Diocese depends on its Bishop; we were, therefore, filled with joy when we heard of your appointment to the See of Sandwich. For your Lordship's known ability, zeal and prudence are sure guarantees for the future welfare of this Diocese. We are truly thankful to God for giving us a Bishop so endowed with talent and virtue; and to you, my Lords [Baillargeon, Horan and Farrell], we are grateful for selecting one so capable of advancing the interests of our holy religion, which is dear to us all.[9]

With a promise of "cheerful cooperation," Crinnon gave way to Mayor Smith, who spoke on behalf of St Peter's congregation. His words of welcome told of the "unalloyed pleasure" they felt due to the new bishop's "advent" among them. He expressed their sincerest thanks to God for this appointment, and promised their full cooperation along with a pledge to do anything necessary to make the former episcopal residence in London agreeable. These words expressed the hope of the Catholics that the bishop would re-establish his permanent residence there. After Walsh gave a pontifical benediction, the large assembly dispersed. Walsh celebrated Mass the following morning – his first in his new diocese – and then boarded the train for Sandwich.[10]

At the official installation in the cathedral at Sandwich the next day, Baillargeon presided with the assistance of Horan and Farrell. Also present were the several priests who had been in London the previous day, along with George Baby, the mayor of Sandwich. The official record of the installation included all of their signatures.[11] By the end of the day, 14 November 1867, John Walsh was officially the second bishop of Sandwich.

Among Walsh's first juridical acts was to appoint Jean-Marie Bruyère as his vicar general. Bruyère had filled that position under Pinsoneault, and had proved himself to be a most competent assistant to the bishop; as well, Bruyère was a francophone. By his appointment, Walsh signalled not only his affirmation of Bruyère's talents, but also the importance of the French-speaking population in his diocese. This clearly pointed to his high regard and support for them and their culture.[12]

Traditionally, a new bishop would publish his first pastoral letter at the time of his consecration. Walsh followed that custom in a letter dated 11 November. In the usual fashion, he addressed his letter to the clergy, Religious, and laity of the diocese. As de Charbonnel had done before him, Walsh likewise chose to publish his letter in the *Canadian Freeman* on 19 December. By then the new bishop had been a full month in his diocese, and many would already have come to know him personally. His pastoral letter gave Catholics further opportunity to learn more about the man who had come to lead them in such trying times, and about the style of leadership he would bring to his new responsibilities.

His letter was filled with many quotations from Scripture, and alluded often to events in history, especially that of the Catholic Church. It began, however, with a sober recognition of the burden of office he had taken up:

> We accept the burden imposed upon us by Christ's vicegerent
> [Pope Pius IX] with fear and trembling, – conscious alike of
> its weight and our weakness. The grave responsibilities, the
> momentous interests connected with the sublime office of
> the Episcopate may well inspire with diffidence and fear him
> who is called upon to undertake the arduous duties of that
> office. Still the great Shepherd of our souls works through

human instruments and it is our consolation to believe that
He frequently chooses for the execution of His work on earth
instruments and means which, humanly speaking, would appear
least adapted for His purpose.[13]

Walsh also pointed to the unity brought about by the Roman Empire
of ancient times throughout the then-known world. In that context, he
reminded his readers that St Peter first preached at Rome, which for
Walsh was an example of the "foolish things that confound the wise":

Peter began his mission in haughty Rome and the result is
known. The folly of the Cross converted the world. The mustard
seed grew up and became a mighty tree, overshadowing the
earth and sheltering peoples, tribes, and tongues beneath its
protecting branches. And so it has been in the whole history of
the Church of Christ. The – humanly speaking – disproportion
and inadequacy of the means employed by the Church to
produce the mighty results history records, attest the presence
of Divine power and wisdom, guiding her counsels, ruling
her destinies, and working through her for the happiness and
salvation of the human race.[14]

God's work continued through the apostolic successors of St Peter;
Walsh himself shared in that apostolic succession:

[It is an] inestimable privilege and happiness to be in communion
with that Chair ... and to receive our mission from the illustrious Pontiff who now so worthily occupies it. Through Pius IX we
received our commission from Christ Himself. A long unbroken
chain of Pontiffs stretches away into the venerable past, uniting
Pius IX, appointing Bishops and commissioning them to go
and teach, with our Divine Lord sending St. Peter and the other
Apostles to go and teach the world.[15]

Having established his credentials, Walsh exhorted the Catholics to
good works and to a devout life, especially to "worthy and frequent
reception of the sacraments, assisting at the holy Mass, devotion to the
Most Blessed Sacrament, and to the ever Blessed Virgin the Immaculate Mother of God, &c., &c." He closed his letter with a sincere promise to visit all the parishes and missions of the diocese that winter, and
also confirmed the naming of Bruyère as his vicar general.[16]

These early indications of Walsh's character showed the Catholics in the diocese the truth of their new bishop's reputation. They soon recognized how profoundly knowledgeable he was about the Scriptures and about history, and that he was able to be instructional without being overbearing. His personal devotion to the Blessed Sacrament and to the Blessed Virgin were also evident; these would play a significant role in his pastoral letters and sermons over the years. Probably, too, the most obvious threads running through that first letter, which would be constant throughout his life, were his total dependence on God and his unswerving loyalty to the pope, two traits he likewise encouraged in his people.

Walsh's pastoral care and sense of duty were apparent also in his promise to visit the parishes and missions: "Should God spare us, it shall be our pleasing duty, during the coming winter, to visit the various missions of our diocese, to share the labors of our beloved Clergy, and to contribute, as far as we may, to the spiritual welfare and happiness of the faithful people committed to our care."[17] Such words, no doubt, would have greatly consoled the Catholics so hurt by the former bishop, especially because of his insensitivity to their needs and his estrangement from them.

Almost at once, two major problems faced Walsh, problems which were longstanding and which were at the root of considerable anxiety and unrest: the location of the episcopal seat and the crippling debt which Pinsoneault had incurred. It was to those that Walsh immediately directed all his administrative skills and pastoral discretion.

Even before Walsh had been named a bishop, letters had been sent to Propaganda Fide by some of the lay Catholics of the diocese asking that the seat not be moved from Sandwich. On 20 April 1867 Baillargeon had forwarded to Alessandro Cardinal Barnabò, prefect of Propaganda Fide, a petition from parishioners in Sandwich expressing their agitation over a rumour that the seat would be restored to London. One month later, Barnabò acknowledged receipt of their petition, without, however, commenting on its content.[18] Propaganda Fide's files state that the rumours of a change were not well founded; but the petition shows that the subject was a matter of concern even while Pinsoneault was still in the diocese. Ironically, many people had been opposed to the original move from London to Sandwich in 1859 as well, seeing it as only a personal convenience for Pinsoneault, while he ignored the real pastoral needs of London and the central and northern parts of the diocese.

As a confidant of Lynch, Walsh would have been apprised of the London situation during his tenure as vicar general in Toronto. Upon becoming bishop, he definitely wanted the seat to return to London. The reception which had been given him in London by the clergy and laity, including people of various denominations, had impressed him greatly, and only confirmed his desire to translate the seat back to where it had been originally envisioned and established in 1856 by the bishops of Canada with the approval of the Holy See.[19]

To that end, Baillargeon wrote to Barnabò on Walsh's behalf, affirming that Walsh had the approval of the bishops of Ontario for translating the see. That letter was dated 14 November 1867, the very day of Walsh's installation at Sandwich. Clearly, Walsh had made some preliminary inquiries among the bishops from Ontario gathered in Toronto for his consecration. While there, Baillargeon would have been able to canvass and find a consensus among the bishops present.[20] That fact was confirmed in Walsh's letter to Barnabò, his first formal request to have the seat translated, in which he also assured Barnabò he was seeking the provision of clergy for the Sandwich parish:

I take advantage of this occasion to mention to Your Eminence, another very important subject for the interest of the Church and of Religion in the Diocese of Sandwich. It is of the greatest importance, I would even say, of the greatest necessity, for me to move my residence from Sandwich to London. On the occasion of my consecration, the Archbishop of Quebec said to me that it was the unanimous opinion of the bishops of this Province that I remain in London. The central position where this latter city is situated, whereas Sandwich is found at the extreme end of the diocese, the considerable expenses incurred by the need to travel the length of the diocese, the importance and other numerous advantages offered by London as opposed to Sandwich – which is a second- or rather a third-class mission – and many other reasons too long to list, requiring that the Bishop of Sandwich make London his place of residence. I am not asking that the name of the See be changed, but I wish at present to declare my intention to reside in London in the future. I will add that the communities in Sandwich and in the environs expect as much, and that they will be satisfied, if they can once again have in their midst, the good Jesuit Fathers, to whom they are sincerely attached. I must inform Your Eminence that I have already undertaken measures in this regard, and that I will write to the general of the Jesuits in Rome, in order to obtain for Sandwich a small band of this excellent society.[21]

By the time he sent his request to Rome, Walsh had received a letter from Lynch, who was not adverse to the idea of the move but rather wanted to propose two practical considerations for Walsh to ponder: first, the residence in Sandwich might make "a very nice country place for Summer, whilst London might be one for the Winter"; and second, a move to London would mean displacing the Dominicans who staffed the London parish.[22] Walsh did not entertain those or any other considerations for long (if at all), as his letter to Barnabò showed. He was determined to move. It was, in his mind, a very important issue for the Church in his diocese. As for the Dominicans at St Peter's parish, on the other hand, he was well aware of the potential loss their departure would be and, not wanting to lose them from the diocese, he offered them instead any other parish they may have wanted. In fact, the Dominicans found it a most opportune time to leave the diocese; their missions in the eastern and central United States were short-staffed. Regrettably, therefore, they severed their connection with the diocese, and returned to Springfield, Kentucky, whence they came.[23] Walsh handled the case with great sensitivity, in marked contrast with the way Pinsoneault had dealt with Dean Kirwan and the Sisters of Loretto when he had arrived in London, or with the Jesuits when he moved his seat to Sandwich.[24]

By mid-January 1868 Walsh had received word from Baillargeon that there was little opposition to his desired move. All the bishops of the ecclesiastical province had approved.[25] Mere days later, on 19 January 1868, Walsh moved to London.[26] After that, it was simply a matter of waiting for the official approval from Rome, during which period Walsh continued to sign his name "Bishop of Sandwich." He had not sought to change the name of the diocese, but only the seat.[27]

Four months after his move to London, Walsh received word from Barnabò that his request was still under consideration. It would take two more formal requests and eighteen more months before the matter would finally be resolved.[28] In his second request, Walsh assured the prefect that he had the support of the people of his diocese for the move, and that he had already made arrangements for the Basilian Fathers to take charge of the mission of Sandwich and its college. He further emphasized that his being in London, because it was more central, would make it much easier to attend to the affairs of the diocese, a fact he had certainly proved in the short time between moving and making this request. His third request reiterated these same points.

Propaganda Fide finally considered the matter during its General Congregation of 27 September 1869, and issued the decree on 15 November, making London once more the episcopal seat of the diocese, some twenty-three months after the subject had been first broached, and twenty-one months after the bishop of Sandwich had made his first formal request. Walsh could easily echo the words of de Charbonnel, the former bishop of Toronto, who, in the early 1850s, had waited for an answer to his repeated requests to retire or to have the diocese of Toronto split: "Three months are three hours for Rome, but they are three years for us."[29] In the end, Propaganda Fide approved the translation of the seat and also renamed the diocese "London," even though the change of name had not been requested. These decisions were approved by Pius IX in an audience with the prefect on 3 October. It would take another ninety days before the official decree was finally issued, and some time yet before the decree would reach Walsh.[30]

His first unofficial notice that the translation had been approved came from Lynch, who was in Rome for the First Council of the Vatican. He wrote to congratulate Walsh on his success with Propaganda Fide, and he indicated that Walsh had probably already received "la nouvelle officielle."[31] In fact he had not, and would not until the official notice came from the archbishop of Quebec, which notice, when he did receive it, Walsh acknowledged with a letter of thanks to Barnabò. This news, he assured the prefect, was a great pleasure for the clergy, the laity, and himself, and the transfer would greatly advance the temporal and spiritual interests of the diocese.[32] He still awaited, however, the official decree from Rome.

When in the spring of 1870 Walsh continued styling himself "Bishop of Sandwich," Baillargeon questioned him on the usage. Walsh responded that he was still awaiting the arrival of the decree. Baillargeon suggested that he contact his new metropolitan, Archbishop Lynch.[33] Later that month, the decree arrived in London, and John Walsh was thenceforth known as the second bishop of London.

During the period of negotiations with Rome concerning the translation of the seat, Walsh was also coping with the state of the diocese's finances. In 1866, within days of the resignation of Pinsoneault, Bruyère had written to Bourget of Montreal concerning the gravity of Sandwich's financial situation. According to Rome's custom, a pension for the bishop was to be paid by the diocese, but the amount had yet to be determined. Bruyère confessed to being unable at that time to provide a complete financial assessment, but indicated some of his continuing concerns. In a later letter, in January, he gave Bourget an accounting prepared by the diocesan treasurer, Joseph Bayard. Both letters gave a complete picture of what Walsh was facing.[34]

Bruyère's first letter indicated that the debt was nearly $30,000, that the cathedral's revenues were only $2,000, and the revenues from parishes amounted to a mere $1,000. He cited the need to maintain the orphanage, the cathedral's clergy, and the episcopal residence, as well as to continue the necessary ecclesiastical work and to pay the mounting interest on the debt. The diocese would receive, he added, a small allocation from Propaganda Fide. This allocation had been discontinued while Pinsoneault was in office.[35]

Bruyère suggested a modest pension of $250 *per annum* with a promise to raise it to $400 when the financial situation improved.[36] Pinsoneault had actually requested a pension of $1,200 to $1,500. Bruyère "observed that Pinsoneault administered [the diocese] in a cavalier fashion and that the pension of $1,200 to $1,500, which he requested of the bishops was exaggerated. There is not one priest who did not find it exorbitant."[37] The retired bishop obviously considered himself far above the station of most of his former flock.[38]

In January, Bruyère began his second letter to Bourget by excusing Pinsoneault's maladministration. He had fallen into several errors, Bruyère argued, because he did not envision the practical realities in London which he had inherited, nor those which he had created himself. Bruyère stressed that he did not want to insinuate that Pinsoneault had knowingly erred. He also referred to the seriousness of the loss of Religious orders and congregations to the diocese, and mentioned that there was only one seminarian studying for the diocese at that time. In view of the situation, he felt, the pension requested by Pinsoneault was not only exorbitant but also unreasonable. He pointed out that the retired bishop of Toronto took no pension, and retired bishops in the United States took only $400 or $500. The diocese could not afford to pay more than that amount, but he would increase the pension, he told Bourget, as soon as the situation improved.[39] In the end, however, the Holy See determined that the pension would be $600 *per annum*.[40]

Sometime later, in February, Baillargeon offered Walsh his assessment of Pinsoneault's problems. He had dispensed himself, the archbishop noted, from formalities and so accumulated personal debt without concern for the abilities or the good of the diocese. Nevertheless, Baillargeon insisted, regardless of how the debt had been incurred, it was a problem that Walsh had to face. As Baillargeon understood the matter, the underlying concerns of Bruyère's two letters were the need for a judgment on the payment of debts and the necessity of a pension for Pinsoneault.[41]

The information about the large debt was widespread. That was why, before accepting the nomination as bishop, Walsh wanted to determine the extent of the problem. His first letter to Horan of Kingston, after receiving the nomination, revealed his investigations: "Before accepting the Bulls I have written to his Grace the Archbishop [of Quebec] requesting of him to inform me if the Holy See has granted an annuity to the retiring bishop and, if so, how much and what may be the amount of debts due by the diocese of Sandwich. I will come to no decision before learning all that may be learned regarding the real state of matters in that diocese."[42] So serious was the debt, in fact, that after learning the state of things Walsh at first hesitated to accept the nomination, but his sense of duty and obedience led to his giving consent. What complicated the matter further was that the estimates of the debt varied greatly, from $40,000 to $35,000 to $30,000. The actual figure presented later by Walsh in his 1870 report to Propaganda Fide was $32,324, with accumulated unpaid interest of $2,259.32, bringing the total debt to the enormous sum of $34,581.32.[43] In addition, it was necessary to consider the urgent need for new construction throughout the diocese, and the money needed for maintenance, as had been outlined by Bruyère to Bourget. What was yet to be discovered only gradually, however, was the full extent of private loans taken out by Pinsoneault. These did not appear in the ledgers of the diocese, and were considerable: one was to a priest from Montreal, another to the Sulpicians of Montreal, among others yet undisclosed at that point.[44] Baillargeon wrote to Walsh about one: the Hôtel-Dieu hospital in Montreal had been experiencing financial difficulties and one of their outstanding loans was one made to Pinsoneault. Lack of full disclosure by Pinsoneault, he stressed, could only aggravate the problem for Walsh.[45]

Walsh immediately decided on three ways to assess and address the situation. The first was to support the work of Bruyère, who had begun to resolve the debt on becoming the administrator during the *interregnum*. Walsh prudently allowed him to continue his regimen of reform, retrenchment, and economy.[46] As a second step, Walsh undertook the visitation of the diocesan parishes and missions he had promised in his first pastoral letter. "The prelate visited every mission and studied their needs carefully even though at great inconvenience to himself. On such visits, Bishop Walsh appealed to the people to assist in removing financial obligations which prevented him from giving himself primarily to spiritual works as he so desired."[47]

For his third step, Walsh appointed William Flannery as a kind of goodwill ambassador for the diocese. A priest of the diocese of Toronto, Flannery came with Walsh to London, living and working in and around the city of London with the bishop. During a two-year period from 1867 to 1869, Flannery made trips to large centres like New York, where he collected funds to be applied to the debt. "His genial manner made him eminently successful in this difficult work and to his efforts is due, in no small degree, the removal of the crushing debt which paralysed the activities of the infant diocese."[48]

The bishops of Canada noted how successful Walsh had been in mastering the debt. The archbishop of Quebec enthusiastically reported to Propaganda Fide in January 1868, less than three months after Walsh had taken possession of his see, that the new bishop was making great progress with its reorganization:

> The worthy Bishop, out of a sentiment of confidence which I
> do not deserve, has just written me to report to me on what he
> has already done to reorganize His diocese, and to liquidate
> the enormous debt weighing on His Church. And I am happy
> to have to inform Your Eminence that this "report," as he calls
> it himself, is completely reassuring, and manifestly proves that
> the new Bishop possesses all the qualities required in His truly
> difficult position, with all the confidence of His people: this will
> ensure the success of His ministry.[49]

Baillargeon then expressed his sentiments to Walsh directly, congratulating him on his spiritual and temporal progress.[50] By that time, too, Walsh had begun consulting the bishops of Canada for ways to pay down the debt.[51] This was his final step to deal with the disastrous financial situation.

Throughout these discussions with other bishops, the matter of Pinsoneault's pension arose again and again. Since it was Pinsoneault himself who put the diocese in such dire straits in the first place, and because he expected such an exorbitant amount, Walsh saw the request as an injustice to the diocese and its people. Baillargeon cautioned his young colleague to adhere to the civil laws regarding the payment of his debts, and also advised Walsh that a pension had to be paid to his predecessor regardless of the financial situation of the diocese. It was necessary, Baillargeon reminded Walsh, to follow "l'esprit de la loi" as regards canon law so as to safeguard the rights of the bishop for the good of his successors, or face rejection of his plan by Propaganda Fide.[52] Walsh responded to this letter immediately. He told the archbishop that he was resolved to pay all the debts of his predecessor, with one exception that he would reveal to the archbishop only, when they met in person: "I believe the honour of our holy religion requires me to pay all when circumstances will permit. If your Grace were to know the desolate state of this diocese your heart would be sorely afflicted."[53]

By early 1870, Walsh was attempting to launch another initiative to deal with the now-diminishing debt. This time his plan was to order every family throughout the diocese to make an annual donation, which would be applied to the debt along with the proceeds of a special monthly collection taken up in each parish and mission. He earnestly sought approval from Propaganda Fide for this, for he feared a repercussion among the laity. It was his intention to use the weight of Propaganda Fide's authority if people refused to cooperate.[54] Before the laity could react, however, and presumably before the idea was publicized in London, Lynch wrote one of his regular letters to Walsh from Rome, apprising him of the events of the Vatican Council. In the letter, Lynch expressed his concern about Walsh's proposed regimen for bringing down the debt. He thought it necessary to caution Walsh about it, for he feared not only the repercussions among Catholics in London, but also the hardship these compulsory contributions would bring them, since very many were poor or without ready cash. To strengthen his argument, Lynch recalled a bishop who had used censure in a similar situation:

> I received your very kind letter, and thank you for it. I lost no time in handing yours to His Eminence Cardinal Barnabò, adding my earnest recommendation, as you requested. The Cardinal answered in the first place, that Mons[igno]r Rapp[e] of Cleveland was forcing his priests under censures to collect for his seminary; and, where the people refused to pay, were punished by the withdrawal of their priest. That this was a great evil, and that the Bishop was persisting &c. we agreed that you were not in that case.[55]

The prefect feared, the archbishop went on, that were he to give approbation to such a collection, Propaganda Fide would be inundated with similar demands, and also pointed out that the cardinal could do nothing anyway without reporting to the Congregation of Cardinals. Instead, Barnabò suggested an intermediary step: that is, for Walsh to get the support of the other Canadian bishops in his endeavour. As a result, Lynch advised that "the first thing to be done was, to consult the Bishops of the province, as it was a matter interesting the whole Province, as an example; and then to have the demand strengthened by their signatures." At the same time Barnabò assured Lynch that Walsh "did wonderfully well … and with time and patience [he] would overcome all difficulties."[56]

Lynch took the opportunity to offer his advice as a friend and mentor to Walsh, clearly suggesting that he needed help with such matters, but that he should rely on an annual collection:

> My humble advice would be, in the first place, not to annoy or harass yourself too much. Your health is delicate. In fact you want such a man, as I have, to make money, and to dispense it, Fr [Jean-François] Jamot. See what a load I have thrown off, that would certainly crush me, but where find such a man? A diocesan Procurator is a necessity with us, to get the Cathedraticum, superannuated fund, students fund, &c. In the second place, to quietly, firmly, and perseveringly urge an annual collection, to pay the old debt, and to pay the annuity to your Predecessor; and that this collection be made by the Parish Priests; that you can rely upon, or by another, deputed ad hoc yearly.[57]

Almost immediately Lynch began gathering the opinions of the bishops of his ecclesiastical province. He did not readily find, however, a consensus amongst them, but was still able to report to Propaganda Fide by July that he had garnered the support for an alternative plan. In writing to Barnabò, Lynch spoke on behalf of all the bishops in his province when he indicated support for Walsh. The bishops wanted to ensure there would be no obligatory tax. Instead, they suggested a five-year pledge be made by each family. In addition, the bishops indicated an interest in raising money for their own coffers through a voluntary annual collection for the future needs of their respective dioceses.[58]

In Walsh's opinion, however, all his efforts toward payment of the debt were compromised by the pension he was required to pay Pinsoneault. Of course, he accepted that it was customary for a retired bishop to receive a pension. Yet the amount requested by Pinsoneault, and the precarious financial situation in the diocese, raised many concerns for him.

Earlier, the archbishop of Quebec had reported to Propaganda Fide on 1 January 1868 that Walsh found it an impossible burden to pay the requested pension to his predecessor "who ruined the Church of Sandwich, and left a crushing debt."[59] Shortly thereafter, he also wrote to Walsh that he and all the bishops agreed that the pension was too high, considering Pinsoneault's needs and Walsh's own means. Baillargeon had suggested to the pope, he assured Walsh, that $500 *per annum* was sufficient for Pinsoneault, but the pope still awarded him $600.[60] Walsh appealed that decision in June. He wrote directly to the prefect, and gave him a financial statement in which he pointed out the great expenses the diocese faced with the debt, and his need to spend more money in education and construction. He listed in a table all of his revenues and expenses. He then summarized:

> The above picture gives but an incomplete idea of the sad condition of the Diocese. I must add, Eminence, that my Predecessor, while leaving me such a considerable debt to pay off, was not able to establish any truly diocesan work such as a College, a Seminary and a Hospice. I find myself obliged to build and to establish everything from scratch. At the present time I must enlarge the church in London, which is entirely too small for the population; to build an Episcopal residence, since the one that I now occupy is totally inadequate for present needs; to build a hospice to save the numerous Catholic orphans who, in the absence of a shelter of this kind are exposed daily to coming into the hands of those who are in heresy.[61]

With all those concerns, Walsh rightly queried how it would be possible to pay the pension: "Of the services rendered to the Diocese by my predecessor, they may be expressed in two words: ruins and debts." If Pinsoneault were struggling to live a moderate life, as had been reported to Walsh, he wondered why Pinsoneault would refuse the generous offer of the bishop of Montreal to live with him. Walsh's final appeal to the prefect was to ask him to consult the bishops of Canada and the bishop of Detroit, who, he added, was perfectly "au courant" with the state of affairs in the diocese.[62]

Meantime, aware of the negotiations and the charges made against him, Pinsoneault wrote from Albany, New York, where he was the guest of Bishop John Conroy, to the prefect of Propaganda Fide in October of that year, defending his administration and the amount of his pension. He had begun, he insisted, his tenure as bishop with a large debt, and had done much to augment the diocese with various constructions. Pinsoneault claimed that he was a victim of misunderstanding at the time of his resignation, but that at age fifty-three, having given twenty-eight years of service to the Church, it was enough.[63]

It was Bourget in Montreal who received the definitive answer from Barnabò in a letter dated 24 November 1868. The bishop was instructed by the prefect to ask Walsh to pay the pension assigned by the Holy See for Pinsoneault. Bourget wrote accordingly on 22 December 1868.[64] In his reply to Bourget eight days later, Walsh thanked him for conveying this information, and graciously gave his consent:

> To that decision I submit most willingly and with a good heart. Animated by a sense of the duty which I owe to this diocese I wrote in Spring last to Cardinal Barnabò, stating it as my sincere conviction that the annuity of six hundred dollars was too large considering the resources of this diocese and the numerous and heavy debts we have to pay ... Now that this decision has come I accept it with the respectful submission becoming a Catholic bishop no matter how severe the privations it may impose. Deus providebit [God will provide]. As to your Lordship's share in this business I am sure it was dictated by a sense of duty and by your love for holy Church.[65]

Walsh still felt deeply that it was an injustice to his diocese. His final attempt to lessen the cost of the pension was to enquire of Baillargeon in January 1869, whether he had to pay it from the time of Pinsoneault's resignation or from the time Walsh had received his own brief of nomination. To this the archbishop replied that the pension was to be paid from the time of the resignation having been accepted by the Holy See.[66]

The diocese of London continued to support Pinsoneault until the day of his death, seventeen years after his resignation.[67] Near the end of Pinsoneault's life, in January 1883, the bishop of Montreal at the time, Édouard-Charles Fabre, with whom Pinsoneault had taken up residence, wrote to tell Walsh of his predecessor's precarious health. In reply, Walsh thanked Fabre, and offered these sympathetic words: "It was a wise thing for him to have resigned the Episcopal office and its responsibilities; for I am sure that he is much better prepared for death now than he would have been had he lived up to the present amid the cares, distractions, and anxieties of the Episcopate. I will cause prayers to be offered up for him in the congregation here and in our communities."[68] Pierre-Adolphe Pinsoneault died twenty-one days later, 30 January 1883, in his sixty-eighth year.[69]

The debt and the pension had absorbed a considerable amount of Walsh's time and energy. Except for his astute administrative skills and strength of character, and the able assistance of Bruyère, he would never have been able to carry out a successful plan of debt-repayment and thus rescue the still-young diocese of London. The debt was totally liquidated by the end of three years. It was a remarkable feat by all accounts. A memoir written to honour Walsh at the time of his twenty-fifth anniversary of priestly ordination paid this tribute: "When assuming the government of his diocese ... vast amounts of arduous and constant labor awaited his Lordship. He grappled earnestly with the difficulties that presented themselves in all directions. Nobly seconded by his generous flock, he succeeded within the incredibly short period of three years in paying off to the last shilling the large debt which had encumbered the diocese."[70]

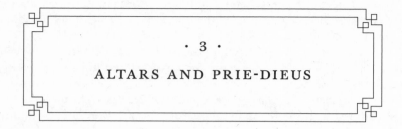

· 3 ·

ALTARS AND PRIE-DIEUS

[T]he great Shepherd of our souls works through human instruments and it is our consolation to believe that He frequently chooses for the execution of His work on earth instruments and means which, humanly speaking, would appear least adapted for His purpose.

BISHOP JOHN WALSH, 11 NOVEMBER 1867

A CATHOLIC BISHOP IS RESPONSIBLE FOR THE SPIRITUAL LIFE OF the people entrusted to his care. His closest collaborators must be the priests and Religious who, by their vocations, have likewise dedicated their lives to the spread of the gospel in parochial work or in other apostolates such as charity, health care, and education; their work is essential to the growth of the Church. Bishop Walsh felt this deeply. It was necessary for him to improve relations with the clergy and the female and male Religious in order to bring about the spiritual and administrative renewal his diocese needed. Only with their help and with his own personal strength of character, wisdom, and spiritual example could he hope to garner the support of the Catholic laity.

At the time the diocese of London was established in 1856, it included forty-eight parishes and missions, of which only twelve were canonically erected as parishes, cared for by twelve priests. When Walsh arrived in the diocese, there were thirty-one priests.[1] By 1877, when Walsh submitted his first report about the diocese to the Holy See, there were seventy-six parishes and missions served by fifty-two priests, of whom he had ordained twenty-three. Meantime, the Catholic population had reached 57,000, and increased again to 62,677 by 1885, at which time the diocese had sixty-eight priests serving seventy-eight parishes and missions. Three other priests were considered invalids. Before his transfer to Toronto in 1889, Walsh would ordain an additional fifteen priests.[2]

Although the number of Catholics in the province nearly doubled in the years between 1851 and 1881, their increase in the diocese of London was less dramatic, but nonetheless was still impressive.[3] That was precisely why Walsh increased the number of parishes and missions, and as well sought out priests from outside the diocese. In the first ten years alone, he oversaw the construction of twenty-eight new churches and the enlargement or improvement of five others. He gladly remarked that "these edifices, with few exceptions, are of brick and stone, and many of them are splendid and costly structures." Additionally, seventeen new presbyteries were built to accommodate the clergy in various parishes, while in 1874, Walsh had a new episcopal residence constructed next to his cathedral in London.[4] By 1887, there were an additional twenty-two new churches built in the diocese, bringing the total to fifty built during Walsh's years there.[5]

He also established twenty-two new parishes, which included raising four missions to the status of parish. It is interesting to note that of the twenty-two parishes, nine were given over to the patronage of the Blessed Virgin under various titles, not surprisingly in the years following the declaration of the Immaculate Conception; two were given to the patronage of the Sacred Heart of Jesus and one to the Holy Name of Jesus, again, two popular devotions of the day; one was erected under the title of the bishop's own patron saint, John the Evangelist; while the remainder were given to the patronage of other saints, all of whom reflected various aspects of the bishop's personal devotions.

Walsh personally dedicated the majority of the new churches, though on occasion, when he was unable to officiate, he deputed the task to a visiting bishop. At the dedication of the church of St Matthew in Alvinston, Walsh spoke in his sermon about the reason for building such grand edifices: "The object they sought to realize in the building of this temple, and the motive of their conduct were to promote the glory of God, and the salvation of souls, in other words, to fulfil the destinies for which they had been created. The salvation of the soul should be the work of life, the master action to which all other actions should be subordinated. Man was created by God that he might know and serve Him here and by this means, attain to his last end, the enjoyment of God in Heaven."[6]

Such occasions, however, were not only celebrations of the dedications of new buildings, but also opportunities for the bishop to instruct the people of the diocese. That point he clearly demonstrated while dedicating a new high altar in 1879 in the church of All Saints in Strathroy, a parish he had established ten years earlier. He was at his eloquent best, delivering a sermon on the necessity of sacrifice and the need for an altar to offer the sacrifice of the Mass. "Tracing from the very beginning, where Cain and Abel offered their sacrifices ... His Lordship took his hearers through the whole pages of Biblical History up to the sacrifice on Calvary, making some masterly comparisons, showing clearly how the spirit of the old law was completely fulfilled and interwoven in the Sacrifice of the Mass as performed in the present age."[7]

Earlier, in 1867, Walsh had raised the mission of St Philip the Apostle in Petrolia to the rank of a parish, and twenty years later, he dedicated its new church. Such was the occasion for another of his articulate sermons, this time as an *apologia* for the Church, in which the bishop vindicated her against "the unsupported charges advanced against her, and traced her history from the days of Christ and His apostles, down through the centuries of opposition and bloodshed to prove that through her zeal, her suffering, and the bloodshed of her priests and teachers, the Bible has been transmitted to the present generation."[8]

One of the finest examples of Walsh's oratory at a church dedication, according to reports, was given at St Joseph's parish in Chatham. This was one of the original twelve parishes in the diocese. The church was remarkably beautiful.[9] At its dedication on 23 October 1887, Walsh movingly spoke about how such a grand new church represented the Catholic Church as "the house of God and the gate of heaven."[10]

In the construction of church buildings, Walsh showed himself to be not only at his pastoral best but also very astute in his business dealings. His correspondence indicated how he made specific demands on the priests and parishioners to ensure the legal protection and the good of both the parish and the diocese. When writing to the members of the parish of St Philip at Grande Pointe, as they prepared to build their new church in 1882, he set forth plainly his carefully reasoned conditions: first, the deed for the church had to be in the name of the Roman Catholic Episcopal Corporation; second, the plans had to be submitted to him in advance; third, the construction would be under the jurisdiction of the pastor; and finally, the recipients of the letter were officially appointed as trustees for the church.[11]

His astuteness was also evident in the caution he exercised and even forced upon the parishioners of Essex Centre, who asked to build a new church in 1882.[12] He insisted the timing was "premature." They were a mission of Maidstone, served by visiting priests from there. They would have to wait another five years, he informed them, before the mission would become a parish with a permanent priest, and only then would they be allowed to build a new church. Walsh pointed out also that they were so few in number that they could not afford a new church without the financial help of the people of Maidstone, who were unable to give such help. As well, he told them, a new church at Essex Centre would be useless unless a second priest were stationed at Maidstone. That was not about to happen. Instead, he suggested that they wait and see what influence, for better or for worse, the new railroad would have on their village.

The bishop did not want to discourage them, of course, and assured them that the pastor of Maidstone, Joseph Molphy, would continue to attend to their spiritual needs: "Rest assured, Gentlemen, that your spiritual welfare is very dear to me and that your wishes and praise-worthy views regarding your religious interests shall not fail to be car-ried out so soon as time and circumstances will permit."[13] Five years later in 1887, as he had promised, Walsh authorized the parishioners to draw up plans for a church, but within strict limits: the dimensions were to be 18.75 by 9.5 metres, and it was to be a frame or brick church, or else none would be built. They were to obtain "reliable" estimates. In June that year he allowed a contract to be given for the building, but warned that he accepted no legal obligation.[14] He was determined they would build only what they could afford.

On other occasions Walsh simply counselled caution when there was a shortage of funds in parishes. When Patrick O'Shea, the pastor of St James at Seaforth, wanted to build a new presbytery, Walsh called for moderation by limiting the spending to $3,000.[15] On another occa-sion, he wanted to ensure that the cemetery in Wyoming parish would generate enough revenue for its own upkeep. To that end, through a letter sent by his secretary, Joseph Kennedy, Walsh instructed the parishioners that the cemetery was the property of the Episcopal Cor-poration, that its mortgage was discharged, and that those wanting plots should come to an agreement with the pastor for a reasonable price that would ensure the continuing care of the cemetery. The sec-retary sharply concluded that "the Bishop is sorry to add that some people in Wyoming by their habitual grumbling and insubordination to pastoral authority has [sic] given more trouble and annoyance than has been given him by any other parish in the diocese."[16]

Walsh also bargained astutely for loans when construction projects were undertaken, and was careful to get the best rate of interest. Once, he even suggested to a pastor where he could find a specific rate of interest, seven per cent at Dominion Loan Security, but the pastor was permitted to get the money elsewhere if he could equal or better the rate. The bishop also put a $3,000 spending ceiling on the project to finish the interior of the church.[17] Earlier, when writing to the manager of Dominion Loan Security, Walsh thanked him for his offer of a loan at eight per cent; he declined it, however, saying he had found a better rate elsewhere.[18] It is likely that that refusal to do business led to Walsh getting a better rate with Dominion Loan Security later.

There were times when Walsh did not hesitate to demand payment on a loan made in the name of the Episcopal Corporation, even to the point of threatening the delinquent debtor with a collection agency.[19] He was very conscious of his responsibilities to the diocese: "I could not in conscience forgive that amount [of debt] because it is not mine, it is the property of the Church of which I am simply the steward and guardian, but not the proprietor."[20] Such were the shrewd business practices that not only allowed the payment of the diocese's debt within three years, but also made possible the construction of fifty new churches and the establishment of twenty-two new parishes and missions.

The last mission Walsh established in the diocese was for a group of people who attracted his special attention and pastoral care: people of African descent, specifically runaway slaves from the United States of America and their descendants.[21] Many had settled in the diocese of London, mostly due to its location on the border of the two countries, in places such as Windsor, Sandwich, Amherstburg, Shrewsbury, Dresden, and Chatham. It was the community in Windsor that especially came under the bishop's care in the 1880s, mostly through the initiative and work of Dean James Wagner, who recognized the need not only to evangelize the black people of the city, but also to offer basic education, health care, and a community centre. He opened the first Catholic mission for black people in Canada during 1886.[22] To extend further care for the community of black people, the Sisters of Hôtel-Dieu of St Joseph opened an orphanage in Windsor with Walsh's approval in 1888.[23]

Because of Walsh's encouragement and Wagner's work, the community grew. The report about Holy Saturday in 1887, for instance, indicated that the latest additions of newly baptized brought the total congregation in Windsor to nearly one hundred persons. With each report was an appeal for funds to support this mission and those for other ethnic groups.[24] These appeals were raised in stature by a letter from the prefect of Propaganda Fide, given to Wagner when he accompanied Walsh on his 1887 *ad limina* visit. Giovanni Cardinal Simeoni congratulated Wagner on establishing the mission and encouraged the Catholics of the diocese to support the cause.[25]

Walsh had always shown a keen interest in fostering vocations and educating candidates for the priesthood. One letter to Cardinal Simeoni revealed his ardent desire to have young men studying in Rome. In late 1887 Walsh wrote to the prefect requesting spaces be reserved for two or three students from London at the Collegio Urbano, the seminary under the jurisdiction of Propaganda Fide. He listed four reasons for his request, all of which spoke of the pastoral needs of the diocese and its particular situation in the province of Ontario. First of all, he wrote, the diocese lacked the resources to educate seminarians and therefore it would be a long time before he could hope to establish a seminary. As well, the youths studying for the Church were generally children of poor parents who were unable to defray the expenses of their sons' education. Further, he wrote, it was desirable that a number of priests be instructed in the sacred sciences at the type of school that already existed in Rome, "the Mother of all Churches, and who by the same capacity will be able to give off the Roman spirit among the other priests and the faithful of our Diocese." Finally, he pointed out that in numbers the province was Protestant and therefore it was necessary to have priests of superior education who could explain the doctrines of the faith clearly to the satisfaction of the Protestants. His venture was successful, and his request honoured – not his first such request – as a number of seminarians studied in Rome for his diocese and were ordained, including Joseph Kennedy, who later acted for a time as the bishop's secretary; James Walsh, the bishop's own nephew; and Thomas Cornyn.[26]

To further the promotion of priestly vocations, Walsh often preached on the subject of the priesthood, and encouraged Catholics to give their support to seminarians by prayer and by financial donations. In one of his pastoral letters he addressed that topic directly: "All who have at heart the good of our holy religion; all who desire the solid establishment of the holy Church of God in this free and happy country; all who value the salvation of immortal souls purchased by the precious blood of our Redeemer, will not hesitate to give largely of their worldly means to enable the Bishop to educate a holy and efficient priesthood for this large and growing diocese."[27] He went on to admonish parents to encourage and to support their sons who aspired to the priesthood as they would their sons who aspired to medicine or law. He also exhorted them and all pastors to encourage vocations, and called on all to make a success of the annual collection for the seminarians, which he was establishing with that pastoral letter.

Walsh decreed that this collection must be taken up each year on all the Sundays of October; that his letter was to be read in all churches as soon as it was received; and that it was to be retained and read every year for that occasion. With considerable insight and prescience, he concluded:

> It can truly be affirmed that the Church will never be firmly established in this country until it possesses a native Priesthood – until it is interlaced with the feelings, affections, and national habits and traditions of the people – until, in fine, it is made 'race of the soil,' like some giant oak that has grown gradually up in our forests, spreading its roots abroad, and driving them deep into the soil and deriving therefrom its sap and nourishment, until it has acquired the sturdy strength and magnificent proportions that bid defiance to the fiercest storms.[28]

Like other bishops, Walsh also encouraged men from other countries to come to his diocese to be missionaries. It was a practice that he carried out for years, whenever he visited Europe and especially his homeland. He had some success. Two priests, Patrick Costello and Thomas Noonan, were ordained in Ireland, at the College of St John, Waterford. They would serve the London diocese for many years to come.[29]

It had also been the custom, ever since the establishment of the dioceses of Kingston and Toronto, to attract priests from dioceses in Quebec to minister to the needs of Catholics in Upper Canada. That custom continued after London was established. Pinsoneault had had recourse to it, and immediately after his departure, Bruyère, as administrator, appealed to the bishop of Montreal to send priests. In a "sad dissertation" about the number of priests, he told Bourget that he needed about six good priests immediately, and asked if he could send some, or even some seminarians. He also indicated that he would write to other bishops in Canada asking help for his poor diocese.[30]

Walsh continued that practice, and likewise implored the help of other bishops. Often he received requests from people in his diocese for priests who spoke their language, such as the Gaelic-speaking Catholics of West Williams, near Parkhill. When they first made their request in 1883, Walsh was unable to supply such a priest, but in the next year found Donald McRae, who originally had been destined for a mission in the diocese of Detroit. Instead, McRae was appointed in October 1884 as the assistant in Parkhill and West Williams, with additional responsibilities for the parish of Forest. In his letter to the pastor of Parkhill, Patrick Corcoran, the bishop expressed his hopes that the Catholics of West Williams would show their appreciation by increasing their dues.[31] In some places, such as Zurich and Blenheim, German-speaking priests were needed. Walsh was able to appoint some German-speaking Franciscans to St Joseph's, Chatham, in 1878, to serve the needs of those Catholics in Blenheim.[32]

By far, francophones were the largest non-English-speaking group in the diocese, and therefore called for much more attention on the part of the bishop.[33] His early attempt to address their need was to train one of his seminarians in the French language at the Collège de Saint-Hyacinthe in Quebec. He entered into an agreement with the superior there to arrange French lessons for his seminarian, by the name of Kelly, in exchange for Kelly conducting a class in English. Through some misunderstanding, however, the plan did not come to fruition; instead Kelly carried out his studies at the Basilian college in Toronto.[34]

A typical request for a French-speaking priest came from the parishioners of Amherstburg in 1874. Walsh wrote to tell them that their demands were reasonable but that the nearest French-speaking priest was occupied elsewhere.[35]

At one point, Walsh appealed to the archbishop of Quebec. In his reply to Walsh, Baillargeon offered to send Félix Gauthier, one of his younger priests, who was a doctor in theology and who spoke English well. He expressed a hope that Walsh would be content with Gauthier as he himself had been since Gauthier's ordination.[36] It is interesting to note that despite Baillargeon's willingness to help in this matter, there is no record of Gauthier ever being assigned to the London diocese.

In 1881, when preparing to establish the mission of Ste Claire at Ruscom River, Walsh turned for help to Édouard-Charles Fabre of Montreal, who, early in the following year, responded favourably. Walsh wrote to thank him and to describe the new mission. He promised a salary of $300 *per annum* and made arrangements for the priest to live with another pastor in an already-established parish eight kilometres distant. With that, Antoine Lorion came to work in the diocese of London in February 1882 as the first pastor of Ruscom River. Two years later Walsh wrote to assure Fabre that Lorion was doing well, and at the same time unabashedly asked Fabre to send four more French-speaking priests.[37]

In late 1885, the parishioners of Grande Pointe were seeking a French-speaking priest. Walsh again wrote to Fabre and, by December, had his reply.[38] The priest who was proposed, however, was not considered so favourable. Walsh wrote again in January and questioned Fabre's selection: "The mission of Grande Pointe is a difficult one and is in debt, and it would require a strong, active and zealous priest to do the duty that would devolve upon him as its Curé." Walsh also wrote that he was ashamed to trouble the bishop of Montreal, but that he was moved by the charity of Christ in this concern.[39] By August, however, the first priest sent from Montreal to Grande Pointe, Joseph-Louis-Marie Lévesque, had come and gone. Nonetheless, the bishop was pleased with his work during his short stay, and wrote to Fabre to commend Lévesque "as a good, laborious and zealous priest," and to thank him for sending a replacement, Anthème Carrière. Carrière stayed fourteen months in the mission and was replaced by Pierre Langlois on 10 October 1887.[40]

When in 1885 Walsh was seeking a francophone priest for the newly established parish of Notre-Dame-du-Lac-Sainte-Claire in Walkerville, he turned to the bishop of Saint-Hyacinthe, Louis-Zéphirin Moreau. As dean of Windsor, James Wagner wrote the official request to Moreau, while Walsh enclosed his own letter. Wagner described the parish, highlighted all of its assets, and pointed out that the pastor's salary would be $600 *per annum*. He mentioned, too, that the parish was situated on a beautiful site and was considered one of the most enviable appointments in the diocese. Walsh lamented that he could send only an Irish priest whose French was "slightly comprehensible." He was limited to reading a short meditation in French, Walsh reported, emphasizing his need.[41]

By return post Walsh had his response. Moreau said he would do his best to procure a priest by Easter. Then, "in the week of Quasimodo," Moreau wrote to say he had a priest who was willing to go to Walkerville, and expressed his confidence that Alfred Lapierre would do well, and that the parishioners would like him. The priest, however, was not only to be loaned to the diocese, but to have Moreau's *exeat* to remain in London, if Walsh so desired. Moreau preferred to give priests working elsewhere their *exeat*, since he considered it more normal that they remain in their new dioceses.[42] Presumably Walsh did not answer directly, for in March 1886, Moreau wrote again asking if he would like to retain Lapierre in the diocese. Walsh was quick to respond this time and, within a few days, he wrote to the bishop of Saint-Hyacinthe that he was pleased to accept the offer and to affiliate Lapierre with the diocese. He thanked Moreau for his kindness in giving the diocese "such a good priest."[43]

Other letters, however, clearly indicated that Walsh, despite the serious shortage of priests he faced, was not willing to accept every priest who asked to work in the diocese. That is evident in the case of several priests from Montreal. One of those, a Father Hogan, suffered from alcoholism and, even though he was a classmate of Walsh in the seminary, he was not welcomed in London. Another was S. Laporte, for whom Fabre would not provide a recommendation or an *exeat*. In consequence, Walsh refused his request. This was also the case with a J.F. Tourmentin, who had applied for a position in London.[44]

While supplying priests for francophone congregations was an important preoccupation, Walsh, as bishop, also needed to tend to other concerns for those parishioners. His francophone vicar general, Bruyère, often accompanied Walsh on visits to these parishes. Though Walsh himself was fully bilingual, having studied at Le Grand Séminaire of Montreal, he would preside at Confirmation ceremonies in these parishes greeting the people and mingling with them while speaking French, but he would give his sermon in English. Bruyère would follow the bishop's address with one in French.[45]

In many of these parishes, however, a particular problem had arisen involving marriages. Among the early French-speaking settlers, due to a sparse and scattered population, it was common to marry one's first cousin, in order to preserve the population, language, and culture. That practice had continued into Walsh's time. He had to appeal to Propaganda Fide about the matter:

> In one part of my Diocese there are several Canadian parishes populated by descendants of French families. In these areas, an abuse has arisen against which I have often protested. We are often importuned by requests for <u>dispensations</u> for marriage between <u>first cousins</u>. If I refuse to send their request to the Holy See, the parties are tempted to have recourse to a Protestant minister. Often with the aim of forcing the Ecclesiastical Authority to grant their request, they do not hesitate to commit the crime of incest. I have reason to believe that, if these marriages between <u>first cousins</u> had been forbidden from the beginning, these troubles would not exist or at least would be very rare.[46]

As a result of this appeal, thenceforth Walsh received the necessary dispensations; and thus the francophone Catholics would not have to be lost to the Protestant churches.

Certainly, over time, Walsh came to appreciate the French-Canadian culture in his parishes more and more, and committed himself to encouraging it. With his approval, there grew up, in many French-speaking parishes, societies named in honour of Saint Jean-Baptiste. In granting permission to establish one such group in a parish, Walsh wrote that he approved of "your Society and its objects and I hope its members will always be true to their faith and country and loyal to the glorious traditions of their Catholic fathers."[47]

With few exceptions, John Walsh enjoyed cordial and affectionate rela-tions with the priests, Religious, and laity living and working in his parishes. The great respect and near-universal admiration shown him while a priest in Toronto continued through his tenure as bishop of London and to the end of his life. The words of welcome addressed to him at his installation in the cathedral of Sandwich by the priests made this clear. Their words, "we beg to assure you that we will cheer-fully co-operate with you in all you undertake for the glory of God and the salvation of souls," indicated the very positive relationship Walsh would have with his priests from the start.[48] This was demonstrated time and again throughout his years in London, when the priests, Religious, and laity expressed their unwavering support and great admiration for Walsh as their spiritual leader. Many of these occasions were celebrations of special anniversaries of the bishop's ordination or consecration.

For his tenth anniversary as a bishop, for example, celebrated in November 1877, Walsh was the recipient of a very generous purse of $3,000 from the priests, an ostensorium from the young priests he had ordained, and an episcopal chair from the Sisters and students of St Mary's Academy, Windsor, along with other gifts not recorded. Among the addresses offered him that day, these warm words best summarize the affection felt for him by the people:

We, the priests of the Diocese of London, beg leave respectfully to address you, not alone for ourselves, but also in the name of all the laity of our various parishes, on the occasion of the tenth anniversary of Your Lordship's elevation to the Episcopacy. We desire to congratulate you on the success which has attended your administration of this important part of the Lord's vineyard during the past decade ... Your Lordship has been able to reconcile the successful administration of an important charge with a suavity of manner which has endeared you to all, so that you are regarded by all as a kind father; and it is this quality, more especially, which has secured to you the filial affection of both clergy and laity in the Diocese, and the respect and admiration of all with whom you have intercourse.[49]

Two years later, when celebrating the twenty-fifth anniversary of his priestly ordination, Walsh was once again warmly complimented with good wishes and gifts, further signs of the high esteem in which he was held. All the priests of the diocese who could be, were in attendance, in company with Peter Crinnon, the bishop of Hamilton, and several senior clergy from the surrounding dioceses. The occasion was marked by a banquet and a presentation to Walsh of a set of the Greek and Latin Fathers, edited by the famous Abbé Jacques-Paul Migne, and estimated to be worth $700 at that time. The gift itself was expressive of his intellectual curiosity and his love of history and of the Fathers of the Church. Dean James Murphy spoke enthusiastically on behalf of the assembly:

In union with the bishops and dignitaries of other Dioceses, who are gathered here to do you honor; in unison with the numerous bodies of the Laity all over the province who send to your Lordship their felicitations; and in concert with the *Religieuses* of different communities to whom you have been so long a time, a kind father, a wise counsellor, and prudent director, – We, the priests of your Diocese (on the greater number of whom you conferred Holy Orders), come one and all, proud and joyous to claim you especially as our own Bishop and Father, endeared to us as you are by the sacred ties of paternity and disinterested devotion to our welfare.[50]

The accolades continued. Indeed, so great was the general affection for Walsh that, when he had been away from the diocese for any length of time, he was met with a tumultuous reception on his return. One such occurred after a visit to his homeland in 1882, an absence of two months. Partly for the restoration of his health, but more to visit relatives, to renew acquaintances, and to be present for the dedication of the monument to Daniel O'Connell, Walsh went to Ireland at the beginning of August that year.[51] Even the two-week ocean voyage was helpful for him, as his dispatch from "on board the Servia, out at sea" indicated that he was in good health and receiving much benefit from the trip.[52] The *Catholic Record* reported regularly during this period about the bishop's vacation, and reminded readers when he would be returning.[53] It seemed everyone followed the bishop's progress with great interest. On his way home, after landing in New York (the usual port-of-call for his European voyages), he made his way to London by way of Hamilton. Anticipating the day of his arrival at the train station in London, an immense crowd, estimated at 3,000 persons from a total population in the city of approximately 20,400, gathered to greet their bishop.

> The spacious platform was filled to excess by an eager throng, which endured with perfect good humour and equanimity the jostling, elbowing and pushing inseparable from a large assemblage, while they anxiously strained their eyes eastward in an effort to obtain the first glimpse of the incoming cars. At length the whistle was heard, and as the long train dashed up to the depot the band of the Seventh Fusileers, which was stationed upon the platform, struck up "Home, Sweet Home". The appropriate character of the selection gained the approval of the audience, and as the venerable prelate, rejuvenated by his brief sojourn in the land of his nativity, emerged from the car, and stood for a moment with uncovered head, cheer after cheer went up from the immense concourse of people, while at the same time a stream of fireworks shot heavenward.[54]

The enthusiastic crowd followed him in a long procession to the episcopal palace and gathered on the front lawn while the bishop entered his palace. He hurriedly climbed to the second floor and then stepped out onto the balcony overlooking the front, to the applause and cheers of the people. John Wright, a prominent broker in the town, delivered an affectionate welcome on behalf of those present:

> May it please your Lordship, – We, the undersigned citizens of London, comprising not only those whose privilege it is to follow your spiritual guidance, but also many who, though not of the flock you rule with such paternal solicitude and success, fail not

to admire your exalted qualities, most respectfully tender you a very hearty welcome on your return to your episcopal city. We hope in all sincerity that your Lordship's health has been permanently benefited by your brief sojourn in the old land. We earnestly trust that you may be long spared to the Diocese of London, upon which your virtues and talents shed such lustre, and beg of you to accept the accompanying testimonial as a feeble token of that regard in which we and the many on whose behalf we may on this occasion justly presume to speak, sincerely hold your Lordship.[55]

The "feeble token" to which Wright referred was a remarkable purse of $1,000. Profoundly touched at their generosity, Walsh spoke extemporaneously, thanking everyone for their warm and unexpected welcome and for their generous gift. He went on to extol the values of this "Canada of ours," and encouraged everyone to be good citizens. He was glad, he assured them, to be home again, in good health, and to continue working among them. The celebrations continued. A few days later, he was fêted at a dinner at the posh London Club by leading citizens of the city. The address, again profuse in its respect and admiration, is noteworthy since it represented the thoughts of laity, both Catholics and members of other churches.[56]

Their love and esteem for him never seemed to waver. Five years later, on the occasion of Walsh's twentieth anniversary of episcopal consecration, there was once again a great outpouring of affection for this outstanding man. In his honour, the parishes of the diocese collected a gift of $5,200 to be presented to the pope, to help support his work. As well, the priests presented the bishop with a personal gift of $1,000.[57]

Even when one makes allowance for the unctuous language of the Victorian era, therefore softening the titles of respect and the superlatives used, a clear picture still emerges of the high esteem in which Walsh was held by clergy, Religious, and laity. Adding to that the value of the gifts offered – more than "feeble" tokens – it is correct to say that the sentiments expressed truly reflected the feelings of those who had come to know and love John Walsh. He was a man who enjoyed their affection and even their veneration, more for his person than for the office he represented. In fact, it was Walsh's human qualities that most endeared him to people. Such public displays of fondness and high opinion, especially when not easily given or expected from those of other churches, showed that even Protestant Ontario had a place for the Catholic Church, and especially for her leaders such as Walsh. He had won everyone's heart.

When Walsh made his farewell to the diocese on being named archbishop of Toronto in 1889, he was presented with the final accolades of his beloved people. The fulsome words spoken on behalf of the priests at that time paid tribute to the respect and admiration given to him, and showed clearly why he had won their hearts: "Your life and labors as priest and Bishop for thirty-five long years are before the country, and form a bright chapter in the ecclesiastical history of Ontario wherein your honored name has long since been a household word."[58] Similar warm sentiments were expressed by the laity on that occasion as they bade him farewell.

Given the energy he expended on behalf of his diocese, it is not hard to understand why Walsh was so highly regarded. Everyone knew that he had worked tirelessly for them to establish parishes and missions, schools and hospitals, and to build new churches wherever needed, while his principal concern was always for his people and for their spiritual benefit. That point the priests clearly confirmed on the tenth anniversary of his consecration: "Amid all these important works, the sanctification of the clergy and your beloved people have been foremost in your mind. Hence to your ability and zeal for religion we must chiefly attribute the present satisfactory condition in which the Diocese stands, for the Bishop is the directing mind of the Diocese."[59]

Bishop Walsh gave much attention to the importance of "the sanctification of clergy and people." Practically, for him, it meant providing retreats and theological conferences for his priests. The purpose of these events was to provide continuing education and spiritual formation for them, with the expectation that their parishioners too would be beneficiaries. These retreats, lasting, for the most part, from a Monday evening to the following Saturday, were held annually, usually in London. The bishop paid close attention to those who led and attended the retreats. Attendance was not optional, yet, each year, through a circular letter, the priests were "invited" to attend. The invitations would be worded in such ways as "You are required to take part in the spiritual exercises" and "You are requested to be present thereat."[60] He referred several times to these annual retreats, in letters to other bishops, in such terms as "the ecclesiastical retreat had just finished," or "the retreat was going well and the preacher was good," or, on one occasion, "the retreat was the best they had ever had."[61]

Walsh likewise held regular theological conferences for the clergy. These provided opportunities for the priests to learn about and discuss theological topics as a way to continue the learning they had begun in the seminary, by bringing to their attention contemporary moral, canonical, dogmatic, and historical subjects. One such conference was advertised by Walsh's circular letter in the *Catholic Record* during October 1878, in which the priests were informed that the "ecclesiastical conference" would be held in London on the following 29 January. The topics to be addressed included *De Scriptura Sacra*, *De Theologia Dogmatica*, and *De Historia Ecclesiastica*.[62]

In such retreats and conferences, Walsh was among other leading bishops breaking new ground with his approach, and proved himself to be not only a man of learning, but one who encouraged learning in others. By making attendance compulsory at retreats and conferences, he meant to show his priests the importance of their developing greater insights into their personal spirituality as well as into theological subjects. In that way, they could better serve their people. His pastoral concern was clear. His priests recognized it and expressed their understanding to him on the eve of his departure for Rome in 1887: "With the clergy your Lordship's relations have ever been those of a father and friend rather than of a superior. Your anxiety for our spiritual welfare has been manifested by the fact that during every year of your episcopate you have afforded to us the inestimable blessing of a spiritual retreat, and by establishing theological conferences you have fostered our love for the study of the sacred sciences."[63]

Like many of his episcopal contemporaries and Protestant leaders in Canada, Walsh was alarmed at the growing popularity of certain staged theatrical performances. Such entertainments were often as bawdy as the plays of Shakespeare, without their redeeming literary value. So important to Walsh was this matter that he addressed a circular letter to the clergy of his diocese in 1886. By virtue of this decree – formally issued *ex aedibus nostris episcopalibus* [from our episcopal palace], in Latin, and signed by his secretary – the priests of the diocese were forbidden to attend dramatic and operatic performances. It was, Walsh pointed out, with great sadness that he had learned some priests had attended such performances in London and even in Detroit, and that, to him, was a cause of grave scandal. Such activity was to cease.[64]

Walsh may have seemed to some to be somewhat prudish or even Jansenistic in his approach to such theatrical performances. He lived in the nineteenth century and was educated – at least for a short time – by Sulpicians in Montreal. Certainly Jansenism was common among bishops and other clerics at the time. Perhaps, too, he worried too much about his priests and their behaviour, but there may have been other reasons for the decree.

Generally, priests were not well-educated, nor would all have had the natural interest in or commitment to continuing their education after ordination. That was the main reason that Walsh instituted the annual retreats and theological conferences, and why he wrote so many pastoral letters to educate his priests so that they, in turn, could educate their parishioners.

He was concerned above all about scandal, especially as it related to the public personae of priests. He felt strongly about that. While some theatrical and operatic performances of the day may have been of good quality and subject, many of those performed in London, or across the river in Detroit, were burlesque-type shows. These certainly would have raised eyebrows – and questions – among the laity, Catholic and Protestant alike. Any bishop, therefore, would think this type of performance unseemly if not scandalous. The strong-willed John Walsh thought it necessary to take action and give direction when needed. It was his duty.

What seemed severe was, in fact, an expression of Walsh's love and pastoral care for his priests. He never wavered in his care for them, especially showing solicitude for the sick and aged clergy. That point was emphasized, among his many accomplishments, at the tenth anniversary celebration of his episcopate: "Not least amongst the religious works your Lordship has called into being, is the creation and establishment, on a permanent basis, of St. John's Society, which provided for the decent support of the infirm and aged priests of the Diocese."[65] Officially named the Society of St John the Evangelist, in honour of the bishop's patron saint, it was the first established fund to provide a pension for priests. Begun on 12 July 1872, it was eventually incorporated by an act of the provincial Parliament, and by the time Walsh was transferred to Toronto, the fund was considered "signally successful and productive of untold benefits. Several of the clergy who, through age or infirmity, were incapacitated and forced to abandon active mission work, were made comfortable and independent, while several thousand dollars [were] still in the reserve fund."[66]

By 1889, there were at least three priests benefiting from this fund. One of them was John Carlin. He received the news of his pension from Walsh when resigning the pastorate of St Mary's parish in Wood-stock. At the time, the bishop assured him of an annual grant of $300, the average salary of a parish priest then, "so long as the state of your health will not enable you to perform the labors of your holy min-istry." Walsh made it clear, as well, that if it was possible for Carlin to return to active ministry, a place would be found for him. The bishop, however, added a condition that Carlin must continue to conduct him-self "in a manner begetting the sacred character of the priesthood." Walsh expressed confidence that he would always do so.[67]

Despite Walsh's ever-present concern and care for his priests, things did not always go smoothly. The majority were well-adjusted and served their people well, but there were some problems. Walsh had to deal with alcoholic priests, priests guilty of fiscal mismanagement or sexual scandals, and priests who were simply disruptive in one way or another. Often personal situations needed to be examined, since at the root of these problems were priests who were generally unhappy.

Much attention had to be given to intemperance in the use of alco-hol. Having come from Ireland, Walsh knew well about the problems associated with over-indulgence, especially among priests from his own country, where it was described merely as "the failing," which label, in practice, tended to justify alcoholic abuse. Many church-affiliated and non-affiliated groups sprang up in the nineteenth century to con-front over-indulgence. Although the consumption of alcohol was strict-ly forbidden in most Protestant churches, it was not so with Catholics. Walsh, however, was determined to address this problem: "Both as bishop of London and as archbishop of Toronto, John Walsh required of all children he confirmed a pledge of abstinence until the age of majority."[68]

As well, it was not uncommon for the bishop to invite a speaker to address the problem of alcohol abuse, and to urge temperance on his listeners.[69] For Walsh, the problem became more serious once such abuse by priests led to ill or devastating effects on parochial life. He had little tolerance for such behaviour. Within four months of arriving in London, he had suspended six priests for alcohol abuse, and expressed his fear that another was not far from suspension. He wrote to the archbishop of Quebec of his deep concern:

All these priests gave awful scandal by their public drunkness
[sic] and one by drunkness [sic] and immorality. There are at
present here two large missions without resident clergymen and
I have no priest to send them but it is far better to leave them
as they are than to send them scandalous clergymen. I believe

however that with the exception of one or two, all the priests who remain are good and virtuous men. One of the sad consequences of the scandals which have occurred here, is the suspicion and distrust with which many of the faithful regard the entire priesthood. But I trust with the help of God these sad feelings will gradually pass away.[70]

One such errant priest with whom Walsh had to deal was John Coffey. He was ordained 19 December 1875 by Walsh, and his problems with alcohol seem to have started soon afterwards. There are no records of appointments for Coffey, but for some of the time after ordination he was living at the cathedral. Somewhere in that period, he went to Ottawa for a time to recuperate. At one point, in 1881, while he was living at Almonte in the Ottawa diocese, Coffey was recalled to London under a command of obedience from Walsh.[71] When he returned, however, it seemed that his problem with alcohol was not under control. Thus, writing to the bishop of Ottawa, Joseph-Thomas Duhamel, Walsh attempted to get Coffey a permanent placement in Ottawa so that he could remain close to his family. Walsh called upon "His Lordship's charity and kindness" in asking for this posting, telling him that Coffey had "many excellent and estimable qualities, his moral character as regards purity is above suspicion," but that he had "a failing" with alcohol. Walsh felt that an assignment for Coffey near his parents, relatives, and life-long friends – and with a good pastor – would greatly benefit him.[72] When no appointment was given in Ottawa, Coffey was named the editor of the *Catholic Record* from 1883 to 1887. Walsh's hopes for Coffey's reform seemed never to materialize.[73]

Typically, full of care and concern, Walsh sought to give such priests as Coffey a fresh start if they wished, tried to find a supportive environment for them, and allowed them the freedom to move in and out of the diocese as necessary. His compassion for them, however, was not unlimited; offending priests would be suspended if they did not eventually reform. Yet, even though suspended, they received financial support from the diocese, and in that way Walsh still expressed his hope that they would change their lives. In this manner he dealt with William Dillon, the pastor of LaSalette and Tillsonburg. In February 1889, Dillion was suspended, deprived of his faculties, and deposed of his pastoral charge. At the same time, though, Walsh allowed for the possibility of his returning to ministry if he repented and amended his life.[74]

Another troubled priest was Nicholas Gahan, who had been ordained by Walsh in 1869, and who had worked in the diocese twelve years before his problems with alcohol led to his suspension and the removal of his priestly faculties. Nonetheless, Walsh offered him financial support, provided he amended his life and lived with a good priest approved by Walsh or the vicar general.[75] Gahan did not abide by these conditions. He was later excommunicated. Eventually, he moved to the diocese of Peterborough, seeking assistance from its vicar general, Pierre Dominique Laurent, who had expressed a willingness to help him "out of the abyss into which he plunged himself." With forceful language, Walsh responded to Laurent's offer:

> This man has been sinning most grievously for years and ruining the souls of those committed to his pastoral care. I could never have believed, until his case was made known to me, that a priest could be so [illegible]. Since his suspension, now more than six years ago, he remained in the midst of his former mission and in sight [of the parish] – without having ever made any effort to reconcile himself to God whom he so grievously offended and to the Church whose sacred cause he so outrageously betrayed!! It was proved by a crowd of witnesses and by irresistible evidence that he was in the habit of absolving "complices in peccato turpi" and in soliciting penitents "ad turpia."[76]

Walsh went on to explain to Laurent that, under such circumstances, he was convinced that it was contrary to the rules of Christian prudence, and to the mind and the spirit of the Church "and to the usual course adopted by holy Bishops and advised by holy Confessors and Directors of souls to relieve this poor priest of the ecclesiastical censures and penalties which he has incurred so soon after he has made his first step towards repentance and amendment of life.[77]

Sometimes it may have seemed that, where scandal was involved and harm to religion was caused, Walsh showed little compassion. Yet that was not so. In every one of those situations, with Coffey, Dillon, Gahan, and others, he was willing to make concessions, but he always laid down conditions for the priests to meet. In time, when those were met, as was the case with Gahan, Walsh would absolve the priests from their suspension and excommunication.[78]

Though it may have seemed less serious, fiscal mismanagement by priests still grieved Walsh. Often he would have to write a letter to a priest asking for a clear financial accounting, or reminding him of his obligation to pay his dues to the diocese, or to render the *cathedraticum*. In May 1880, he sharply called to task Henry Japes, the pastor of LaSalette, for that reason:

You are one of the few who neglect this [financial] duty in this
respect. I hardly need say that this is very wrong and very unjust
towards me. Local improvements are no reason why pastors
should fail to do their duty in this respect ...

If every priest of the diocese would consider himself free
to set this law [of paying the *cathedraticum*] at defiance as you
have done thus far, what would have become of the law and the
authority of the bishops? It seems to me that your conscience and
the obedience which you owe to your Bishop ought to be sufficient to induce you to do your plain simple duty in this respect.[79]

By September of that same year, when Japes had still failed to render
his financial account to the bishop, he was summoned to see Walsh in
London. Within days, however, and not having gone to London, Japes
wrote to the bishop of Detroit, Casper H. Borgess, begging for a pastoral assignment. Japes claimed in his letter that he had Walsh's consent to move once he had given a financial accounting for the parish.
Borgess agreed to take Japes, he assured Walsh, providing "there
[was] nothing crooked in his case."[80] Once again, Walsh was willing to
allow the offending priest a new beginning, but not without alerting
the next bishop to potential problems. Japes was replaced in LaSalette
and there is no further record of him in the diocese.

Sometimes the heartache of the bishop over financial mismanagement was compounded by legal action taken by third parties against
priests. In one case, for instance, the priest Patrick Corcoran was
charged with land-speculation, and with cheating a businessman
named Peter Mitchell in the process. Corcoran was cleared in court
of the charges of cheating Mitchell, but he was guilty of much wrong-
doing in the eyes of Walsh. In an 1881 letter, he made it clear to
Corcoran that *negotiatis clericorum*, the buying and selling of property
by clerics, was, in his mind, a mortal sin for which a priest should
incur suspension and even excommunication. Walsh was also annoyed
by the way Corcoran had lied to him:

I ask you, after this, what confidence can a Bishop have in you
and what reliance can he repose in your veracity and in your
trustworthiness as a pastor of souls? ...

I write these things more in sorrow than in anger because I
had once hoped better things from you and because it is still my
earnest wish that you would make up your mind to live and act
as a good zealous priest and would cease meddling with worldly

transactions that can bring nothing but trouble and dishonour to you as a priest and can be of very little avail to the eternal interests of your soul.[81]

One of the more colourful characters to trouble Walsh was Richard Beausang, a native of Ross, County Cork, Ireland. He was the pastor of Sarnia, but was removed from that assignment in February 1874 as a result of gross fiscal mismanagement and pastoral failure. In one letter, Walsh referred to "scandalous rumours ... so well authenticated that [he could] no longer remain silent or inactive in regard to them."[82] Beausang had had permission from the bishop to buy a building for a school, which he had purchased with diocesan funds, but failed to register it as property of the Episcopal Corporation. Rather, he had registered it as his own. He then rented out the top floors, keeping the money for unknown uses, and consigned the children to the basement for their classes. The parents quickly objected, and asked for the intervention of some local doctors, who declared the basement unfit for children. After repeated pleas went unheard, the parents withdrew their children from the school, and Beausang in turn refused the sacraments to the parents.[83]

Beausang, consequently, was appointed to Ashfield and its mission of Wawanosh, and Bartholomew Boubat was assigned in his place to Sarnia. When asked by the bishop to report on the finances of the parish, Boubat admitted that Beausang had kept the accounts in "an irregular and confused manner," but believed that he had not intended to defraud the parish. Boubat also pointed out that Beausang was held in high esteem by the clergy and the laity in Sarnia. The move to Ashfield may have given Beausang a fresh start, but, unfortunately, it was only a fresh start at more "irregular and confused" accounting. He also stole the horse and buggy from the mission of Wawanosh. Walsh wrote to him and demanded that he return them to John O'Connor, the new pastor responsible for that mission.[84] It did not end there.

Beausang's next scheme, in early 1880, with the mission of Kingsbridge by then added to his pastoral charge, was to "augment" the pastoral dues, by which means he hoped to raise his personal revenue. Walsh informed him in May of that year that he was not authorized to do so, and that they would discuss it *vive voce* at the annual retreat. The bishop later asked, in September, for a complete accounting of the parochial finances in writing and, after receiving it, informed Beausang that he was forbidden to add a new tax to the parishioners, since his own books showed there were sufficient funds to support him:

You state there are about one hundred and fifty families in your mission. This number of families paying annually, at the rate of four dollars per family, would pay six hundred dollars per annum or thereabouts. The Christmas and Easter offerings amount, according to your own returns, to one hundred and twenty-five dollars. Your pew rents amount at least to forty-five dollars. Now this sum is, in my opinion, more than amply sufficient for your decent support especially when we take into consideration the fact that you have a presbytery rent free and eight acres [3.2 hectares] of excellent land that can be utilized for your sustenance.[85]

Paying no attention to the bishop's instructions, Beausang began to harangue his parishioners by demanding more money from them in the collection, since he was forbidden by the bishop to raise the pastoral dues. In an April 1881 letter marked "Private and Confidential" to a J.T. Egan of Kingsbridge, Walsh responded to Egan's charge that "Father Beausang is accustomed to indulge in violence and extravagance of language even in his addresses from the holy altar." The bishop assured Egan of his right – even his obligation – to speak up regarding such improper conduct by a priest, and asked that he get signatures of aggrieved persons and present those to him.[86] Matters had taken a turn for the worse by June of the next year; at that time, Walsh, in the strongest terms possible, declared certain unspecified acts of Beausang "null and void and illicit": "I consider it my duty to declare to you, as I do by these presents, that any acts done by you in violation of diocesan law in defiance of your Bishop's authority are null and void and illicit, and that I will hold you strictly responsible for them. On the occasion of my visitation to Ashfield Mission I intend, with God's blessing, to do justice to you and justice also to that portion of my flock intrusted [sic] to your temporary charge."[87] The bishop added that he would entertain no more correspondence on the matter.

Nothing changed, for fourteen months later, in August 1883, while still in Kingsbridge, Beausang informed the bishop that he was too sick to participate in the annual diocesan retreat. Walsh immediately wrote to say he regretted hearing this news about Beausang's poor health, and that he feared Beausang would no longer be able to discharge his pastoral duties. He also pointed out that Beausang had failed to pay his dues to the diocese. In fact, the *cathedraticum* had not been paid for six years, since 1877, nor had he paid anything toward the cathedral, nor dispensation money, nor even the $40 for the fund to support the infirm priests. He was the only priest, Walsh emphasized, who failed to pay his dues, and he had until 22 December next to come to some sort of satisfactory agreement with the bishop or lose his faculties as pastor of Ashfield.[88] Walsh had to iterate this demand in a later letter, but with even more forceful language:

> I cannot tolerate the scandalous state of things any longer ... You may rest assured that no subterfuges and no [effic]acious claims on me for a special and exceptional legislature in your favour will save you this time from the consequences of your habitual violation of ecclesiastical law on the Episcopal rights in the matter of my cathedraticum authorized and regulated by the Holy See and sanctioned by Diocesan and Provincial law ... What I want from you is obedient and loyal action and not empty words quae ad rem non pertinent [which are not pertinent to the matter] ... In conclusion let me indulge in the hope that you will consult your own true interests in this business and that you will spare me the performance of an unpleasant although necessary duty.[89]

The bishop's firm demand for payment still fell on deaf ears. He was forced to reiterate his demands in yet a third letter, dated 7 December 1883, which was personally delivered by the chancellor, Michael Tiernan, who also carried a fourth letter that day. In that, Beausang was informed that Tiernan, by special faculties granted him by Walsh, was taking control of the parish for a week. He was to take up a collection for the cathedral, officiate at Mass, preach, hear confessions, and carry out "other duties of ministry proper to a priest." He was also to examine the financial accounts of the mission and report about them to the bishop. For his part, Beausang was to repair to Ashfield for the week. After reviewing the parochial records, and recognizing the parish's financial limitations, Walsh wrote to Beausang later that month in a characteristically generous gesture, telling him that he had forgiven the *cathedraticum* and that he could continue his duties as pastor "usque ad revocationem et salve meo jure [right up to the revocation taking into account my right]." The bishop expressed surprise at the parish's limited finances, and promised to review matters again when he would visit there personally. In anticipation, Beausang was to prepare the children of the parish for the sacrament of Confirmation.[90]

Later that month Beausang found another method for "irregular and confused" accounting when he claimed personal ownership of a legacy left to the pastor of the parish. A parishioner, in his last will and testament, had expressed his desire that the money be spent by the pastor for "pious uses." In fact, instead of adhering to those instructions, Beausang was planning to leave the diocese and take the money with him. Walsh wrote to a barrister for legal advice, querying whether he could force the pastor in question to spend the money for "pious uses" before leaving, or if the pastor was within his rights to take the money. Walsh followed up with a letter to the prefect of Propaganda Fide, Giovanni Cardinal Simeoni.[91]

In the end, advice from neither counsellor was necessary. Beausang decided not to leave the diocese. Instead, the following July he tendered his resignation to Walsh, who accepted it immediately. By virtue of Walsh's letter of 20 July 1884, Beausang's appointment to the mission and his priestly faculties were withdrawn. Walsh also informed him that he would receive the pension for infirm priests, $300 *per annum*, beginning the day he handed over the parish to his successor. Yet this still did not settle the matter. Beausang's final attempt to exert his control in the parish was to make a declaration, sometime in August or early September, that his health had improved. In return, Walsh wrote in September to express gladness at this news, but insisted that Beausang vacate the presbytery immediately so that the current pastor could take possession of it. The bishop also advised a move to Sarnia or Goderich "before the bad weather [set] in, where [he would] receive better attention and better medical treatment than [he could] in Ashfield."[92]

Ever kind but also ever vigilant, John Walsh wanted to balance the needs of individual priests, especially those troubled by physical or moral weaknesses, with the needs of parishioners, the diocese, and the Church. Always, such problems called for great wisdom, prudence, patience, compassion, and strength of character, which he showed in abundance when making difficult decisions that affected the lives of many.

After Pinsoneault's impetuous treatment of the Jesuits at Assumption parish and college in Sandwich, it was not surprising that they had left the diocese, with the exception of those few who remained at St Joseph's parish in Chatham. When Walsh decided to move the seat of the diocese back to London, he tried to have the Jesuits return to Assumption. Originally, they seemed in favour, as indicated in a letter from Charles-François Baillargeon of Quebec. Stating that God had blessed Walsh's enterprises, the archbishop assured him that he had the favour of Peter Jan Beckx, superior general of the Jesuits, but their low numbers and commitments elsewhere led to a negative answer.[93] The Jesuits eventually left Chatham, thus completely withdrawing from the diocese in 1874, after over one hundred years of service in the southwestern peninsula of Ontario.[94]

In light of that, Walsh appealed to the Basilian Fathers to take charge of the parish and college in Sandwich. After he began negotiations with their superior general, Jean-Mathieu Soulerin, two Basilian priests, Denis O'Connor and Charles Vincent, visited there. Soulerin himself later visited in July 1868, and as a result, he signed an agreement with Walsh on 27 September 1869, enabling the community to take control the following year of the parish, the college, and the eight acres of land on which they stood. O'Connor was credited with negotiating the agreement, which was recognized as successful in reconciling the views of the bishop of London and the superior general in France.[95] The Basilians would not disappoint either their superior general or the bishop. They soon began serving missions outside of Sandwich, including Dresden, Wallaceburg, Blenheim, and Raleigh. When the Jesuits could no longer continue at St Joseph's parish in Chatham, the Basilians also took charge there, and served there for four years, from 1874 to 1878. From Chatham, the Basilians would also accept responsibility for the parish of St John the Baptist in Amherstburg.[96]

On 20 January, the same day the Basilians left St Joseph's, a group of four Franciscan Friars took charge of Chatham's parish under the leadership of Eugene Butterman, OFM, who remained as pastor for a time. He was replaced by William Gausepohl, OFM, who continued there throughout the remainder of Walsh's episcopacy in London. The Franciscan Friars had come from Cincinnati, Ohio, originally to serve the German-speaking population that had settled in Kent County, and had then overseen the construction of the new church in Chatham in 1887. The previous year, the provincial superior of the Franciscans, Jerome Kilgenstein, OFM, had written to Walsh questioning how long the Friars would be allowed to stay in Chatham; a new friary was required and he needed to make long-term plans. In reply, Walsh assured Kilgenstein that the Friars could continue in Chatham as long as he lived. There was, however, one consideration: "[I]n a new country like this, with the prospect of great developments before it, I would not feel justified in tying the hands of my successors and depriving them of freedom of action in a matter of such importance."[97] Being a man of broad vision, and having learned from his experience on arrival in the diocese, Walsh would not make a decision that could have difficult repercussions for his successors. By then, he also had hints of a possible move to another diocese. In the same letter, though, he gave the Friars permission to proceed with their building plans, and to hold a bazaar to raise money for the building. However, Kilgenstein's request in an earlier letter to make an appeal for funds – the kind "published in some American papers" – was denied.[98]

Unlike the male Religious orders, most of the women Religious from the years of Pinsoneault had remained in the diocese, however troubled their relations with the first bishop may have been. Right from the very beginning of Walsh's episcopate, and mindful of the great service rendered by women Religious to education, health care, and spiritual growth in the diocese, Walsh paid close attention to their welfare and work.

The Madams of the Sacred Heart were among those who had remained. Though they had been abruptly forced by Pinsoneault in 1857 to relocate from Sandwich to London, they re-established themselves in a vacated convent there. Four years later, they opened their new convent and a new school, Mount Hope. They acquired more property to expand, and then built a completely new school, now called the Academy of the Sacred Heart, on the property in 1886.[99] Eventually, by 1888, due to a decrease in the number of students, the Madams of the Sacred Heart decided to leave the diocese. Greatly concerned at losing such an important institution and the contribution of the Sisters, yet having failed to persuade them to remain, Walsh obtained a rescript from the Holy See to keep them in London. Thus the Sacred Heart Madams remained, but the school was not overly prosperous.[100]

Meantime, in nearby Chatham, the work of the Order of St Ursula was continuing to prosper and increase from the days of Pinsoneault. As a result, during Walsh's time, the Ursulines became an important educational presence. They enjoyed a good rapport with him, turning to him for wise counsel and direction throughout the years, while he was appreciative of their contribution to the spiritual life of his diocese. Right from the beginning of his episcopate, he encouraged the building of their new convent and school at Chatham. In 1868 a contract for a new building, costing $18,000, was signed and the foundation was dug. Charles Conilleau, SJ, the pastor of St Joseph's parish there, tried to stop the construction, fearing the escalating expenses.[101] The Sisters ignored him, knowing that Walsh supported them, and continued construction.

Despite his personal opposition, Conilleau authorized a collection in the parish for the new building, and on 13 May 1870, though the building was not yet completed, fourteen Sisters and twenty-one boarders moved into their new quarters. The local townspeople came with horses and wagons to assist with their move.[102] The Ursulines' motherhouse was finished in 1872, though the grounds were left untended. The people of Chatham and the surrounding rural area again responded generously by landscaping the grounds. Among the variety of trees planted, pine trees dominated, from which the motherhouse and school took their name, "The Pines." Five years later, on 16 November 1877, Walsh blessed the completed monastery, the school, and a new cemetery.

The Sisters often relied on Walsh's counsel, especially in practical matters. In 1871, he was asked to intervene regarding a Sister who wished to leave the Order and be released from her vows. He wrote to Elzéar-Alexandre Taschereau, the archbishop of Quebec, for canonical advice and clarification of the process, then made the necessary ruling for the Ursulines.[103] When the matter was raised again in 1883, regarding another Sister, Dean Wagner wrote to Propaganda Fide on the bishop's behalf and in his own role as spiritual director of that community.[104]

The Ursulines also asked Walsh for assistance in choosing a competent mistress of novices. He again wrote to Taschereau, praising the Sisters for their accomplishments in Chatham, and asking that the Ursulines in Quebec city send an able Sister.[105] Taschereau replied within a week that the superior general, Mère Saint-Georges, agreed to send a mistress, but asked for time to make the best selection.[106] In the end, no one from Quebec city was appointed. Two years later, Mother Xavier Le Bihan, OSU, signalled her intention to the bishop to give up the role of superior; he consented provided that she at least accept the office of mistress of novices.[107]

The motherhouse continued to be augmented as time passed, with property, cloister gates, recreation rooms, sleeping quarters, and a wing for a music hall including an auditorium and music rooms. An interesting letter from Walsh to the superior in 1886, Mother Baptist O'Grady, OSU, showed his practical concern as well as his personal interest in their welfare. When presented with the architect's plans for the new academy, Walsh insisted that they install two fire escapes because of the size of their convent, "as they should be attached to every College and Academy."[108] Later that autumn, further demonstrating the excellent rapport between the Ursulines and the bishop, Mother Baptist sent a barrel of apples to him in London as a gift, and he wrote to thank her.[109]

The bishop paid a great deal of attention to this growing Order by encouraging them as much as he could, through his frequent presence at their "Annual Exhibition," a custom Mother Xavier inaugurated based on an American model. The "Annual Exhibition" was the closing exercise each school year, when graduates were crowned and received medals, diplomas, and prizes for academic excellence and for other competitions which had been held throughout the year. The event always included musical presentations and literary recitations, since Mother Xavier realized that if the parents did not see what the pupils could do, the school would lose its popularity.[110] Walsh happily accepted that it was his duty to be present and to confer the honours upon the graduates. Indeed, his presence, seen as a "usual" thing, was so taken for granted that he had to write to the Sisters to excuse himself whenever he needed to be absent.[111]

One of his final acts for the Ursulines before he moved to Toronto was to approve their new rule for Religious observances. In granting his approval, Walsh recognized their capability and the suitability of their rewriting their own rule, and to that end, he also offered his encouragement: "The rules are of course all there, only changed a little as to the time of their observance. I hope all will observe them ... and will not allow the modifications aforesaid to result in any laxity as to their observance or in any tepidity in the religious spirit of the Community. This would be a result deplorable beyond expression."[112]

Such was the affection and concern they had for each other, it was hardly surprising, then, that when Walsh was named to the see of Toronto, the Ursuline Sisters had their own private farewell for him at the Pines. Their address at the time to the archbishop-elect pointed out to him that "sorrow mingles with our joy today, when we remember that Your Grace's promotion in the Master's vineyard calls from our midst a devoted prelate and a kind father."[113] The warmth of their personal relations over the years was reflected to the end.

Of course, those were not the only women Religious orders who enjoyed close relations and collaboration with Walsh. The Sisters of the Holy Names of Jesus and Mary, who had also come to the diocese during the time of Pinsoneault, were likewise warmly supported by Walsh in their efforts to build up and serve the various educational needs of young people in Essex and Lambton counties. This was especially important for young girls from poor families, who had to rely on the generosity of the Holy Names Sisters, who operated "select" and free schools at Amherstburg and Sarnia as well as St Mary's Academy in Windsor, which had opened in 1865.[114]

It was, however, the academy in Amherstburg which would cause some friction between Walsh and the Sisters. He refused approval to expand their convent there. Ever vigilant about fiscal responsibility, he was uneasy that the cost of such an expansion might revert to the diocese. In addition, the Sisters had asked to have an annual bazaar to augment their income. That, too, was refused. Walsh knew that the people of the parish of St John the Baptist there were already taxed for the building of the new cathedral. A bazaar, he felt, would conflict with the cathedral's tax and would "serve to irritate and discontent the congregation at what would be considered too heavy a tax for religious purposes not directly connected with parish interests."[115] He was also somewhat angry that the Sisters had added a boarding school there without his approval.

In the end, consistent with his usual manner of governing, Walsh did not entirely prevent their project. Instead, he insisted that the Sisters could enlarge their convent only at their own expense. He added, however, that if perchance they were to leave the diocese, he would reimburse them for the amount they spent, providing they sought his approval on the cost of the construction before any further expenditure of funds. At any rate, and despite the occasional point of disagreement between them, the Holy Names Sisters continued to express their deep affection and admiration for their bishop. These were always reciprocated.[116]

The Sisters of Loretto, also known as the Ladies of Loretto, or the members of the Institute of the Blessed Virgin Mary as they were more formally named, were not so fortunate as the Ursulines or Holy Names Sisters had been; they were the first congregation dismissed by Pinsoneault after his arrival in the diocese. It was not until 1878 that they returned, at the invitation of Edmund Kilroy, DD, pastor of St Joseph's parish in Stratford. Walsh was very happy to endorse Kilroy's request, as he himself had been a spiritual director for one of their convents in Toronto. Later, Walsh gave permission for the Sisters to teach in the parochial school at Stratford. A small group under the leadership of Mother Evangelista O'Sullivan, IBVM, came to the diocese at the direction of Mother Teresa Dease, IBVM, the founder of the Institute in Canada. By 1881, their convent became too small to accommodate them and their students, so two wings were added, one for a chapel, the other for a boarding school. The Sisters continued working in the Stratford area throughout Walsh's years in London.[117]

Like the Sisters of Loretto, the Sisters of St Joseph had also been expelled by Pinsoneault, but were invited back to the diocese by Walsh. Originally the Sisters had made their home in Amherstburg from 1853, prior to the establishment of the diocese, when they were first invited to teach there, until 1857 when they left. They had also, at that time, been invited by the pastor of Chatham, Jean Jaffré, SJ, to open a hospital there. All came to nought in Amherstburg and in Chatham, however, and the Sisters returned to Toronto when Pinsoneault dismissed them from Amherstburg to make way for the Grey Nuns from Montreal.

Shortly after his installation as bishop of London, Walsh invited the Sisters to return to the diocese. He specifically asked that they take responsibility for St Peter's school in London and that they establish an orphanage in the city. When there was opposition among some Catholics, especially among the lay teachers who feared they would be displaced, the vicar general, Bruyère, intervened on the bishop's behalf, and forcefully quieted any opposition with the threat of excommunication. Five Sisters arrived on 11 December 1868 under the leadership of Mother Theresa Brennan, CSJ. They immediately took charge of the school and, on 2 October 1869, opened Mount Hope orphanage in the former Sacred Heart convent, earlier vacated by the Sisters of the Sacred Heart and purchased by Walsh from J.C. Meredith. Seventeen orphans were admitted that day, fifteen of whom were transferred from the House of Providence in Toronto since they had been born in the diocese of London.[118]

Within two years of the Sisters' return to London, Walsh wanted them to establish themselves in the diocese independent from Toronto. Yet, unlike his predecessor, he first approached his colleague in Toronto, Lynch, to obtain his permission for the severance of the Community. Lynch willingly consented. In his letter to establish the new congregation in London, the archbishop cautioned the Sisters not to lose their fervour nor to fall into tepidity. He commended them to the care of Walsh: "In your doubts and difficulties, in your joys and successes, let your Bishop be to you after God, your guide, your councillor, your friend, as he is your spiritual father ... May our Blessed Lord, His Blessed Mother and St Joseph continue to bless and keep you."[119]

Walsh celebrated a Mass at Mount Hope orphanage on 18 December 1870, at which time he renewed the Sisters' vows and received their promise of obedience as a new congregation. At the time, he named Mother Ignatia Campbell, CSJ, the superior general. The novitiate was opened that day, and three postulants were admitted.[120] After that, Walsh sought legal incorporation for the Sisters through the assistance of Justice Hugh McMahon. By an act of the provincial Parliament, the congregation was declared to be "[a] body, politic and corporate under the name of the Sisters of St. Joseph, of the Diocese of London." Royal assent was given on 15 February 1871.[121]

Within six years of the Sisters' arrival, because the orphanage was no longer able to accommodate its needs, Walsh encouraged them to construct a larger building. On 20 June 1876, he blessed the ground and turned the first sod at the site. Later, in a handwritten note in the official record of the event, he invoked the Divine Providence: "May our most merciful and loving Saviour Who dearly loved the little children, and Who is the Father of the Orphans, bless and save for eternal life, all who will have any share in bringing this good work to a successful issue."[122] The next year, he dedicated the new orphanage on the feast of the Holy Rosary, 7 October 1877. It was a memorable event, not only for the Sisters, but for the city and the diocese itself, as the dignitaries for the occasion included the Right Honourable Sir John A. Macdonald, former prime minister of Canada; Colonel Walker and Major Leyes from the local regiment; Sir John Carling, a leading citizen of London, knighted by the Queen and a cabinet minister in Macdonald's second ministry; and Josiah Blackburn, first owner and publisher of the *London Free Press*.[123] The Sisters continued to expand their work and, during Walsh's years in London, established convents and schools in Goderich, St Thomas, and Ingersoll. As well, in 1888 they opened the first hospital in London, named in honour of St Joseph. It had the capacity for twenty-five patients, but its expansion was immediately planned so that many more patients might be accommodated.[124]

Unlike those women Religious who had their roots in the diocese from the time of Pinsoneault, one Religious congregation was personally invited by Walsh: the Sisters of the Religious Hospitallers of St Joseph, or the Hôtel-Dieu Sisters as they are often called. In 1887, at the instigation of Wagner, dean of Windsor, Walsh invited the Hôtel-Dieu Sisters to establish an orphanage for black children in Windsor. The first five Sisters from Montreal arrived there on 13 September 1888, and a week later, Walsh travelled to Wagner's parish of St Alphonsus, where he officiated at the ceremony of installation of the congregation as a community in the diocese of London. On that day, Mother Josephine Paquet, RHSJ, was confirmed as the superior general. This made the new community independent of their motherhouse in Montreal.[125]

Immediately work was also begun on their new hospital in Windsor, and Walsh blessed the cornerstone on 29 November 1888. To help meet the expenses for the project, the Sisters were dispensed from the rule of the cloister so they could solicit funds throughout Essex County. Though their resources were limited, they "could not shrink from the challenge posed by the bishop. It was clear that the sisters had in this bishop a sympathetic friend, supporter, and collaborator, someone who would serve their needs so that they might serve others in need." Walsh continued to interest himself in this project, though it was not completed before he transferred to Toronto the following year.[126]

Meanwhile, another congregation that found a friend in Walsh, though from a distance, were the Precious Blood Sisters. Louis-Zéphirin Moreau, bishop of Saint-Hyacinthe, had supported their establishment as a new congregation in his diocese in 1861. In a circular letter to the bishops of Trois-Rivières, Rimouski, Kingston, Peterborough, and London, and to the administrators of Toronto and Chicoutimi, Moreau asked assistance in seeking approbation for the institute from Pope Leo XIII. He emphasized in his letter that the Precious Blood Sisters had already existed for twenty-seven years: "I do not believe I am fooling myself, by saying that this new Religious Institute, which is totally devoted to penance and prayer, is very useful for religion and for souls. God has made it prosper to such an extent in every respect that I do not doubt that it will please Him, and that it will be the source of great good for the Holy Church."[127] Like his episcopal colleagues, Walsh well knew the spiritual value of having such a cloistered community, devoted solely to prayer and to the ascetical life, in a diocese. He was happy, therefore, to petition the Holy See for their cause, and sent an appropriate document to Moreau which was forwarded with his request.[128]

Later the next year, when the news of Walsh's appointment to Toronto was breaking in various quarters, the foundress of the Precious Blood Sisters, Mother Catherine-Aurélie Caouette, RPB, wrote to offer her congratulations. Walsh sent his thanks, and expressed the care he would have for them should he be sent to Toronto:

> Although I have as yet received no official intelligence of my appointment to the Metropolitan See of Toronto I cannot refrain from thanking you most sincerely for your very kind wishes and congratulations. Should it please God to send me to Toronto

I shall consider it a duty to be a father and a protector to your Community in that city as far as circumstances will allow, and I am sure your Sisters will, by their devotedness, their fervour, and their prayers be a source of encouragement and comfort to me.[129]

Official approbation for the congregation came several years later, and eventually, long after Walsh had departed London, they were established in that diocese as well.

The "father and friend" that John Walsh proved to be to his own diocesan priests, he was as well to the men's and women's congregations that laboured and increased in the diocese throughout the years of his London episcopate. That good relationship highlighted for them the contrast between Walsh and his predecessor. While the Dominicans and Jesuits did leave during Walsh's time in London, it was with considerable regret, since they suffered from small numbers, rather than with relief, as under Pinsoneault. For over twenty years in London, Walsh actively encouraged priests and Religious in their work, supported their endeavours, and frequently sought to increase their numbers throughout the diocese.

"Friend," "protector," "advisor," "beloved," "illustrious" – all these, and more, were words used by so many people to describe him. Indeed, the word most often used, by those who came to know and love him, was "father." Priests, Religious, and laity alike saw in him a kind father who truly cared for their spiritual needs. It was universally felt that he was close to all and available to all. Certainly, in his work of establishing parishes and missions, building churches and hospitals, encouraging Religious congregations, and the like, better than anyone else, he knew that as bishop he could not care for the diocese alone. He had been commissioned by the Church to lead the diocese, and he proved himself to be a most able spiritual leader.

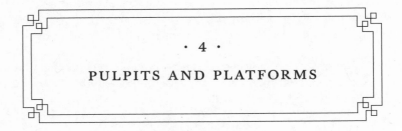

[The apostles and their successors'] teaching is divinely guaranteed; they
rule the Church with the authority of Christ, and through them the voice
of God is heard by the faithful of today, even as it was 1,800 years ago,
proclaiming to the world, in unerring accents, the truths of eternal life.

BISHOP JOHN WALSH, 13 MARCH 1887

ONE OF A BISHOP'S MAJOR ROLES IS THAT OF A TEACHER OF THE
Catholic faith. Bishops are the voices of Christ the Teacher, and therefore the interpreters of the Church's Magisterium in each locale.[1] John
Walsh, always a diligent student, was well prepared for this role both
in his priestly ministry and, later, as a bishop. He excelled as a great
orator and teacher in his many sermons and speeches. He was also a
renowned theologian, as manifested in his several pastoral letters, and
he played an essential part in fostering Catholic education in the diocese of London, and in vigorously promoting it throughout the province of Ontario.

For Walsh, being an orator was of utmost importance. In fact, from
the time he became a priest, he was perceived as a convincing teacher,
edifying his hearers and leading them to better understand the Catholic Church. His early studies in Ireland and then in Montreal, as well
as his continuing personal studies, developed in him a type of scholarship and a way of thinking considered to be "in the classical tradition":
"He was very fond of using brief Latin quotations. He would quote
from Pliny, Seneca and others of the Roman writers, and spoke much
of the Empire in the course of his sermons and lectures. Evidently he
was a deep student of Roman history and perhaps this was the out-

standing feature of his scholarship. But we must not forget his patristic and theological lore, so be-mindful of the Fathers and Billuart and Ligouri and Perrone and many others."[2]

It was for these reasons, along with his cheerful and outgoing disposition and his respect for his audience, which he always felt would understand and appreciate such classical learning and erudition, that Walsh was often sought after to preach or to speak on special occasions; this was also why, when speaking in his own diocese, he held audiences or congregations with rapt attention. Always they listened enthusiastically to him the many times he was called upon to travel throughout Canada and even to the United States, to speak at a memorable event such as the dedication of a new church or the blessing of a cornerstone. He was invited to Guelph in 1876 and again in 1888; to Charlottetown in 1879; to Far Rockaway in the diocese of Brooklyn, New York, in 1885; and to his old parish of St Paul in Toronto in 1887.[3]

The blessing of the famous Church of Our Lady Immaculate, in Guelph in 1888, was one such event. This building was designed by Joseph Connolly, noted architect of the time, under the direction of the Jesuits, who served the parish. The church, a magnificent example of neo-Gothic architecture, popular in Ontario in the mid-nineteenth century, was at the time the largest building in English-speaking Canada. In 1876, Walsh had been invited by the Jesuits to preach at the laying of its cornerstone; now, he was back to celebrate the church's completion eleven years later on 10 October 1888.

Walsh's sermon for that dedication was particularly noteworthy. It typified his style of weaving a tapestry of scriptural and liturgical images with history, in the most eloquent language. He first compared the sacrifice of the Mass with the sacrifices of the Old Testament, showing humanity's longing to "reach" God, something now made possible through the Mass and the sacraments:

> We are not surprised to find men in every age exhibiting the need they feel of reaching their Creator, and, as it were, of localizing God ... To satisfy this craving of the soul, God has more than once come down, marking spots made forever glorious by His actual presence ... God is here by His Eucharistic Presence. Here is His mercy seat. Here is offered to appease the wrath of an offended God that the most precious blood overflowed the world and cleansed it of its impurities ... It is to this august sacrifice that in a Catholic church the architect's every thought is directed ... Here, through the agency of a living priesthood, all saving

doctrine is taught and the sacraments administered for the sanctification of souls.[4]

Following this, he spoke of the need for architects to design churches as the places, or temples, where prayer is offered up: "A Catholic church is really a constant prayer and a perpetual act of worship to the living God. Priests and people may perish, and the Bishop who speaks to you may be gathered to his fathers, but this magnificent temple, raised by your piety and your zeal for God's honor, shall stand for ages a monument of your divine faith, and shall draw down untold blessings on this city and this parish." Touching on his own mortality and that of the bishops who had been present for the laying of the cornerstone, he went on to remind his congregation of the transitory nature of life and of the need for a proper disposition of the human heart:

> When I preached eleven years ago at the ceremony of blessing
> the corner-stone of this church there were present His Excellency
> Bishop Conroy, the Legate of His Holiness; Archbishop Lynch
> of Toronto, Bishop Crinnon of Hamilton, and Bishop Jamot of
> Peterborough. These venerable and saintly Prelates have since
> all passed away and are gone to their reward. So we too, beloved
> brethren, shall soon experience how passing and transitory are
> the honors and joys of this world, and how necessary it is that
> our treasures be laid up where thieves may not break into and the
> worm may not consume. For the true temple, dear brethren, is
> the human heart, where God loves to dwell by His saving grace,
> where alone He can be adored in spirit and in truth. Without this
> veritable worship of the heart all else is of no account.[5]

Other grand occasions which he graced with his preaching included the fiftieth anniversary of the presbyteral ordination of Patrick Dowd, ss, on 26 May 1887 in Montreal. A well-known social activist in Montreal who had established orphanages and homes for the poor, Dowd had preached at Walsh's own consecration. Walsh returned the favour twenty years later for Dowd's jubilee. The bishop gave a stirring sermon at St Patrick's Church on priestly service, spiced with historical references and well-crafted phraseology, all reflecting his deep piety and love for the priesthood.[6]

The *Catholic Record* acknowledged Walsh's oratorical skills in particular on 16 May 1879 at the dedication of the new high altar at the church in Strathroy: "Taken as a whole, the instruction was one of the most eloquent and masterly productions of our beloved Bishop."[7] Similar praise, however overstated, likewise was given after Walsh dedicated the new church in Petrolia: "After Mass, His Lordship Bishop Walsh delivered what was considered by all who had the gratification of being present, one of the most powerful and interesting discourses ever heard in Ontario ... The address was listened to most attentively."[8]

Two years later, on 1 May 1889, Richard O'Connor invited Walsh to preach at his episcopal consecration in Peterborough. As he had done at so many previous events, Walsh articulated the role of bishops as praying and sanctifying, teaching and guiding, governing and ruling. In that sermon, he explained – as he would in many of his pastoral letters – the meaning of the apostolic succession in Christianity, in the florid language of his day:

> [T]his long, unbroken line of Popes and Bishops, who in each succeeding generation have stood up for right and virtue, who have lived for God's glory and man's salvation, who by their teachings and virtues have made a track of light through the centuries, who like watchful sentinels on the watch-towers of Zion, have challenged and condemned every form of religious error and faithfully guarded the citadel of divine truth, who preached the Gospel of Jesus Christ to the savage as well as the civilized races of man, illuminating their intellect with the light of faith, softening and Christianizing their hearts by the graces of prayer and sacraments, refining their manners by the gentleness and sweetness of charity, teaching them justice, mercy, charity, and peace.[9]

Walsh's oratorical skills were used not only on such official occasions but also to preach retreats. Casper Borgess, the bishop of Detroit and Walsh's close personal friend, invited him to preach the retreat for the priests of Detroit in 1876. Borgess made arrangements with the Basilians to hold the retreat at Assumption College in Sandwich, to take place during the students' vacation period. Undoubtedly, with his popularity as a speaker and his love for priests and the priesthood, Walsh received many similar requests over the years.[10] Besides sermons on special or memorable occasions, the bishop would often give lectures on topics of interest. It was not unusual, for instance, for him to give a series of lectures during the season of Lent at the cathedral in London. During Lent of 1887, Walsh focused on the articles of the Creed. Even the title of the article in the *Catholic Record*, "A Brilliant

and Masterly Lecture on the Catholic Rule of Faith" concerning his
lecture on the catholicity of the Church, revealed his popularity: "His
Lordship the Bishop of London lectured on 'the Catholic rule of faith'
in St. Peter's Cathedral on last Sunday evening [13 March]. The noble
church was crowded to the doors by an eager and attentive audience,
fully one third of which consisted of Protestant citizens. So great was
the hush of expectancy that a pin could have been heard to fall amid
the vast audience as His Lordship ascended the pulpit."[11] Not only
was the reaction of the audience remarkable, but so was the fact that
a third of the audience was Protestant, gathered to hear a Catholic
bishop lecture about the catholicity of the Church. That was a rarity
in nineteenth-century Canada. Not only was Walsh well ahead of his
time by attracting Protestants to hear a Catholic prelate, but they had
turned out because of his profound knowledge and very deep faith.

    As usual, Walsh began his lecture by reminding people what he had
taught them about the Bible in a previous lecture, "that it is the word
of God, that every line of it is inspired by the Holy Ghost and that it
is to be regarded with the greatest reverence." Contrary to what most
of his audience would have believed, he went on to remind them that
the Church encouraged their reading and meditating on the sacred
Scriptures, and thus to nourish their souls with "the divine truths and
heavenly doctrines therein contained, but ... with docile dispositions
in submission to the magisterial authority of the Church and under
the guidance of her teaching. The Bible is the book of the Church and
by right belongs to her."

    While these words would have been astounding for Protestants to
hear, believing as they did then that Catholics did not sufficiently
revere, read, and hear the Scriptures, his lecture would have been just
as astounding for the Catholics in the audience. In fact, what Walsh
was really presenting was the teaching of the First Vatican Council
(1869–70) in *Dei Filius,* a document which had been promulgated on
24 April 1870. His knowledge of conciliar documents, reflected in his
preaching and teaching, placed him at the forefront of contemporary
theological thinking.[12]

    The next part of the lecture, and really its focus, would also have
been a reflection of the council, specifically the doctrinal constitution
Pastor Aeternus, issued on 18 July 1870.[13] Based on those documents,
Walsh emphasized the role of the Church as the official teacher of
God's word. Jesus revealed the saving truths of the Christian religion
and founded the Church to be the "oracle of His truth, and the treas-

ure house of His graces forever." Walsh referred to the text of Matthew chapter 28, on the apostolic commission to teach and to baptize.[14]

At the risk of leaving his Protestant listeners feeling uncomfortable, the bishop continued his line of thought by indicating that Protestants would dispute what he had said. Yet, he insisted, undeniable proof was found in the text of Matthew's gospel, which stated that authority in the Church was given by God Himself: "From the moment the commission [to preach the gospel and to baptize] was issued, the ministry of apostles and their successors bears with it the seal of heaven. Their teaching is divinely guaranteed, they rule the Church with the authority of Christ, and through them the voice of God is heard by the faithful of today, even as it was 1,800 years ago, proclaiming to the world in unerring accents the truths of eternal life."[15] His conclusion was that no one could take only their personal interpretation of sacred Scripture as the norm for the Christian life, since Jesus had also sent the Holy Ghost to be the animating soul and indwelling life of the Church. Thus, Christians must listen to the pope as the successor of Peter and the head of the teaching body, the Church.[16]

It was not only for stirring Lenten lectures that people would turn out in such large numbers to hear Walsh speak; even other lectures, such as one on the evils of divorce, resulted in the cathedral being "well filled." So did a lecture on "The Philosophy of Ancient History in Relation to the Coming of Christ," for which, "[n]otwithstanding the tempestuous character of the weather, a crowded audience greeted His Lordship, amongst whom we noticed many of our most respectable and intelligent Protestant fellow-citizens."[17] That was always true for his lectures on religious and profane subjects alike.

As bishop, Walsh was also occupied with issues beyond theological and ecclesiastical matters, including such profane concerns as politics abroad, when he felt the effect on the people of his diocese. One topic he often addressed publicly, which was especially close to his heart, was Irish "Home Rule," a matter of considerable concern in Canada in the latter half of the nineteenth century. The basis of the movement for Ireland's growing independence from Great Britain was that it wished to be ruled not from the Parliament of Westminster, but rather from "home," in the Dail, its own Parliament. The Dail, however, would have become subservient to Westminster in the plans of certain proponents of variations on Home Rule, such as Isaac Butt. Clearly concerned about the debate, Walsh issued a pastoral letter in 1880 on Ireland's problems, in which he asked the priests of the diocese to take up a collection for the relief of the Irish people.[18] He himself had firsthand experience of the people's needs, growing up there and having returned to visit in later years. After one such visit, upon his return to London, Walsh gave an eloquent lecture in his cathedral on 8 October 1882, entitled "Ireland and the Irish," which summarized the sufferings of the Irish people during the centuries of English rule. He began by referring to his 1864 visit to Ireland, during which the cornerstone of the monument to Daniel O'Connell was laid. In describing the finished "masterpiece" he focused on the actual statue of O'Connell, clearly displaying his own sympathies:

> He stands there the embodiment of a crushed and enslaved people's cause, the fearless advocate of their rights, the emancipator of their conscience and their altars, and the prophet of their coming liberty, prosperity and happiness. He found Ireland a crouching and chained slave; he broke her chains, he lifted her up, he inspired her with the spirit of his own manhood and with the love of liberty, and he looked defiantly into the face of her oppressor, and shamed her into a partial justice.[19]

Three years later a meeting of Irish citizens was called in London to discuss the Irish problem on 9 November 1885, when Westminster debated Home Rule. Walsh could not attend. Nonetheless, because his position on the matter was considered important, the organizers still sought his advice. In a letter, he made it clear that he was entirely in sympathy with the purpose of the meeting, and believed it the duty of every Irishman in Canada to give "practical sympathy" to the Irish people working so hard to win back the right of self-government for their country. Three years earlier he had spoken on this matter, and now he reiterated his message: "I venture to think that Home Rule, such as we enjoy here in Canada, is what Ireland wants to make her a prosperous and contented country. Every free people ought to have the right to manage their own affairs, and to make the laws that govern them."[20]

Though Home Rule was defeated at Westminster the following year, Walsh continued to speak out on the question. On his return from his *ad limina* visit and the celebration of Pope Leo XIII's jubilee at the end of 1887, he wrote to Archbishop Lynch from Paris. He referred to the fear of the Irish that the Vatican would interfere in the Irish question in favour of England, and suggested that all the Canadian bishops must demonstrate clearly their support for the Irish people. Since many Catholic countries had supported the Catholics in Germany "suffering under the lash of Bismarck," so they could now campaign to help the Irish. He wanted the archbishop to initiate such a campaign, and wanted him also to urge James Cardinal Gibbons, archbishop of Baltimore, to do the same throughout the United States:

> English influence is at this moment forceful and active in Rome and Irish churchmen throughout the world should take steps to counteract it in the interests of our poor people and in the interests of Religion itself. I am sure if the movement were once well initiated by Your Grace in Canada, and by Cardinal Gibbons in the States, it would rapidly spread and would be taken up by Irish priests and Bishops throughout the world and would have the most beneficial effects in favour of our poor people.[21]

Walsh continued to support Irish Home Rule for his remaining years.

Walsh's intelligence and erudition were reflected in his speeches (both religious and profane), in his sermons, and in the many talks he gave on various occasions; not surprisingly, these qualities were also found in his pastoral letters. He wrote many letters. In fact, he seemed able to touch on every possible subject of the day: his personal devotional life and that of his people, the Blessed Virgin Mary, the commemoration of the dead, the season of Lent, devotion to the Sacred Heart of Jesus, and his personal allegiance to the Roman Pontiff. "Replete with Sacred Scripture, the holy fathers, the history and practice of the Church, [his pastoral letters] are pregnant with instruction upon the various subjects treated. Practical in their bearing, a spirit of earnest piety, so natural to their author, breathes from every page; and their language is that of a kind father teaching his children the most important lessons of life, and bidding them love God, the Sacred Heart, the Blessed Mother, the Church, the dead."[22]

Devotion to Our Lady was especially prominent in his letters. He took the opportunity, at the end of his 1876 *ad limina* visit, to make a visit to the shrine of Our Lady of Lourdes, in France. This was the site of the personal revelations of the Blessed Virgin as the Immaculate Conception, a dogma which had been proclaimed only four years before by Pope Pius IX. Walsh's visit to Lourdes was not only a personal pilgrimage; it was, as he expressed in his pastoral letter of November 1876, his sacred duty as bishop "to visit for [his] instruction and edification, and in order to supplicate our heavenly Mother to extend her special protection and favor to her children of the Diocese of London, and to obtain for them the graces and blessings they [stood] in need of in the all-important work of the salvation of their souls."[23]

In his letter, in order to help people understand the significance of an apparition of Our Lady in the Christian life, the bishop carefully outlined the procedure through which the Church gave official approval to such, and how after suitable inquiry, the Church authorized belief in such a case, but never obliged it. In the conclusion, he decreed four directives for priests to promote special devotion to the Blessed Mother with a view to placing his diocese under her protection: the celebration of a triduum prior to the feast of the Immaculate Conception on the next 8 December; the celebration of a public Mass on those three days at all the principal churches of the diocese; the hearing of Confessions throughout the days of the triduum; and special evening devotions in each church to include the Rosary and a sermon, and Benediction of the Blessed Sacrament, if they chose. Parishioners receiving worthily the sacraments of Penance and the Eucharist would receive a forty days' Indulgence.[24]

Another one of his pastoral letters on devotion to the Blessed Virgin Mary was published nine years later, on 25 April 1885. It too encouraged personal devotion to the Mother of God, and emphasized her role in intercessory prayer. At the same time, his letter was remarkable for two things in particular. Along with his usual quotations from the Scriptures and the Doctors of the Church, Walsh also quoted John Henry Cardinal Newman and the Protestant poet, Henry Wadsworth Longfellow. Of note too was Walsh's use of a beautiful image comparing the month of May to the Blessed Virgin, expressed in his own exquisite style and the fulsome literary style of his contemporaries, and especially of Newman:

> What the month of May is in the order of nature, that, in the mind of the Church, the Blessed Virgin is in the order of Grace. May is the Springtime of the year, the month of hope and promise, the harbinger of the bright Summer, the fairest and most beautiful queen of the year, decked out in all its fresh young beauty, and fragrant with blossoms and flowers ... The cold, stormy Winter is past, Nature has risen from its tomb, and has awakened into a new life. The voice of Spring is heard on the hills and in the valleys, and behold the fields are robed in bright-

est green, the trees bring forth leaves and blossoms, the gardens
are fragrant with flowers, the woods are vocal with the sweet
music of singing birds, the air is resonant with sounds of joy and
gladness, and all nature is clothed with a vesture of varied beauty
... [The Blessed Virgin is] the Springtime of that season ... and
the fairest flower in the garden of God.[25]

As formerly, he instructed his clergy to hold Marian devotions
throughout the month – every evening in the cities and at least twice
each week in the rural areas – for the edification of the people.

The commemoration of the faithful departed, a belief promoted
among Catholics of the day, received attention in a pastoral letter from
Walsh on that subject. In consecrating the month of November to the
holy souls, he reminded people that the teaching of the Church was
"in harmony with the lessons of decaying nature": "This advanced season of autumn with its gloom and sadness, with its weeping skies, and
moaning winds, its bare forests and withered leaves, speaks to us in
accents that reach the heart, and preaches a solemn sermon worthy of
the deepest consideration; and that sermon is on the subject of death,
and the certain ending of all mortal things. As God has revealed Himself to us in the order of grace, He has also revealed Himself to us in
the order of nature."[26] Walsh wrote poetically, even on topics which
might not lend themselves easily to such expression. Indeed, it was
hard for him not to do so, even when he was recommending that death
be the subject of his parishioners' frequent meditation, that they cultivate a devotion for prayers for the souls in Purgatory, and that they
pray especially the Rosary for the souls of the faithful departed.

Walsh also wrote several pastoral letters to the people of his diocese
during the season of Lent. The letter of 1881 was a meditation on the
life of Christ, which he concluded with five lessons drawn from the life
of the Lord. These were: loving the Lord Jesus Christ with one's whole
heart and soul; valuing the salvation of one's immortal soul above all
things and labouring each day for that salvation; embracing poverty,
toil, sorrows, and afflictions as coming from the hand of God and,
with humility and patience, being resigned to the will of God; being
charitable, tender, kind, and forgiving; and, finally, detesting and ab-
horring sin with all the energy of one's being.[27]

It was Walsh's hope that God, in his mercy, would grant to the
people of London the grace "to practise these salutary lessons and to
carry them out" in their daily lives, but especially during the holy season of Lent. In encouraging them to follow the usual Lenten practices

of prayer, fasting, and almsgiving, he emphasized a Lenten fast similar to that suggested by Isaiah chapter 58, that is, fasting from "all dishonesty, calumny and detraction; from immodest words and acts; from reading bad books and journals; from drunkenness and rioting; in fine, from every thought, word and action that would offend God and transgress his Divine law."[28]

In the conclusion the bishop reminded the people of their Easter duty, and encouraged them to receive worthily the sacraments of Penance and the Eucharist and to attend to daily family prayer, especially the Rosary. Priests were requested to hold public devotions in the churches, including the Rosary or the Way of the Cross, and to give appropriate instruction. Permission was given to have Benediction of the Blessed Sacrament as well. Finally, priests were reminded to visit their people during the season of Lent, "especially the lukewarm and the sinful, with the view of inducing them to give up the evil of their ways and return to God and the observance of their religious duties."[29]

Walsh aimed to stir the consciences of many. Truly he hoped for spiritual growth in his diocese; he gave attention to the ways of the Christian life that could assist this growth, such as the worthy reception of the sacraments of Penance and of the Eucharist, and the daily recitation of the Rosary. In his role as teacher, too, he tried to lead people to know and love God better. His timely admonitions for the priests were very practical. As well, they emphasized his own role as teacher of the teachers in the parishes, and as a father to all his people. The *Catholic Record* made reference to other Lenten pastoral letters of his, though not all were published in full. Often throughout the Lenten season, the regulations for the diocese were published separately there; for Lent of 1882 they were published a week after the printing of the pastoral letter, which was, in fact, a repeat of the letter of 1881.[30] Walsh wrote a new pastoral letter for Lent of 1885. He began with a reminder that "Mother Church called her children" to sincere repentance during the season of Lent. He pointed out that the people were created for an immortal destiny, but that, for sinners who had lost their baptismal innocence, the only way to that destiny was to return "by the thorny road of penance." As usual, he quoted extensively from sacred Scripture and from the Doctors of the Church, but included as well a quotation from Pope Benedict XIV.

In calling for fasting and abstinence he applied those practices to the widespread evils of drunkenness and to the vice's deleterious effects on families, which he had witnessed in his diocese, and which therefore led him to use the most vigorous – even forceful – language possible to draw attention to them. This was a major moral issue of the day, and various Protestant and Catholic organizations promoting temperance were springing up in Ontario and elsewhere. Walsh recognized how "the fearful sin of drunkenness" was common among the Irish, and brought "sorrow, desolation and death unto numberless families" like a deadly plague. As bishop, he strongly believed that he had to face the issue head on, and therefore he hammered home the evils of alcoholic abuse:

> It brings a curse upon all who are guilty of it; it maculates and defaces the image of God stamped on our souls; it dethrones reason and reduces man to the level of the brute creation; it darkens the intellect, weakens the will, blunts the conscience, and smooths the way to an impenitent death. It squanders the savings of years of toil; it plunges multitudes in misery and want and sorrow; it wastes the energies of the mind and the body; shatters the constitution and drags its victims' bodies into a premature and dishonored grave, and casts their souls into the everlasting flames of hell. Woe to the world because of this wide-spread and hateful sin! ... O, dearly beloved brethren, let us conjure you to shun this gigantic evil which deluges the world with a tide of miseries, which is so offensive to God, and so destructive of our happiness, both here and hereafter.[31]

In conclusion, he drew attention to a spiritual way forward to overcome this gigantic evil by reminding people to fulfill their Easter duty, and he included a catechesis on the sacraments of Baptism, Penance, and the Eucharist from the Fourth Lateran Council of 1215. As he did every year, he then listed the Lenten regulations for the diocese, important among which was that the clergy were required to provide spiritual exercises and instructions for their parishioners. In addition, Walsh encouraged the priests and people to promote Catholic education and Catholic schools. While not related to the season of Lent, this last point was an important concern at the time.[32] This letter was issued again during Lent of 1887 and yet again of 1889. There was no substantial change, except the date.[33]

Among his other pastoral letters was an important one on devotion to the Sacred Heart of Jesus, issued on 21 November 1873, the same day that he consecrated the diocese to the Sacred Heart in a solemn ceremony. Nine years later in May, he re-published it with a circular letter to the clergy asking that they read it again from all the pulpits of the diocese, and that all parishes and missions be consecrated to the Sacred Heart. In these ways, he believed the priests would renew the devotion to the Sacred Heart among their people.[34]

Following on that, two years later, he published a theological work with two treatises, one on devotion to the Sacred Heart, the other on the life and work of Jesus Christ. This latter treatise was a synopsis of stories in the gospels. In his own words, he emphasized the two natures of Christ, human and divine. Such treatises were commonly written throughout the nineteenth century to counter rationalism, and to make up for the fact that many people did not ordinarily read even the Scriptures, let alone other books.[35]

In his treatise on the Sacred Heart, he explained the relationship of that devotion to the theology of Christ's Incarnation.[36] He delineated the reasons why the Church established and fostered this devotion: "to promote God's glory, to destroy the reign of sin, and to inflame the hearts of men with the fire of divine charity. This devotion is also intended to make reparation to the Lord, for the cold neglect and ingratitude with which He is treated in the Blessed Sacrament. But its principal aim is to cause His love to be loved."[37] Fully a third of this treatise dealt with the problems experienced in the world at that time, as he understood them. These included attacks on the Church, on religion, and on the pope.[38] His remedy for these was to turn in prayer to the Heart of Jesus "and implore it to cast its divine fire of love on the frozen earth once more, so that the winter of our desolation may pass away, and the springtime of our holy hope and fervor may come back again; we must implore it to breathe the breath of life into the numberless souls that, Lazarus-like, lie dead in the grave of sin, that they may arise to a life of grace and virtue."[39]

Since this treatise was also meant for a wider audience than his own diocese, Walsh did not decree that his readers follow specific recommendations or requests. Rather, he suggested that they exercise the apostolate of the Sacred Heart: that is, that they pray for the reparation of sin in the world.[40]

As well as manifesting his ability to teach, his letters and treatises reflect how thoroughly well-read Walsh was. He was part of a long tradition of intellectual bishops. Among his contemporaries was Henry Cardinal Manning, archbishop of Westminster, England, whose writings were as popular in North America as in Britain. There was a similar approach in the development of their writings. In fact, the bishop had very likely carefully read Manning, and based his own later work on the Sacred Heart on the cardinal's work. There is a convergence in two areas of their writings; both believed that there was a relation between the mystery of the Incarnation and devotion to the Sacred Heart, and both saw the devotion to the Sacred Heart as the remedy for the ills of the world of their day.[41]

The fact that Walsh's various letters, instructions for the faithful, and other teachings appeared in London's *Catholic Record* indicated how he used the press to carry out, in part, his mandate to teach. He was very much aware that newspapers were a principal means of social and religious communication. From the beginning, therefore, he had supported and promoted the *Catholic Record,* which came into existence during his years in London. Though the newspaper was not an official organ of his diocese, it served a function much like the *Canadian Freeman* in Toronto, in that it made known to a wide audience the diocesan-related events as they were about to happen and then reported on them afterwards. It also recorded many of Walsh's sermons and pastoral letters, and made them easily available to the entire diocese and to others across the country. Reporting regularly on events such as the blessings and dedications of churches and schools, pastoral visits to various places in the diocese, and the bishop's comments on events across the country and around the globe, the *Catholic Record* gave the people of London diocese an opportunity to know firsthand the thoughts of their bishop, which was especially important in an age when travel to diocesan events and the diocesan seat would not have been easy.[42]

Walsh's hopes for the newspaper were in keeping with early Catholic thought about the press, and with that of its first owner and publisher, Walter Locke, that every family would know "the triumphs and trials of the Church both in this and other countries the world over, and of furnishing its younger members with a literature which will train them in the path which will make them fervent and well-instructed Catholics able to give a reason 'for the Faith that is in them' and which will make them good citizens as well."[43] Locke's ambitions were lofty. As a result, the paper enjoyed a wide circulation and a very good reputation.[44]

The praise given Walsh for his sermons, lectures, pastoral letters, and other writings was well deserved. He approached that part of his work and ministry as a teacher of the Catholic religion in a scholarly and faith-filled manner. As a result, his influence extended far and wide, and his work was always appreciated. The following words, taken from a memoir written at the time of his silver jubilee of presbyteral ordination, expressed well the common sentiments about his sermons and pastoral letters:

As a pulpit orator, Bishop Walsh has achieved a high reputation. His sermons betoken plan, thought, study, and are ever practical. His style is ornate, eloquent, full of point, logical and impressive. He has easy command of the choicest language, illustrating his subject with a suitably applied imagery. The attention of his audience never wearies. The pastorals of His Lordship – always opportune and welcome – are models of composition and pregnant with instruction. In their valuable pages he dispenses to his clergy and people the treasures of his well-stored mind. In all truth it may be said of His Lordship's literary productions, *"nihil tetigit quod non ornavit,"* whatever subject he handles he embellishes.[45]

As an extension of his teaching ministry, Walsh recognized that schools were an important instrument for protecting and promoting the Catholic Church, at the level of both parochial schools and higher education. Walsh's endeavour to improve Catholic education was catalyzed by the arrival of Denis O'Connor and the Basilian Fathers in Sandwich on 20 July 1870 to take over Assumption College. O'Connor had moved from Toronto to be named the superior in Sandwich and the president of the college. Under his leadership, it took on a second life.

O'Connor's success in revitalizing Assumption College was attributed to his own strength of will, and to the obedience and help of the other Basilian teachers. The result was that, with strict attention to administrative matters and his hard work, he overcame every difficulty associated with re-establishing the school. It expanded with two new wings, while the parish church gained a new sanctuary and bell tower.[46] The success of the college under O'Connor continued during the years of Walsh's episcopacy. The college developed a good academic reputation. That was further emphasized when Propaganda Fide conferred an honorary title, "Doctor of Divinity," on O'Connor, and had it presented by Walsh on 20 September 1888, along with a scroll from Giovanni Cardinal Simeoni and the doctor's cap which Walsh had brought from Rome earlier that year.[47]

During that same period there were various congregations of women Religious working in the diocese, dedicated to education. The Sisters of the Sacred Heart continued to offer their services in the school in London, which they had done since 1861. Walsh made several visits to the school for official purposes and for social occasions. The prestige of the school was greatly enhanced when the Sisters and students received a visit from the governor general and his wife, the Marquis of Lorne and Princess Louise, in September 1879. The governor general was making an official visit to London, and the school was included in the itinerary so he that could see the progress of education in that city. The fact that he would visit a Catholic school was considered an especially great honour.[48]

The Ursuline Sisters continued operating The Pines at their convent in Chatham. In 1874, a school was established next to St Joseph's church, also in Chatham, and the next year Walsh asked the Ursulines to take charge of the girls' classes there. The superior, Mother Xavier, declined the bishop's request on the basis that they were a cloistered community and should not venture outside the convent. She then changed her mind, in light of the great Ursuline ideal of "the salvation of souls through the education of youth." This, it was believed, had to rank above that of the ideal of the cloister. "[S]he acceded to the Bishop's request, and on his advice procured a closed carriage in which the nuns would drive to and from school. She also arranged that four religious would be appointed for the work, two to go in the morning and two in the afternoon, in order that all might have 'the opportunity to observe their holy Rule.'"[49] The Sisters began teaching at St Joseph's school that year.

Similarly, St Mary's Academy in Windsor remained the largest school under the care of the Holy Names Sisters. There was greater emphasis there on learning languages than at other schools. St Mary's grew rapidly, with the enrollment becoming so high that the Sisters were forced to build another addition in 1884. In time, it became more than a school; it developed into a centre for religious and educational life in the city. "It was here that colourful Church events, cultural and social affairs and musical concerts were sponsored. Strategically situated, in the heart of the growing metropolis, St. Mary's opened its doors to both civic and diocesan functions."[50] The Sisters also expanded their work to include a private school for girls, Our Lady of Lake Huron, in Sarnia. This convent school offered "a solid, useful and refined education" with emphasis on vocal and instrumental music. Tuition and board were the same price as at the school in Windsor.[51] In 1878, at the request of O'Connor, the Sisters began teaching at the parochial school in Sandwich. They also had a school in Amherstburg by the 1870s, which continued to expand and increase its numbers. Due to its success, however, it outgrew its facilities, and the bishop requested the boarding section be closed in 1881. Two years previously, the Sisters had opened a new select school for girls in Amherstburg and, by 1881, they were considering a similar one for boys. Four years later, the Amherstburg convent school was operating as a boarding school once again.[52]

By this time, too, the Sisters of St Joseph had opened schools in London, St. Thomas, and Goderich, while the Ladies of Loretto had charge of a school in Stratford. With that, there were five congregations of women Religious operating twelve schools in the diocese, in nine different cities or towns. Added to that was the boys' college of Assumption.

All in all, in Walsh's mind, the education of youth was a primary concern, and he gave unfailing support to all educational endeavours in his diocese, because these aimed to strengthen the Christian faith and morals. With the Religious of the various congregations of women and men, great progress had been made in Catholic education all during his years as bishop, and continued in the years following his transfer to Toronto.

Providing schools, and Religious men and women to teach in them, was not the bishop's only concern. The broader question of establishing the Ontario separate school system was of great importance. During Walsh's years in London, there was a concerted effort on the part of the Ontario government to curtail the rights of Catholics regarding their schools. Walsh and his episcopal colleagues in the other dioceses of Ontario had to confront, and overcome politically, this major obstacle to Catholic education.

A public system of education had been established in the united province of Canada principally as a result of the work of Egerton Ryerson, who envisioned a public system for elementary and secondary schools and denominational universities. Ryerson was noted for being a popular but extreme Protestant, often given to inflammatory outbursts of anti-Catholic agitation and rhetoric.[53] He never questioned the necessity of religious instructions in the schools; he took it for granted that this would be part of the structure and curriculum. In his plan, Catholic ratepayers would have the right to withdraw from the system and establish their own schools, yet his hope was to eliminate the need for such a withdrawal. This right was seen as a privilege, against which some Protestants agitated, calling it "unreasonable and harmful."[54]

The rights of Catholics were guaranteed in the Scott Act of 1863, passed by the united province of Canada. Richard William Scott, a Catholic representative in the legislature, directed the bill through the legislature after receiving the support of the Church and of Ryerson, who had become the superintendent of schools. The act guaranteed the establishment of Catholic schools and funding for them by the government. Catholics would be taxed for these schools instead of for the public schools. Although Ryerson saw this as a satisfactory solution for Catholics, the Catholic bishops held to the possibility of further negotiations to give Catholics a share in corporate taxes and secondary schools. At the time of Confederation, the British North America Act (1867) confirmed the rights of the Catholics in each of the four provinces to publicly funded education. Contentious issues regarding schools and funding remained at the forefront throughout Walsh's time in London. Often, fair solutions put forth by various provincial governments were sabotaged because of political interference along Catholic and Protestant lines.[55]

Two specific issues challenged the Ontario Catholic bishops in matters of education: an attack on the credibility of the archbishop of Toronto regarding the use of school funds and the secret ballot, and the obligatory use of Protestant prayers and Protestant Bibles in the public schools which Catholics attended. John Lynch was quite public about his political contacts with and support of the governing Liberals. By contrast, John Walsh maintained an aura of privacy and greater discretion in his political contacts and dealings. He, therefore, was called upon to play an important role in both these matters, through his quiet diplomacy and support for Lynch behind the scenes: "Although Walsh saw his way clearly on every aspect of the separate school issue, he purposely maintained a secondary role in the ongoing drama about the painful lack of parity between Catholic schools in Ontario and those in Quebec. He usually deferred to Lynch before expressing his own mind or making a public statement."[56]

In the heated debates of the day, it was one thing to have Protestants attacking Catholic bishops, but quite another for Catholics to fight amongst themselves. Particularly galling was an attack by some Catholic lay people on the credibility of the archbishop of Toronto himself. Walsh saw this as an attack on the archbishop's authority, and quickly rallied to his defence.

The problem began in 1876 when the chairman of the Toronto Separate School Board, Remigius Elmsley, charged the episcopal corporation with mishandling school properties, and held the archbishop personally responsible. The *Irish Canadian* and the *Canadian Freeman* entered into the debate. Since the *Canadian Freeman* enjoyed a wide readership across the province, the matter quickly turned from being a local issue in Toronto into a provincial issue. Underlying it all was the desire of some laymen and priests "to wrest control of school affairs from the imposing tough-willed Archbishop of Toronto." This was expressed especially regarding his use of certain funds for the archdiocese which they considered to be meant for the schools.[57]

Thoroughly disgruntled at the attacks and always quick to react, Lynch decided to launch a public defence of his actions, sending a letter to all the bishops of Ontario. Upon receiving it, Walsh was happy to pass it along to his priests on 2 December 1878, issuing a circular letter in which he added his own defence of the archbishop, instructing that the letters were to be read in all the churches. Walsh was unambiguous in his support. Lynch's letter, he wrote, was "a thorough and triumphant vindication of His Grace and of his clergy from the false charges and the calumnies so persistently uttered against them by certain persons in that city." Since these "charges" and "calumnies" were found in journals and newspapers circulating in the diocese, Walsh was obliged, as "a matter of justice," to make known the archbishop's position, for, he wrote, it was time "that the scandalous school agitation were dead, and like a putrid carcass buried out of sight."[58]

The agitation, however, did not end there. It erupted again the following year with the question of secret ballots for school trustee elections. The lay people on the board and many in the community saw the secret ballot as a proper means of exercising their franchise, allowing supporters of separate schools to freely choose their trustees without ecclesiastical pressure. Their thinking was also to pursue a better approach to education, sometimes stymied by Lynch, who held the post of superintendent of education, the equivalent of Egerton Ryerson's position on the public board.

The secret ballot was still seen by many at that time as an innovation, having been introduced into provincial and municipal elections only five years previously. Walsh – and Lynch as well – believed it to be an unnecessary and radical innovation, as well as an attack on the Church's influence in education. They saw it as something proposed by anti-clerical lay people who wished to eliminate the authority of the clergy in school affairs, the very basis of the separate school system as both Walsh and Lynch understood it. Lynch feared, as well, that secret ballots would be used to promote Irish nationalism and allow trustees to grow rich because of their influence. In opposition to Lynch, local newspapers, including the *Irish Canadian,* lobbied for the secret ballot.

Robert Bell, a Conservative member of the Ontario legislature, who was an Orangeman and vigorously anti-Catholic, introduced a bill on 4 March 1879 calling for the secret ballot in separate school board elections, with the support of many newspapers in Toronto and many

Catholic lay people. Premier Oliver Mowat was reluctant to support a bill that was contrary to the wishes of the archbishop, whose support he had and appreciated. In turn, Mowat was attacked in the press not only for being inconsistent but also for giving in to ecclesiastical pressure.[59]

Lynch turned to Charles F. Fraser, the minister of Public Works in the Mowat government and a prominent Catholic, for advice. Fraser counselled the archbishop to circulate a petition to counter the bill. Lynch then consulted Walsh and Crinnon of Hamilton, along with prominent priests in a number of dioceses. They agreed with Fraser's suggestion, and the petition was circulated, simply calling the secret ballot "inopportune" at the time. The bill was defeated, receiving only thirteen favourable votes.[60]

The debate continued during the subsequent years.[61] Walsh wrote in January 1883 to his own member of Provincial Parliament, Ralph Meredith, who was also the leader of the provincial Conservatives, in support of Lynch. He listed his reasons why he did not support the secret ballot. First of all, he wrote, the bill originated in a spirit of hostility to Catholic schools because of a discontented few in Toronto. The issue was peculiar to their problems and was not desired or demanded by the great body politic. "In representative forms of government such laws are always absurdities and often wrongs." Such a change, Walsh wrote, "would tend to create and foster agitation and dissension." The "discontented few" would cause mischief rather than leaving "Church and school matters with unquestioning confidence to the care and zeal of their clergy." He continued: "Were Catholics bound by law to support S[eparate] Schools as Protestants are bound to support Public Schools then I, for one, would not have the slightest objection to vote by ballot in the election of our trustees. But as it is the S[eparate] School System has really no foundation (since Catholics are free by law to abandon it at the end of each year) save in the moral influence of the C[atholic] clergy and in the good will and confidence of the C[atholic] laity."[62] In closing, he warned Meredith that Conservative members would lose support in the next election by prejudicing the Catholic clergy and a large majority of the Catholic laity against them. Walsh's support of Catholic education was unwavering. It would take, however, another eleven years before a law was passed, in 1894, which allowed for the secret ballot whenever requested by trustees and ratepayers.[63]

The second and even more contentious issue came to the fore even while the secret ballot was still being debated: that is, the use of Protestant Bibles and prayers in the public schools which Catholics attended. Opposition by the bishops was seen by Protestants as one more example of the Catholic hierarchy trying to force its will on the public and thus unduly influencing the governing Liberals. On the other side, Walsh, along with some other Catholics, saw it as an attack on the consciences of Catholic parents and pupils, because they would be forced to use Protestant Bibles and Protestant prayers. It was also seen as an attack on Catholic teachers, who would be forced either to use the Protestant materials at hand, or to be in danger of losing their teaching positions. The issue even divided the hierarchy of Ontario. Lynch had convinced the government that the readings and prayers could be held during the last fifteen minutes of the day and agreed to the use of specific passages of Scripture, a practice in place in the schools in Ireland. American bishops had come to realize they had made a great mistake, he said, in opposing the use of the Bible in American public schools. "The exclusion of Christianity, [an] American bishop had stated, left the way open to infidelity ... [Lynch also] agreed with Cardinal Manning of England, who repeatedly says, 'better a fragmentary Christianity than none at all.'"[64]

Believing that the new regulation would undermine the Catholic faith and endanger the teachers involved, Walsh disagreed with Lynch on the matter. There were, as well, Catholic parents who objected to such Protestant influences on their children, and they were informed they could write the trustees for an exemption for their children.[65]

In consequence, Walsh, Lynch, and other members of the Ontario hierarchy corresponded on the matter. Writing to Walsh from Buffalo, New York, in January 1885, Lynch tried to convince him of the correctness of his own position, and indicated he favoured a meeting with representatives of the government to resolve the issue. Mowat and his colleagues would meet them "in a most friendly spirit," he assured Walsh, and argued that "in the schools where the Catholics were in a majority the religious teaching should be left to the Catholic Church."[66]

Within two weeks, Lynch wrote again to Walsh, listing the concerns of Mowat, who by then was unable to have the meeting since some government members could not be in attendance. Mowat was also very worried about the reaction in the press, fearing it would injure the cause of giving any support to Catholic issues. Lynch suggested to Walsh that they should address their questions to the Holy See and discover from the authorities in Rome "whether the Catholic School teachers can read the extracts from the S[acred] Scriptures as ordered by the Minister of Public Instruction to [their] pupils whether Protestant, or even Catholic."[67]

Walsh immediately responded to Lynch and made it abundantly clear where he personally stood on the issue, eschewing what he perceived to be too great a compromise on Lynch's part. Concerned about the fourth regulation from the minister of Public Instruction, that the parents would have to write to ask to have their children excluded, Walsh wanted it to be written in a reverse manner: that the parents should write to the trustees to have their children included. He was adamant as well about the third regulation, which allowed teachers who objected to the Protestant lessons as provided to write the trustees for exemption from these: "Now what does this regulation practically amount to? It amounts to the peremptory dismissal of all good conscientious Catholic teachers from the public schools of Ontario. For if the said teachers object to comply with the new regulations and object they will, and indeed several have already objected to do so in this diocese, the trustees have no option but to dismiss them, since they (the trustees) are obliged by Order in Council to carry out the regulations."[68]

The bishop attributed no ill will to the legislators, allowing that they did not perceive the gravity of the situation. "[T]he new regulations," he wrote, "are nothing better than penal laws and we might not and cannot, in conscience, remain content until they are so modified or changed as to be made to harmonize with the civil religious rights of our people in this free Country." Walsh stated that he had the support of his clergy on this question, since it had been made manifestly clear to him at a conference he had held the day before. Knowing full well that any recourse to Rome on this matter would bring a vociferous Protestant reaction and so lose the support of the government for the Catholic cause, he wisely suggested the matter be submitted to Rome only after a meeting between the bishops and the government had taken place.[69]

The next day, 16 January, while visiting the episcopal palace in London, Bishop James Cleary of Kingston wrote to Mowat with Walsh's support, pointing out that the bishops were not trying to embarrass the government, but were acting out of their responsibility to conserve the faith. They were, he insisted, asking nothing from the government that they would not want to see granted to all, "whether as regards the right of the majority to have the method of religious instruction in their school determined in conformity with their faith or the right of the minority to be effectively protected against interference with their creed or religious sensibilities." Cleary went on to suggest that the trustees not be allowed to enforce the regulations until the cabinet and the bishops had met.[70] Cleary and Walsh had also been able, by that time, to win Lynch's support on the matter.[71]

Letters from Cleary to Walsh shed further light on the subject: late in January 1885, Cleary wrote to Walsh apprising him of his meeting with Charles Fraser, the most prominent Catholic in the provincial cabinet. Fraser had made it clear that the hostile regulations were rooted in decisions and procedures established by Egerton Ryerson in 1859, and not in the decisions of the present government. Meanwhile, the government for its part had given a copy of the suggested biblical passages to Lynch, expecting that he would distribute them among the bishops. This he had not done. Together, Cleary and Fraser then drafted new wording for the regulations, which Fraser would present in a memorandum and forward to Walsh. It was decided that Fraser would meet with Walsh within twelve days. If the bishop was satisfied, Fraser would meet with all the bishops and give "a formal guarantee on this basis in the name of the Government." Cleary wrote four days later to say that Mowat was considering the regulations as proposed in his meeting with Fraser.[72]

Walsh received a letter from the bishop of Hamilton, James Carberry, in February, regarding the matter and the meeting that he himself had had with Fraser. The letter confirmed that a compromise had been reached with the government as a result of the meeting: teachers with problems of conscience regarding the Protestant readings and prayers could simply appoint a senior pupil to lead the lessons. "This meets all we want," wrote Carberry. "I don't desire to worry the Government that is so well disposed to us." Interestingly, he also suggested the question not be sent to Rome, as Rome might declare it to be heretical.[73]

While the compromise had been reached, it still needed cabinet approval, which was slow in coming. Mowat continued to delay the meeting with the bishops, something Walsh did not see as a problem as long as the agreement reached with Fraser was accepted by the government. This Walsh detailed in a letter to Lynch in mid-February. He wrote that he felt strongly about the need to hold a meeting of all the bishops to have "a full and frank discussion" about the whole educational system in the province:

> As it is, our Separate School System has a most insecure and
> shaky foundation and if it is to be permanent it must necessar-
> ily have the same legal foundations as the Public School System.

Besides it needs several other amendments ... It would be for us Bishops to enforce on the clergy a certain rule of action in this matter – a rule of action that would have our united sanction and would be uniform in the Province. This is what giant strides the various Protestant bodies are making towards obtaining state grants or endowments for their higher Educational Institutions. The federation scheme for the various universities means practically endowment, by the state funding all. And whilst this movement is going on before our eyes we are at a standstill and our poor Colleges are quietly and contemptuously ignored.[74]

While these debates over the use of Protestant prayers and Bibles were won for the Catholics, the many questions about Catholic education, alluded to in Walsh's February letter to Lynch, would continue to plague the bishops of the province for a very long time to come. Throughout his remaining years in London, Walsh continued to work with the bishops of the province in the struggle for Catholic rights, while all the time working to establish and enhance Catholic schools in his own diocese.

Besides his role as a teacher, Walsh believed fidelity to the Roman Pontiff important for his own spiritual life. From the beginning of his episcopacy under Pius IX, to the end of his life in the time of Leo XIII, Walsh spoke and wrote about the need to defend, support, obey, and pray for the pope. This need was aggravated by the "Roman Question," which had direct influence on many of the pastoral letters and circular letters he wrote. These began immediately upon his becoming bishop when Pius IX issued an encyclical, on 17 October 1867, about the troubles in the Italian peninsula, Russia, and Poland. In it, the pope asked for the prayers of Catholics throughout the world, believing that the invasion of the Papal States and other such troubles were the work of evil that could be overcome only with prayer.

Walsh responded to this with his own pastoral letter, in which he compared the lament of the pope about "the evils that overspread the face of Italy, and that have swept in a devastating tide over unhappy Poland" with Christ mourning over Jerusalem. Walsh wrote that the pope's sufferings were like those of Christ. The pope, he insisted, had been the object of "ingratitude, treachery and hatred," as well as being "maligned and persecuted" and, though he had instituted reforms, "he was repaid by treason and revolution."[75] All of this Walsh saw as part of the "warfare between good and evil" being waged everywhere.

He then traced a very brief history of how the popes came to be guardians of the temporal order after the fall of the Roman Empire, and spoke of the "absurdities of these pretences" to deprive the pope of his temporal power. He went on to give the historical development of papal primacy: "We shall begin by stating that the Primacy of St. Peter and his lawful successors over the Christian Church is an article of faith and a fundamental doctrine of Catholicism. What the sun is to the solar system, that the Primacy of the Apostolic See is to the Catholic system of belief."[76] In this part of his letter, Walsh quoted or referred to the Scriptures, the Doctors of the Church, and the Church councils. He then summarised the implications of the primacy: "Who does not see, therefore, that the doctrine of the primacy involves as a corollary the divine right of freedom of communication between the Head of the Church and its members, the right of the supreme Pontiff of being free and independent of any human power in the discharge of the sublime duties of his office? Such a freedom is an essential element of Church government and discipline, and the Church is in its normal state only when it enjoys it."[77]

Nearing his conclusion, quoting a long section of the encyclical itself, Walsh asked for the prayers of his people, with explicit guidelines to be followed: a triduum of prayer for the "necessities of the Church" was to be established by a certain date; the devotions were to consist of the recitation of the litanies of Loretto and of the Saints, and Benediction of the Blessed Sacrament; Mass would be offered each day at the same time as on Sundays; clergy in coterminous missions would collaborate on times so as to be able to assist each other with preaching and hearing Confessions; and all pastors were to read the letter itself in all churches and missions throughout the diocese.[78]

Pius IX, at a meeting with the Congregation of Rites, had announced on 6 December 1864 his intention to call an ecumenical council at the Vatican. This was to be the first such council since the Council of Trent in the sixteenth century; consequently, all the bishops of the Catholic Church throughout the world were invited to attend. Pius IX's intention was to rally the Church against rationalism, liberalism, and nationalism, which he considered to be the greatest evils of the day. He published his encyclical *Quanta Cura* along with the *Syllabus of Errors* two days later on 8 December 1864, as an attempt to deal with the problems threatening religion and society at that time. *Quanta Cura* became the primary guide for the council's preparatory theological commissions. The convocation was formally announced on 29 June 1867, to five hundred bishops gathered in Rome to celebrate the eighteenth centenary of the martyrdoms of Saints Peter and Paul.[79]

Walsh was not yet a bishop when the convocation of the Vatican Council was officially announced. He was, however, the bishop of Sandwich/London by the time Pius IX published the bull of convocation, or indiction, *Aeterni Patris*, on 29 June 1868. In turn, Walsh wrote his own pastoral letter to publish the bull of indiction in order to announce the jubilee proclaimed by the pope.[80] Walsh sketched the history of the Church from the time of the Reformation to the Council of Trent, emphasizing how that council addressed the errors of that time. He then went on to point out the evils of that period which perdured to his day:

> Yet the evils caused by the teachings of Luther and his followers have not been wholly eradicated, and the seed sown by him is now producing its bitter fruit. The great and fierce battles of error against truth, of Protestantism against Catholicity, which characterized the sixteenth century, have ceased, – infidelity and a general indifference to all religion are the characteristics of our age ... The wholesome restraint of authority removed, toleration was a necessary consequence ... Toleration begot indifference, and indifference in religious matters is the fruitful parent of atheism and unbelief.[81]

The consequences, or ravages, of these errors were outlined by the pope in *Quanta Cura*, the bishop pointed out. The council was called, consequently, to remedy those evils of the day which had threatened religion and society. Walsh quoted extracts from the bull of indiction to emphasize that point, and then gave his rationale for writing his own pastoral letter:

> Considering therefore the solemn nature of this gathering into General Council, no less than the great and momentous objects it has in view, we have thought it our duty, dearly beloved Brethren, following the example of many of our venerable colleagues, throughout the Christian world, to address you, in this Pastoral Instruction, on the magisterial authority of the Church in matters of faith, the rejection of which by Protestants has led to the

sad results we see around us; as also on the nature of the General
Councils, and their great importance and bearing in Catholic
theology, on articles of faith.[82]

He next developed his line of argument by citing the writings of
St Paul, specifically about faith. From there, he traced the theme of
the rule of faith through the writings of several of the Fathers of the
Church. Failure to understand this concept, he believed, had led to
the problems of faith experienced by Protestants, who would accept
no teachings outside the words of the Scriptures. Our Lord himself,
wrote Walsh, never wrote a word of the Scriptures, nor was it recorded
that he ever instructed the apostles to do the same. The Church taught
the faith, therefore, before it was ever confined to the pages of the
Bible. The extrinsic proof of the authenticity and inspiration of the
Scriptures was found, therefore, in the Catholic faith.

Making reference to problems of interpretation experienced by Protestants, the bishop pointed to the difficulties in the Anglican Church
as an example. The loss of the true faith had led to an indifference
that had crept even into England: "[W]e have it on official returns,"
he wrote, "that five millions have never had the gospel preached to
them; have never, consequently, been taught to invoke that *sweet name*,
in which alone is salvation ... The Church of England is torn asunder by contradictory doctrines and contending sects – it is indeed 'a
house divided against itself.'" He went on to cite statistics from the
United States of America and demonstrated how this indifference had
led over ten million Americans to deny the divinity of Christ. Many of
them were members of Protestant congregations that had broken away
from the Church and then formed their own doctrines. Among these
he listed the Spiritualists, the Unitarians, and the Universalists, and
included as well "Jews, Infidels and Sceptics."

In the second part of the letter, Walsh wrote an extensive section
on general councils. He wrote of their need to be convened from time
to time, and the recognition given them over the centuries. Their
decrees were "but the active expression of the passive infallibility of
the Church, and must be themselves infallible and irreformable." The
right to invoke a council belongs solely to the pope, as given in the divine commission to Peter, he wrote, adding that though councils were
useful, they were not necessary, since the pope was the pre-eminent
teacher in the Church and could teach without recourse to a council.
He then gave a list of all the general councils accepted as "ecumen-

ical councils" by the Church, along with the chief matters discussed at each.

The heart of the pastoral letter was the definition of infallibility. Walsh clearly laid out the parameters: the Church could not define a doctrine that had not already been revealed. "Infallibility, regarded in its most elementary light," he wrote, "is freedom from doctrinal error, and this freedom from error the Church claims in virtue of the promises of the Redeemer that He would be with her all days, even to the consummation of the world. Infallibility, then, is not impeccability, or freedom from sin. The two ideas are perfectly distinct." A long quotation from Cardinal Newman, who would turn out to be an important figure at the Council, was used to strengthen the bishop's point. As an example of an infallible teaching, Walsh pointed to the doctrine of the Immaculate Conception, proclaimed in 1854. In it nothing new was taught, but rather an ancient doctrine was confirmed.

The bishop ended his pastoral letter suggesting that people offer a prayer of thanks to God for being members of the Church, and he called for prayers for the Church and the pope, for heretics and schismatics, and for pagans. He added two appendices, one about the unity of the Church, the second an extract from the writings about the Church by another like-minded contemporary, Archbishop Manning of Westminster. The pastoral letter was to be read in all the churches of the diocese.[83]

In that pastoral letter, Walsh not only defined the notion of infallibility as it applied to the Church and to general councils, but he also made it clear where he stood on the question of conciliarism, a debate that was being waged in the Church at that time between those who wanted to give the pope supreme authority over councils and those who wanted to give councils – and therefore the college of bishops – authority over, or at least equal authority with, the pope. This was not the same extreme notion of conciliarism that had surfaced in the late Middle Ages, but rather the view of a small faction eager to promote the infallibility of the whole Church and not just the pope. They saw the authority of the Church resting on the bishops in apostolic succession.

Mixed with that, however, was also the question of "ultramontanism." This movement arose from Napoleon's treatment of the Church in the aftermath of the French Revolution; he increased the power of the state over the bishops, and excluded papal influence in France. Many people responded by choosing not to put faith in the local leadership of the Church, that is, their bishops, but rather to look "over the mountains" to Rome during that time, seeing the state as evil and the papacy as the last protection and stronghold of authority and stability. Attachment to the person of the pope, especially strong since the loss of the Papal States, and emphasis on the gift of infallibility were two hallmarks of ultramontanism in the mid-to-late nineteenth century.[84]

Many, including Canadians, saw ultramontanism as the antidote to compromises of the faith. The bishops of Quebec were especially alarmed with the loss of faith and growing anti-clericalism in France, and wanted to maintain unity and fidelity among their people. That mentality had prevailed since the British takeover of Quebec in 1760. The young John Walsh became attracted to ultramontanism during his years of study in Montreal, and it was reinforced in him later by the growth of Protestantism in Ontario at the time. He was clearly also influenced by the "poor afflicted pontiff" mentality, so prevalent in northern Europe and in the English-Irish Church, in reaction to the political situation in the Italian peninsula.

Such thoughts were evidently at the base of much of what Walsh wrote and preached over the years. In his early years as a bishop, therefore, he favoured a stronger centralization of the Church and papal authority. He found himself in company with many at the time of the Vatican Council who also desired the decree on papal infallibility. His thinking would mature over the years, as he would come to see his role as Christ's representative in his own diocese, and as he would grow in a sense of his own autonomy as a successor of the apostles. He would never suffer a diminished sense of his own authority; neither, however, would he act or write without due deference to and respect for the successor of Peter, chief of the apostles, and Vicar of Christ on earth. Over time, as with many issues, he would "take a middle road" on the question of papal authority, firm in his thinking and understanding, and not tending to any extreme view. In this, he supported the authority of the pope, but not at the cost of his own.

Unfortunately, Walsh was not one of the seven hundred bishops who attended the first session of the Vatican Council when it opened in a solemn ceremony on 8 December 1869, the feast of the Immaculate Conception. Because of ill health, aggravated by the long-term effects of his earlier bout of cholera, he was unable to attend the Council. He wrote to Archbishop Baillargeon of Quebec in October 1868 for a dispensation, but was instructed to ask the pope directly. A later letter to Edward Horan, bishop of Kingston, in May 1869, spoke of his request for the dispensation: "My health was wretchedly bad during the past winter but it is now very much improved. I might say restored, but still I am not able to undertake much as yet. When do you intend starting for Rome? I have written for exemption but have as yet received no answer."[85] The exemption was given, and Walsh did not attend the Council.

Bishop Lynch, however, did attend, and wrote often from Rome to keep his friend and colleague informed of Roman and conciliar matters. He expressed his enthusiasm about what was happening there and encouraged Walsh to come to Rome when his health allowed, to share in the experience. In his first letter, written to Walsh shortly after the first session had begun, Lynch expressed his hope for Walsh to come to Rome the following Easter. It became clear that the Council would proceed more slowly than expected, so it still would have been worth the trip at that point. "I would be very glad," wrote Lynch, "if your Lordship would come here about Easter time. There will be a recess for, I presume three months, July, Aug[ust] & Sept[ember] if the Council do[es] not finish its work before then, as the Pope wishes, if possibly it can be done. I will procure lodgings for you at your command." He pointed out that the unrest in Italy, arising from the *Risorgimento* which had instilled so much fear in people, meant that visitors were few. Yet it was still difficult to get good lodgings that were "clean, exposed to the sun, [with] good board and fair price. The Minerva Hotel is one of the best and most reasonable."[86] Lynch described the situation thus: "There is great display of military at Rome reviews, and marching through the streets with music." These would have been French troops, who, at that time, still protected the Papal States in the immediate vicinity of Rome. The bishop advised a safe route for travel, should Walsh decide to come.

This first letter contained little news of the Council itself. Lynch did report, however, that the archbishops and bishops of Canada were to have a papal audience that day. He indicated that the Congregation concerning the faith had elected its members. These included archbishops Spalding, Leahy, and Manning, but, Lynch added, "Canada was forgotten." The Congregation concerning Church discipline would meet the following Monday to elect its members. He added two notes of interest; the printing press at the Jesuit church in Rome, the *Gesù*, was rendering great service in making up lists; and "Gallicanism and Jesuitism are not dead yet. These extremes never meet."[87]

Lynch's second letter – written in French – reported the slow progress of the Council, adding, "it will be longer than I first thought." About one hundred and fifty Council Fathers had spoken, but, he wrote, he gave better witness with his silence. He added a personal note about his encounters with his predecessor in the see of Toronto: "Bishop de Charbonnel electrified us with a discourse that lasted about twelve minutes. I see him frequently; he is always very affectionate toward the diocese of Toronto and he loves to glorify you. He is always the same, and his vocation as a Capuchin has taken root and developed his former habits."[88]

Lynch cautioned his friend Walsh not to believe accounts given in the *Times* about the Council, where there was much discussion about the role of bishops, but whose outcome remained to be seen. He referred to the Council as being the most worthy of its deliberations of its kind in the world: "We will have an analysis of all that must be believed and practised by the Bishops, by the priests and by the people ... Canon law must be codified. The breviary will probably be reviewed." With those extracts, he added, "like a Bishop of the council, it must not seem [the same] in the journals."

Pope Pius was enjoying excellent health, Lynch also reported, as was Peter Crinnon, the bishop of Hamilton. Crinnon was accepting invitations to dinners given by the bishops from England, and was meeting and discussing issues with them three or four times each week. As for himself, since his health did not permit such visits, Lynch rested in his quarters, which he shared with the bishop of Buffalo, Stephen Ryan. To this, he added a postscript in English: "If the Council should last till after summer, make up your mind to come."[89]

Lynch reported, in his second letter, a ruling that all bishops were to submit in writing their ideas on the discussions of the Council. Since he was not in attendance, Walsh was not expected to do this. Yet long before he had even heard of the ruling, he had been prompted to write his own pastoral letter on the question of infallibility, and thus share with the people of his diocese this longstanding teaching of the Church. There is no doubt he intended to make a contribution to the discussion on the issue in wider circles, since he sent a copy of his letter to Lynch who, clearly impressed by what he read, later wrote and told him "to feel free in the future to speak on behalf of the entire Canadian church whenever writing on infallibility."[90]

Thus it was that on 2 February 1870, Walsh issued his pastoral letter on what would turn out to be the most controversial question addressed by the Vatican Council: "Now that the Council of the Vatican has been inaugurated, amid the greatest pomp and grandeur of ceremonial, we deem it our duty to address you on the thoughts which this august assemblage suggests, and on the objections which are daily urged against it by its adversaries. The doctrine that lies at the foundation of this Council is the Infallibility of the Church of Christ in matters of faith and morals."[91] Faith in the Church and in her teaching role was at the crux of Walsh's arguments. Accepting the pope's ability to teach in these areas followed logically from the first premise, he believed. Faith was a condition for salvation; the nature of faith demanded an infallible witness to the fact of revelation presented, as well as an infallible interpreter of the fact:

> Christianity presents two rival claimants for these distinctions:– the Bible, interpreted by individual judgement and Church authority. Of the claims of the former, we disposed in our last Pastoral Letter to you [when publishing the Bull of Indiction]. [The Bible] is not the witness and interpreter, and for many reasons it cannot be. It does not claim the distinction; it is only a dumb record, and cannot assert itself when belied by false interpretation; ... We come now to consider the claims of the Church to be the infallible witness and interpreter of divine revelation.[92]

God, he went on to write, always made supernatural truths known through a living, teaching authority, as was clearly shown in the writings of the Old Testament. From the time of God teaching Adam, the word of God was handed down by and through living authorities before words were ever written. Moses, other patriarchs, and the prophets wrote down the words, but their interpretation was always the work of kings and judges, later priests, Levites, scribes, and doctors of the Law, who read the word of God and interpreted it for the people throughout the ages. In this, the Catholic Church was foreseen: "Either, therefore, the Catholic Church is the infallible Church foreshadowed in the Old Testament and foretold by the prophets, or the prophecies have been made void, and the promises of God have not been fulfilled – a conclusion which every Christian must reject with horror."

This living, teaching authority was continued through the evangelists who wrote the gospels and through the apostles given the divine commission to teach and gather disciples to Christ. This commission was given also to the successors of the apostles, Walsh wrote, who understood the need for the teaching authority and who shared in it: "The Apostles understood that they had received a power which they could delegate. They did give the power to others, and associated

them to the teaching Church ... They were appointed for the perfection of the saints, for the work of the ministry, unto the edification
of the body of Christ, till we all meet in the unity of faith and of the
knowledge of the Son of God, unto a perfect man, unto the measure of
the age of the fullness of Christ."[93]

Walsh then developed a theology of the Church as the body of
Christ, quoting, in his usual manner, from sacred Scripture and the
Fathers of the Church. There were three conclusions to be drawn from
this conception of the Christian Church, and these, for Walsh, were
the heart of the matter that followed "as streams from their sources":

> 1st. The Church is necessarily infallible in matters of faith and
> morals; for being the body of Christ and the organ of the Holy
> Ghost, she cannot possibly err in her office of teacher, and judge,
> and witness, of the truths of revelation ...
>
> 2nd. The Church is indefectible, or imperishable ... because
> it is the body of Christ indissolubly united with the Holy Spirit,
> and because this indissoluble union is to last for all time ... Now,
> of this indefectibility, this present Council of the Vatican is a
> most striking evidence. After a life of nineteen hundred years of
> terrible trials, of dangers innumerable, of incessant conflicts with
> the powers of earth and hell, the Catholic Church finds herself in
> this nineteenth century as strong and vigorous as at any period
> during her long and eventful existence ...
>
> The third consequence which we asserted flows from the con-
> ception of the Church being the body of Christ, is that of unity
> ... But the Catholic Church is the only one that not only requires
> actual union of faith amongst all its members; but that holds a
> principle of faith that supposes, and even enforces, unity as an
> essential quality of the Church ... we must believe whatever she
> decides, with the assistance of the Holy Ghost.

The bishop then dealt with five objections against the Council that
had been made in the secular press and among Protestants. The first
of these reported, he wrote, was a general indifference to the Council
and its aims and objectives. He countered this with the fact that the
whole world was watching this Council, and indeed that it was being
widely reported.

To the objection that it was not a true ecumenical council, since the
Anglicans and Greek Orthodox were not participating, the bishop responded with an answer from history. In no other council had heretics

and rebels been allowed to deliberate. Citing examples, he explained that in the past, rebels were invited to present opposing views, and so debate them, but the deliberations were left to those in the communion of faith.

Another charge made against the Council concerned the freedom of bishops, with some questioning whether or not they would be forced to say only what the pope wished to hear. Walsh countered this with the understanding that bishops in communion with the pope had a right to speak at councils and synods called by the Church. This right ensured they would be able to speak freely and so allow for free and open deliberations.

Some people objected to a council, the bishop wrote, because it would run counter to the modern age. That, he replied, was the very reason for this council and every council. To be faithful to the gospel, the Church would have to run counter to every age to condemn, he said, their "unchristian and wicked characteristics."

To the final objection, that the Church would define doctrines that had never been revealed, Walsh responded by quoting from Manning, who said that the Church cannot define what has not been revealed. These principal objections, wrote Walsh, could not stand the test of examination:

Truth is mighty, and must ultimately triumph. It may for a time be obscured by the shadows of misrepresentation, its radiance may be hidden by the mists of prejudice, but sooner or later the shadows or mists will clear away, and its light, like the sun emerging from a cloud, will shine on it with greater brilliancy. The Church of God must, however, always expect to be thwarted and opposed; for it is a remarkable phenomenon that God's truth has always been contradicted in the world.

For Walsh, if the bishops were truly united to the bishop of Rome, it would be impossible for the Church to be anything but infallible in matters of faith and morals. This was the way the Church would make real the divine commission; this was the way the Church would be the infallible witness and interpreter of the fact of revelation. Citing several quotations from the Scriptures that spoke of God's truth being contradicted, the bishop concluded with the usual ordinance that his pastoral letter should be read in all the churches of the diocese. It was signed and sealed by him and, as an indication of its importance, it was also countersigned by his secretary, Patrick D. Stone.[94]

Several pieces of information surfaced in the third and final letter written by then-Archbishop Lynch on 13 June 1870 to his colleague, still beleaguered by poor health. In giving Walsh still more encouragement to join the Council Fathers, the archbishop indicated that the Council would continue much longer than expected: "How I earnestly desire that you could take the rest, after your years of hard work, and great success, in comming [sic] to the Council. As there is now no hope of its conclusion this year, try to come here for next winter." Lynch then indicated that he would be speaking a few days later "in the name of the Church of Canada, on the infallibility – rightly understood, affirmatively ... The great question is being debated. About two hundred Fathers are to speak on it. Our session will run in to July for God will direct his Church." He reported his health had improved, thanks to spending a month at the sea, and he promised to write again to Walsh in a few days. He asked the bishop to write to him at the American College, since he would be moving there in a short time.[95]

In just over a month, 18 July 1870, the Council session was ended, and the pope sent the participants home for summer recess. They were dismissed until November, but, with the march on Rome by Italian troops on 20 September, Pius IX declared himself "a prisoner in the Vatican," and prorogued the Council on 20 October *sine die*. The First Council of the Vatican never met for another session.

Though Walsh was not present at the Council, there is no question about his influence in Canada and especially in the diocese of London regarding the teachings of the Council. His objective of educating the people of his diocese had the secondary advantage of making a contribution on the subject of infallibility to a wide audience, providing a "popular" understanding of this doctrine to many.

Walsh addressed the matter of the Roman Question and the defence of the pope again in March 1871. Rome had been overrun with Italian troops on 20 September 1870, "imprisoning" the pope behind the walls of the Vatican, as long as he refused to surrender voluntarily his temporal power. Catholics throughout the world condemned this action, but Italy obstinately refused any outside negotiation. In a circular letter addressed to the clergy of his diocese, Walsh wrote in the bluntest of terms about the situation:

It is unnecessary to inform you that our Holy Father is still a prisoner in the hands of his iniquitous despoilers. The revolution – the abomination of desolation – is in the midst of the holy places, and the heart of Christendom grieves ... In other days, in the ages of faith and chivalry, a *Catholic crusade* would enter the Italian kingdom and would sweep the sacrilegious wretches from the States of the Church which they plunder, and from the holy places which they profane. But as the circumstances of the present time forbid this ... we must make use of the moral and constitutional means left us.[96]

The "moral and constitutional means" included petitions sent by various dioceses in Canada to Queen Victoria, asking her intervention with the government of Italy. The bishop signalled his intention to do likewise in the diocese, and sent such a petition to all the priests. It was to be signed and returned immediately to his residence "so that we may send them without delay to the Governor-General, with the prayer that he will cause them to be laid at the foot of the throne of her most gracious Majesty." To this, the bishop added the need to offer prayer, "as the best efforts are fruitless without God's blessing," and specifically suggested the "Pater," the "Ave," and an ejaculation to St Peter and St Joseph.[97]

Four years later, in 1875, Walsh wrote again on the question of infallibility when he published a seventy-five-page booklet in response to polemical pamphlets written by William E. Gladstone. A Conservative member of Great Britain's Parliament and prime minister during some of the years between 1868 and 1894, Gladstone believed strongly in Christian values having their influence on society. Fearing, however, that the Catholic Church would interfere in British politics by influencing English Catholics, he had wanted to break up the Vatican Council by force of British military power if necessary. He did not, however, due to the influence of his long-time friend, Manning. When Gladstone later wrote against infallibility, in the wake of the Council, Manning and Walsh were among those who responded.[98]

Walsh wrote a defence of the conciliar doctrine of papal infallibility, largely based on his 1870 pastoral letter, in order to challenge the notions put forth by Gladstone. The 1875 "revised and expanded" version included three appendices, one of which was a defence of Catholics, saying they could be faithful to their Church and their state at the same time. The other appendices addressed what the bishop referred to as "certain historical difficulties": the case of Galileo in the late sixteenth and early seventeenth centuries, and the dispute between Pope Liberius and Honorius in the fourth century. This was his last official publication to deal specifically with infallibility and was, in the words of one writer, his "most brilliant polemic and his closest brush with purely political controversy."[99]

Although constitutionally the pope's "freedom" was not changed with the death of Pius IX, his successor, Pope Leo XIII, experienced less tension because of the almost-universal desire to see the issue resolved. It was, after all, a stigma attached to the king of Italy and to his "democratic" government. The freedom and recognition accorded Leo XIII was demonstrated clearly when he celebrated the golden jubilee of his presbyteral ordination in 1887. The bishops of Ontario chose to address that issue as the jubilee approached. Walsh was charged by the bishops of Ontario, the year before the jubilee, to write a letter about the papacy, quite likely because of his literary ability, his knowledge of the issues, and his strong fidelity to the papacy. This assignment indicated the importance in which the opinions of the bishop of London were held, and also pointed to his position as a senior prelate in the ecclesiastical province:

> We deem it our duty to address you with all the weight of our
> combined authority as the Archbishop and Bishops of the
> Ecclesiastical Province ... The whole Catholic world is prepar-
> ing to celebrate the felicitous event ... It will be a joy, as well as
> a duty, for us, the clergy and faithful laity of Ontario, to take
> a proper share in this celebration, and to mark it with substan-
> tial proofs of our Catholic loyalty and heartfelt devotion to the
> august person and the sublime office of the Vicar of Christ.[100]

Fidelity to the pope as the "central figure and Chief Pontiff in the hierarchy of the Spiritual Kingdom" established by Christ was the key to the first part of the joint pastoral letter. It spoke of how the children of the Church looked to the pope for light and guidance, but also of how they were "prepared to make the greatest sacrifices in order to help and uphold him in the discharge of his sublime duties and in his warfare against the enemies of Christ and His Church."[101]

The next section, on the primacy of the pope, quoted and paraphrased the pastoral letter of 1868 in which Walsh had published Pius IX's encyclical and called for a triduum of prayer. It was also similar to a sermon he gave at St Peter's Cathedral on "The Supremacy of the Pope" on 25 September 1887, at the same time that the Ontario bishops' pastoral letter was written and published. For instance, both pastoral letters gave as an example this image from astronomy: "What the sun is to the solar system, that the Primacy of the Apostolic See is to the Catholic system of belief." The letter then followed with a question, also seen before, though now with a slightly different wording: "Who does not see, therefore, that the doctrine of the Primacy involves, as a corollary, the Sovereign Pontiff's divine right to teach and rule and govern his spiritual children in every part of the world with absolute freedom, and consequently, to have unrestricted liberty of communication with them in all that relates to the religious discipline of life without let or hindrance on the part of secular government?"[102]

The next section, about the pope's temporal power being usurped, was taken from the pastoral letter concerning the 1867 encyclical, in which Walsh wrote extensively about the historical development of the Petrine primacy. Next, the letter focused on the accomplishments in international relations credited to Leo XIII since his election. The prelates – or rather, Walsh – pointed out that Pope Leo had strengthened the work of the Church in America and Australia, settled longstanding disputes such as that between the see of Goa and Portugal, established a native hierarchy in India, re-established the hierarchy in Scotland, promoted the study of history, philosophy, and theology, and written masterful encyclicals. "In a word, he has during his short reign raised the Papacy to a greater height of moral power, of commanding influence, and of universal regard than it has ever attained since the dark days of the so-called Reformation."[103]

In conclusion, the archbishop and bishops decided and decreed that the best way to show their love and loyalty to the pope was to make him a "generous large-hearted offering of Peter's Pence." All Catholics had a duty to support the pope, they wrote. The collection was to be taken up in every mission of the province and forwarded to the bishops without delay; the prayer *pro Papa* was to be recited at every Mass to the end of the year, when a *Te Deum* was to be sung in every cathedral "and every place it can be suitably chanted" on 1 January 1888 as thanksgiving to God for sustaining the Holy Father beyond his anniversary; and finally, the pastoral letter was to be read in every mission of the province. The letter was signed by Lynch, Cleary, Carberry, Walsh, and Thomas Dowling of Hamilton.

Walsh's "hand" was seen everywhere in the pastoral letter, including the last part. True to his style, certain actions were "ordained" to be carried out. As well, the four orders were numbered, something he did in his own pastoral letters and in correspondence when itemizing things. Walsh almost always referred to parishes and missions only as "missions," to be inclusive of the two types of establishments without always repeating both words or having to make distinctions all the time. Finally, he often favoured adding prayers at Mass or recommending devotions in his pastoral letters, as this letter did.

Walsh planned his 1887 *ad limina* visit to coincide with the pope's golden jubilee, and many bishops from around the world also gathered for the celebrations at the Vatican. While in Rome, Walsh also presented an address to the Holy Father on behalf of himself, his priests, and the people of London diocese. In it, they expressed their "filial obedience and reverential affection" along with their "heartfelt congratulations." These kind words were accompanied by a very generous gift of $5,200, from the collection taken up at the behest of the Ontario bishops. Clearly that which Walsh felt himself, and that which he expounded in the joint pastoral letter, he had successfully conveyed to his people. Their love and loyalty for the pontiff were akin to their bishop's. Their actions gave meaning to their words.[104] It would take, however, many months before the diocese would hear about Walsh's Roman visit.

He left for Rome in late October and was scheduled to return to London in March 1888. His plans had to be radically changed when he accidentally sprained his knee on arrival in New York, and was hospitalized there. Consequently, he did not reach the diocese until April, and did not return to full duties until 1 July 1888. "It was a source of deep affliction to the faithful people of the diocese, that the accident which happened to His Lordship after his arrival in New York, on his return from Rome, prevented his active work up to the present time. It was, therefore, with great joy that the people of London beheld him once more in his accustomed place in the Cathedral last Sunday."[105] At that time, then, Walsh was finally able to report on his *ad limina* visit and the pope's jubilee celebrations in his own pastoral letter. In it he gave a clear indication that Leo XIII enjoyed widespread recognition and sympathy from world leaders. Walsh listed the many political adversaries that the Church and Pope Leo had had when he first ascended the throne of Peter, and how he had overcome many obstacles with these governments:

This age has not witnessed such another movement of hearts and minds as that which the Papal Jubilee has occasioned. Addresses, presentations and other evidences of respect, esteem and filial devotion came pouring, in a ceaseless tide from the whole civilized world, into the Eternal City for the jubilee celebration. The number, the variety and the value of the gifts offered for the occasion were simply inestimable. Emperors, Kings and Queens, Presidents of Republics, the rulers even [of] Pagan or semi-Pagan states, the Sultan of Turkey, the Shah of Persia, Princes and heads of noble families, Bishops, priests, and religious communities, Catholics, Protestants and infidels – all nations, whether civilized or semi-barbarous, sent their gifts and the expression of their congratulations, esteem and homage to the Vicar of Christ.[106]

The jubilee taught important lessons, Walsh wrote, about the undying vitality and indestructibility of the papacy, and about the universality of the Church. It also gave him an excellent opportunity to make clear that the stature of the Roman pontiff had risen greatly in the eyes of the world, and that the pope was not to be seen as insignificant on the world stage, despite Italy's continued stance of non-recognition. Through this letter Walsh was able to trumpet a cause that was close to his heart and the heart of his episcopate. If loyalty to the pope came through this pastoral letter clearly, then all the more clearly was it stated in the letter issued jointly by the archbishop and bishops of Ontario in advance of Leo XIII's jubilee, addressed to the clergy, Religious communities, and laity of the province to prepare the people for this celebration and encourage their prayers for the pontiff.

John Walsh sought to instruct all the people of his diocese so they could be truly nourished with words of faith and sound teaching. For most, access to books was still restricted, not only because of their shortage and cost, but also because of a widespread lack of education. Walsh's preaching was therefore all the more important. Walsh knew that good preaching was the key to good formation for the laity, and this knowledge was evident in the seriousness with which he approached his own study, reflection, and preaching, and in the importance he placed on the priests' theological conferences. In that he was eminently successful. Ever true to his responsibilities as a teacher, he carefully passed on the Church's teachings with clarity and conviction, and by so doing, he taught his priests and people a better understanding of their role as Christians and Catholics.

DIOCESE AND DOMINION

*The picture you draw of me is not mine, it is the ideal of what I ought to be,
and indeed what I would wish to be, viz., the good shepherd who gives
his time, health and life itself, for the spiritual welfare
and sanctification of his people.*

BISHOP JOHN WALSH, 28 NOVEMBER 1877

LIKE OTHER CATHOLIC BISHOPS, JOHN WALSH WAS CALLED TO BE
an administrator as well as a leader, and to use his influence for the
good of the Church and society not only in his diocese, but also in the
province of Ontario and the country as a whole. This sometimes meant
taking an active part, however discreetly, in the provincial and federal
politics of the day. Canadian Catholics, especially those in Ontario
and Quebec, generally supported the Conservative party in the early
decades following Confederation. On his part, Walsh accepted that
civil government was a means to an end, a social instrument at the
service of the country and its people. Especially it should serve as a
protector of religion. In his mind, therefore, he had to support the
political party and government which best served that end. He felt he
could use his relations with political figures to influence the government's course. Through his actions, he demonstrated that he was in
tune with the time-honoured institution of government, that he knew
how to bring the maximum benefit to Catholics, and that he could
avoid the pitfalls of secularization which he believed threatened the
country. In view of those ideals, he could work with any politician who
would respect the rights of the Church and of individual Catholics.
Nonetheless, he still preferred a Conservative government.

On the other side, a friendly, workable relationship with Catholics
was also important for the prime minister, Sir John A. Macdonald, and
his colleagues in government. Though a Scots Presbyterian, Macdon-

ald relied on the support of Catholics and even greatly depended on them at times, though they were in the minority. Support from Quebec, which had the majority of Catholic voters, enabled him to form four Conservative governments in the years from 1867 until 1873 and again from 1878 until 1891. Early during his first mandate, Macdonald wrote to John Lynch, then bishop of Toronto. In that letter, he indicated his dependence on Catholics, but also his caution. Making reference to a patronage appointment given to "our friend Moylan," who had been recommended for some position by the bishop of Toronto, Macdonald made an unusually frank reference to the political hazard of such favouritism: "I shall steadily pursue a course in the same direction, by which the Irish Catholics shall get their fair share of public employment. Your Lordship understands human nature well enough to know that I must do this with caution, to prevent The Globe getting up another Protestant howl. Mr. [George] Brown is ready enough to coquette with the Catholics, and yet will attack me for any favour done to them."[1]

A similarly courteous relationship prevailed between the prime minister and the bishop of London. It began very early, immediately after the election in August 1867 which had led to Macdonald's first post-Confederation government. At that time he wrote to Walsh, who was still the bishop-elect of Sandwich, to thank him for having supported the Conservative party during the election campaign. The results, the prime minister added, made him happy, especially since some Catholics had been elected.[2] That letter marked the beginning of a long friendship with Walsh which would last until Macdonald's death. Over time, the two men came to rely considerably on each other for support and favours.[3] Their friendship would yield much good both for the Catholic Church and politically for Macdonald and the country. Over the next decades, there were at least four other general elections during which Macdonald greatly depended on Walsh to bring the Catholic vote to the Conservative party. Such dependency ranged far, from Walsh's speaking to a pastor, urging him to assist a local Conservative candidate, to Walsh's contacting a fellow bishop to gain his support for the Conservatives.

During the campaign for Macdonald's third general election in 1873, he candidly asked Walsh to garner the assistance of the pastor of St Thomas, West Flannery, for the local Conservative candidate and sitting member, John H. Munroe. Without a doubt, Munroe needed all the support he could muster to win the riding for Macdonald; the prime minister was in deep political trouble due to the "Pacific Scandal," and needed every one of his sitting members to be returned. He was well aware that the Catholic vote might hold the balance.[4] Some thirteen years later, during the campaign for the election of 1887, the prime minister again unhesitatingly turned to Walsh, entreating him to convince Bishop James Carberry in Hamilton to support Macdonald's party and encourage the Catholics of his diocese to do likewise. Though Walsh had earlier told Macdonald about Carberry's Conservative leanings, the prime minister still feared that, as a stranger born in Ireland, the bishop of Hamilton might not take any interest in Canadian politics.

To prevent that from happening, and to guarantee the Catholic vote in Hamilton, Macdonald urged Walsh to be Bishop Carberry's "guide, philosopher & friend" during the election. He was appealing, therefore, to Walsh's long friendship and "all powerful influence" to help him and his party in the campaign:

> I need not remind you what I have done for the Catholics, but I shall jot down from recollection what has been done, so that you may indoctrinate Bishop Carberry to a certain extent on the subject ... There are many other evidences of my support of Catholic interests which I cannot now recall, or enumerate, without an expenditure of time which I cannot at this juncture afford. The Archbishop [of Toronto] and Bishop Cleary are very friendly and I <u>hope</u> to get actual evidences of it.[5]

In truth, Macdonald admitted (with some small exaggeration), the fate of the government was in the hands of the Catholic hierarchy, especially in western Ontario, Walsh's domain.

At times Macdonald could be very direct when he needed help or wanted to "trade" political favours for assistance: "Sir, I want you to help me. I know your good feeling towards me but I shall be obliged by your giving me an extra push this time among all your people. Be assured that I shall gratefully appreciate your assistance. I'll see London is going to have a cabinet minister in its midst."[6] In turn, Walsh did not hesitate to support that "trade," though he had nothing to gain personally. His motives for political involvement were always to use his influence to secure benefits for Catholics however he could.[7] That became particularly obvious during the general election of 1878. Macdonald had earlier lost to the Liberals in the national election of 1873, which resulted in Alexander MacKenzie forming the government. In the midst of the customary several weeks of voting, Walsh congratulated Macdonald for his "splendid triumph" – that is, his personal re-election – and pledged his support. Macdonald's government lost the election; but MacKenzie's election to office, unfortunately for him, coincided with a national economic depression, and he and his Liberal government received much blame and sharp criticism for their ineffectual handling of economic matters. Walsh himself expressed considerable criticism of them because of how the depression affected Catholics in his diocese: "[O]ur people in Centre Huron," he wrote to Macdonald in October 1878, "have suffered greatly at the hands of the local Grits [Liberals] and will do their utmost to defeat them in this approaching contest."[8]

In the period preceding the 1873 general election, Macdonald toured the country to build support, and Walsh was happy to give it. He wrote to congratulate Macdonald on the "splendid receptions" he had been receiving in the campaign, and added that he was pleased to offer his backing: "I am happy that you have found my advice and influence beneficial to your interests. I can honestly say that my influence, such as it is, has been earnestly exerted wherever it was found that it was needed and would be beneficial – [for] instance Kent, the Ridings of Huron, Perth, Middlesex, etc."[9] Walsh was always discreet, however, about what were, in effect, politically tactical moves which supported the Conservatives while also serving Catholic interests. Prudent he was, of course, and always cautious. He was loath to bring either himself or his clergy into open political conflict or to cause scandal, or (most importantly) to raise the ire of Ontario's Protestants and Orangemen, something which was of as much concern to Macdonald as to the bishop. Later, in a letter to Macdonald prior to the general election of 1882, Walsh carefully outlined the delicate nature of his position as a bishop:

In reply to your favour of the 24th inst[ant], I beg to assure you that I have not and will not forget your interests in the approaching elections as I am convinced that your policy is best for the welfare of the country and also because of your past record as regards our people. Of course a gentleman in my position must act in political matters with much caution and prudence in order not to compromise higher interests. I am confident your party will be fully sustained in this section of the country.[10]

As a realistic and matter-of-fact person, the bishop of London knew how to be supportive while never actually making public his own political allegiance. No doubt many knew where he stood, but he revealed his full allegiance only to those who requested or received his assistance, and to his intimate episcopal colleagues. He was circumspect and expected those whom he favoured or from whom he received favours to be likewise. In the matter, he differed strikingly from the then-archbishop of Toronto. Lynch never made any secret of his political opinions, allegiances, or support: he was always in favour of the Liberal party. He felt strongly on the matter, and once openly castigated Walsh for his support of the Conservatives, something which greatly embarrassed Walsh, who believed that bishops must always operate with discretion in the political realm.[11]

Ever sensitive to the political wind, Walsh knew when his influence would be less effective or even non-existent, as clearly it was on the national level during the five years of the Liberal government under MacKenzie. In 1877, when seeking a patronage position for Hugh McMahon, a lawyer from Sarnia, Walsh directed his request not to Prime Minister MacKenzie – knowing that approach was futile – but rather to the senior Catholic in the cabinet, Senator Richard Scott. It was a reality which Walsh had come to accept. In fact, a year later, he complained to Joseph-Thomas Duhamel, bishop of Ottawa, who had requested help for a certain individual, that he had no political influence which could benefit him: "With reference to the object of Your Lordship's letter I regret to inform you that I am convinced that I have little or no influence with the present government and that in view of that conviction I have ceased to trouble it with any requests. This is of course entre nous."[12]

Patronage, and the ability to control it, was always in the forefront of Canadian politics at all levels of society, and governments depended on it to maintain their own power in office and to hold voters' loyalty. Walsh knew that all too well, and it was for this reason, during the years of Conservative governments in Ottawa, he seemed never to hesitate in placing a whole range of requests before the prime minister or other members of his government. These requests were never directly for himself; the majority of them were for official appointments or other sinecures for Catholics from his diocese, or sometimes even for Catholics beyond his territory. He firmly held that Catholics had a right to patronage in the same way as anyone else did. In his strong opinion, since Catholics had a role to play in society for the betterment of the world, they therefore deserved the opportunity to do so from positions of authority and influence at whatever level. Often he preached about the Christian's responsibility to be the "leaven in the dough," as taught in the gospels, a role which he interpreted could be fulfilled in governmental service and other responsible posts as well as anywhere else, and all under the patronage of governments and their officials. Since Catholics were the minority in Ontario, Walsh felt that they needed someone to promote them and their talents, and that given his position as bishop, his personality, and his political contacts, he was the one best suited to do just that.

Sometimes he was not always immediately successful in promoting someone. When he first recommended McMahon for a judgeship, it was during the MacKenzie years. Not surprisingly, nothing came of it. His second effort was in 1883, and he was directed to Senator Smith, then a member of Macdonald's cabinet. That too was without success. In fact, despite his unwavering support for Macdonald personally, and the prime minister's repeated expressions of gratitude and promises to promote and reward Catholics for their political support, Walsh had to direct no fewer than three attempts to Macdonald himself to be heard, in April, May, and July 1884.[13] In those letters, he used various tactics to win his cause. He emphasized McMahon's Catholicism, which would mean that his appointment to a judgeship would please other Catholics. Walsh also allowed that McMahon's appointment would be, for Macdonald, politically advantageous: "I would be glad to see McMahon on the Bench in Manitoba and I am confident his appointment would be a good stroke of policy for the government apart from the consideration of his legal qualifications which are amply sufficient for this position. The appointment would please our people whilst it would remove a more or less influential opponent from the path of the Government."[14]

Walsh also reminded the prime minister that the number of Catholics in Ontario and Manitoba would be in itself a justification for appointing a Catholic to the Bench, and that it would be "a just and generous recognition of our people as constituting an important element in the body politic of Ontario; and would be sure to bring your Government political strength as it would enable its supporters and friends to appeal to that appointment as an evidence not only of the justness but even friendship of your administration towards our people."[15] Another good reason for appointing a Catholic, he concluded, was that it would blunt the influence of the provincial Liberals in Ontario, who were trying to secure the Catholic vote: "This strong argument would rob [Leader of the Opposition Edward] Blake's rhetorical efforts of their seductive power." Walsh was concerned about keeping a united front among Catholics in supporting the Conservatives, as that would enhance the Catholic strength in numbers.[16]

Yet despite all those efforts and repeated arguments on Walsh's part, McMahon did not receive a judgeship at that time. While vacationing in Rivière-du-Loup during August 1884, Macdonald made the reason for his refusal very clear to Walsh: McMahon was not a supporter of the Conservative party, and Macdonald's friends would not appreciate McMahon being advanced to that kind of a prominent position. Besides, Macdonald added, another Catholic, John O'Connor, had a prior "claim" to such a favour. Walsh gave up his sponsorship of McMahon, although, three years later in 1887, he would receive the news, through a local Conservative member of Parliament for Essex, James C. Patterson, that McMahon was in fact to be appointed a judge. Perhaps Walsh's efforts on McMahon's behalf had paid off in some fashion.[17]

Patterson himself had earlier been recommended by Walsh for a position in Macdonald's cabinet, and Walsh had first petitioned on his behalf in October 1886. For good reasons, including his usual discretion, Walsh marked the letter "Strictly Private & Confidential." That time, for reasons unknown, he felt it unnecessary to stress Patterson's Catholicism: "I make this suggestion entirely in the interests of the Conservative party with which I am now, and always have been, in friendly sympathy. In this connection however I deem it a duty to say that now, as in the past, I do not think that as Catholic bishop ruling over people of different political creeds I should take an active or prominent part in the purely political contests. This letter is intended solely for yourself and I trust to your honour to keep it absolutely secret."[18]

Walsh's willingness to use his political influence for someone's benefit, while also promoting the Catholic cause in Ontario, was never lost on Macdonald, who acknowledged Patterson's "political and personal merits," but insisted that he could not promote him at that time. Perhaps Macdonald was beginning to fear a backlash when he reminded Walsh of the number of Catholics to whom he had already granted patronage appointments. Despite having to turn down Walsh's request, Macdonald still hoped that Walsh would help him keep his "fair share of the Catholic vote."[19] Later, a pending cabinet shuffle in the summer of 1888 prompted two further attempts by Walsh to promote the member from Essex. For his part, however, Macdonald continued unmoved by the pleas of the bishop, although this time he flatly gave the reasons for Patterson's rejection: the man had "no following in the House of Commons. He is disliked and distrusted."[20]

At the time of the 1887 general election, one sitting Catholic, Timothy Coughlin, the Liberal-Conservative member for Middlesex North, was seeking a Senate seat rather than re-election. Believing that Coughlin would render important services in such an office, and would also help to elect another Conservative in his current riding, Walsh wrote to the prime minister in January 1887 to endorse Coughlin's request for promotion. Macdonald was more interested, though, in having Coughlin run in the election for the Commons seat; there was no vacancy in the Senate. To that end, he made a deal with Coughlin, for which Walsh became the guarantor: if he would run and win, Macdonald would keep a Senate seat available for him in the future; if he lost, he would have the third next available Senate seat. "This of course is a secret but I told him that I would make Your Lordship the depository of that secret, that this letter should be his voucher." Walsh accepted the offer to be the guarantor, and Coughlin was re-elected in 1887.[21]

Along with promoting Catholics as cabinet members, senators, postmasters, and judges, Walsh also wrote letters suggesting people for such positions as Dominion appraiser of groceries, revising officer, clerk in Division Court, higher-ranking militiaman, Customs collector, and even warden of a penitentiary. In his promotional efforts, Walsh was successful with some and not with others. Still, he felt it important not to shy away from stating his allegiance to Catholicism, because he believed that this kind of political patronage would make it easier for Catholics to render their service to the government of the day and to Canadian society in general. He knew, too, that in their new positions, they would in turn benefit the Church.

In the beginning of his episcopate, it was simply a matter of trying to give Catholics exposure in such positions as came available. Over time, Walsh's views also reflected the thought of the day, especially in the development of the Church's social teaching, based on the common good, in response to the growth of Marxist ideology and rampant socialism. Many prominent Catholics were writing and speaking in this vein, including Wilhelm von Ketteler, bishop of Mainz in Germany; the Friebourg group spread throughout Europe; Manning of Westminster; and James Cardinal Gibbons of Baltimore. The Catholic Church was discovering the best way to face rampant socialism, through inserting Catholic values in public discussions and policies. Walsh hoped that those he promoted for public office would, in turn, promote Catholic values in their own spheres of influence, corresponding to their vocations and the degrees of influence they wielded in public life.

They were all, more or less, qualified candidates for their prospective jobs. It was less important in Walsh's mind that they be members of the Conservative party, but of utmost importance that they were Catholics with something to offer their country. His position in these

matters was best summed up in a letter of 14 May 1880 when he proposed James Egan for the position of postmaster of the London Post
Office. He was a "fit and proper person" for the position, Walsh wrote,
"a bye-long Conservative and has rendered very substantial services
to the party. He was loyal to it in the days of its adversity as well as
in those of its prosperity ... His appointment would, I am confident,
give satisfaction to every Conservative in this city and would be especially gratifying to the Irish Catholics of Ontario who would see in his
appointment a substantial evidence of the good will of the Government towards them."[22]

There were, as well, a number of pastoral needs which Walsh felt
obligated to address from time to time when writing to the prime minister or to other members of government. Although valuing the justice system and its laws and applications, Walsh also recognized the
need at times for mercy, forgiveness, and clemency. Those he willingly
sought when he felt it necessary. In one such instance, he intervened
for a John Hargraves who was in jail. Walsh and Jean-Marie Bruyère,
his vicar general, believed that Hargraves had served sufficient time
in prison and should therefore be released. They appealed directly to
a judge, John Carling, who subsequently wrote to the minister of Justice, James McDonald. He, however, ignored the judge's entreaties on
the prisoner's behalf. Carling then turned directly to the prime minister. Walsh and Bruyère, he wrote to Macdonald, were "very anxious
for his discharge." Another prisoner who attracted the bishop's attention was a James Wall who was under a sentence of death. Such a con-
demnation could only be commuted by the governor general. Walsh
pleaded directly with Macdonald who, in his reply to Walsh, promised
"to present [the bishop's] thoughts to His Excellency" as soon as the
papers on the case could be submitted.[23]

Likewise, in 1881, pastoral concerns led Walsh to write seeking assistance with governmental pensions for, in one case, the widow of a
judge, and in another, the widow of an army colonel.[24] Walsh believed
that, as a bishop, he had a public duty to guarantee that the Catholic population received just treatment. For that reason, he willingly
took up several causes requested of him, or which he himself judged
deserved attention for the good of the individual and of Catholicism
itself.

One of the more important and complex situations in which Walsh
had to use all his political connections and influence was in defence
of his vicar general. In 1871, Jean-Marie Bruyère became the centre of
a highly unpleasant controversy which had been spawned by the anti-

Catholicism of some Protestants of London over the legalities of sol-
emnizing Catholic marriages. As a result of their complaints, Bruyère
was charged by the local magistrate for having solemnized a marriage
without the publication of banns or a civil marriage license. Bruyère,
in fact, had given a dispensation from banns, in his capacity as vicar
general, according to the norms of ecclesiastical law and respected civil
custom. The charge against him, however, had been brought in compliance with the new civil marriage regulations that had recently come
into effect in the province.

In a circular letter, Walsh brought the matter to the attention of the
bishops of Ontario and Quebec, indicating that this was "a direct
attack on the rights and immunities which the Catholic Church had
enjoyed in this country from its first establishment, which have been
guaranteed by the Treaty [of Paris] of 1763 and confirmed by the un-
disputed usage of more than a hundred years."[25] He sought their
advice for the most prudent way to proceed: should his vicar general
accept imprisonment rather than pay a fine, since such a payment
would be an acknowledgement of guilt? An appeal to a higher court
was another option. Should he take it? Finally, Walsh wanted the bishops of the two provinces to send "a joint remonstrance" to the Dominion government instructing their legal officers not to succumb to the
pressure of anti-Catholic groups attacking the rights of the Church:
"This question directly affects the status of the Church in Ontario and
possibly also, in the Prov[ince] of Quebec; for if the provisions of a
Treaty agreed upon between two Sovereign powers may be set aside
by a colonial law what security is there for the rights and liberties of
the Church in this Dominion in the face of a protestant majority." In
a postscript, Walsh added that he had "just learned from trustworthy
sources that several protestant ministers [were] the prime movers in the
prosecution of the Vicar General. It [was] therefore a protestant movement against the liberties of the Church."[26]

Five days later, on 20 September 1871, Walsh wrote to John O'Connor,
the member of Parliament for Essex and the postmaster general, asking for help and including a copy of his letter to the bishops. Clearly
annoyed at the whole anti-Catholic affair, he bluntly named the individuals involved:

The whole thing is got up by a clique of bigots, amongst whom
figure the city clerk, Mr. Abbot, and deputy clerk Mr. E. B.
Cornwall. These two officials have not ceased, since the new marriage registration law has come into effect, to annoy us in every

possible manner, and have abused their official position to vilify and misrepresent the Catholic Clergy of this city. They have gone so far with this disreputable work, as to slander me publicly in the newspapers, attributing to me words and acts in connection with the registration law, of which I was absolutely innocent, but which were calculated, and doubtless intended, to damage me in public estimation.[27]

As he viewed the matter, Walsh continued, the new law had two main problems for Catholics: bishops would no longer be able to dispense from banns, and all priests would be required to register each marriage. The blessing of a union of previous concubinage, where it might not have been publicly known, could become an especially thorny matter, since registration of such a marriage would bring this concubinage to light, possibly destroying the reputation of the couple and making bastards of the children, not to mention violating confidences given to a priest. The right of the Church to grant a dispensation from banns, Walsh insisted, had been guaranteed in the Treaty of Paris, had been in use both in France and in Canada before the British takeover of Quebec, and had continued since then. In his mind, the new law was tantamount to the state interfering in matters of the Church and determining who priests could or could not marry. That was intolerable. Marriage was a sacrament and could not be controlled by the state, nor could the state legalize the priest as a minister of matrimony, nor therefore prescribe the conditions under which he would be entitled to solemnize it. Without doubt, Walsh recognized the civil nature of marriage, but believed that the civil laws should govern the candidates for marriage, not the priests performing them:

This is strange language to be held in a Country in which it is pretended that all connection between Church and State has been severed. I deny, in toto, the competency of the state in this matter, as far as the Catholic Clergy are concerned. For if the State can legalize a priest as minister of the sacrament of matrimony, it can also legalize him as minister of Baptism, or of Penance, or of Holy Orders, since they are all alike sacraments of the Church; and it can as a consequence, render the administration of the sacraments illegal, for the power to legalize implies the power of rendering illegal. Is not this constituting the State supreme in spirituals as well as in temporals? Is it not arming the civil magistrate with a power and a sway over the consciences of men not different in kind from that exercised by the Autocrat of all the Russias?

He submitted these matters to O'Connor, a prominent member of Parliament and a practising Catholic who would know "what is due to the State as well as to the Church."[28]

The matter of timing was crucial. A court date for Bruyère was expected in October, and Walsh needed timely replies from the bishops. By early October, the bishops of Quebec and Ontario – with the exception of the bishop of Kingston, who responded later – had replied to Walsh. Among the responses, that of Charles LaRocque, bishop of Saint-Hyacinthe, is preserved. He agreed with Walsh that Jean-Olivier Briand, the bishop of Quebec, from the very next day after the signing of the Treaty of Paris, would have exercised the right to dispense from banns. It was, therefore, LaRocque's contention that the case should be presented to the Queen's Privy Council in England, and that Bruyère should not pay the fine. If he were thrown in jail, there would be a great call for justice which would provoke anger and disturb the public peace:

> And supposing – an eventuality which seems to me very possible – that during Msgr Bruyère's stay in prison, public opinion would arise that would be hostile to the judgment which had condemned him there, you would be subject to the accusation, and with apparent justification that would be screamed from the rooftops, that out of religious fanaticism, you wanted, to stir up anger and to trouble the public peace, by his going to prison, rather than having used the right of appeal, which was open to you as to all other citizens.[29]

The consensus among the bishops was that the charge was a direct attack on the rights and liberties of the Church. Clearly, Walsh later reported to Elzéar-Alexandre Taschereau, archbishop of Quebec, "the prime movers made no pains to deny it." The best course of action, Walsh pointed out, was to deny the competency of the courts in the matter, and for Bruyère to submit to imprisonment rather than pay a fine or appeal to a higher court. Walsh assumed the archbishop, after second thoughts, would have come to the opinion that an appeal to a higher court would seem to acknowledge the competency of the lower court. Submitting to imprisonment instead would show the penal character of the proceeding. He explained to the archbishop, too, that he had written to John O'Connor, requesting him to forward his letter to the prime minister, presuming, he added, that his position was in accord with Catholic theology.[30]

Having received the consensus of the bishops, it was hardly surprising then that Walsh sensed it more expedient to write the prime minister himself, who also held the cabinet portfolio of minister of Justice at the time, and thereby would have great influence in how the case might proceed. The result was a telegram from Macdonald requesting Walsh to forward a copy of Bruyère's summons directly. Walsh promptly provided a certified copy to Macdonald. He also informed the prime minister that the trial date had been set for Friday, 13 October, but queried whether it would "not be well to put an effectual stop to the attempts of such people to rob us of rights which we cannot surrender if our church is to be left its liberty and independence in this country – rights which have been exercised without dispute or protest since the first establishment of the colony?" In a closing personal note, he expressed hope that Macdonald's health, "so precious to the Country," would be "quite re-established."[31]

After reviewing the summons, Macdonald arranged to meet the archbishop of Toronto, John Lynch, bishops Edward Horan of Kingston and Eugène Guigues of Ottawa, and Sir Georges-Étienne Cartier, Macdonald's chief lieutenant, to discuss a way out of the entanglement. Subsequently Macdonald wrote to Walsh himself, protesting the "ill-advised proceedings" which in the end would not settle the questions surrounding the marriage legislation. Yet the prime minister nevertheless recognized the importance of the underlying issue involved, specifically the dispensing power of the bishops, which should be addressed, he believed, by the Queen's Bench. That meant, for the moment at least, allowing it to take its course in the courts. If, Macdonald reckoned, a judgment was made against the dispensing power of the Catholic bishops, then an application could be made to the House of Commons for an act confirming their powers. Besides, he added, there should have been legislation protecting these powers long since, both in the Parliament in Ottawa and in the legislature in Toronto.[32] To Walsh's delight, Bruyère's hearing ended swiftly; the charges were dropped, and the dispensing powers of the Catholic bishops left intact. It was a significant victory for Walsh. Not only was the problematic matter of his and other bishops' episcopal powers resolved, but the whole sorry episode unmistakably demonstrated his ability to utilize his extensive contacts quickly to call in support from a broad cross-section of society, including every bishop in Ontario and

Quebec, members of Parliament, and the prime minister himself. His was no mean accomplishment; few of his episcopal colleagues could have done similarly. From one perspective, too, the whole regretful episode surrounding the charge against Bruyère was fortunate inasmuch as it placed Walsh himself squarely in the forefront of those bishops willing to go to great lengths to protect the welfare of the Catholic Church in Canada, especially in Ontario.

At the same time, Walsh was extremely grateful for Bruyère's willingness to be incarcerated if that meant protecting the powers of his bishop. It was hardly unexpected, therefore, that in 1876, in recognition of that, along with Bruyère's enduring devoted and valued service, Walsh petitioned Pope Pius IX to name Bruyère a monsignor. On 12 December 1876, Bruyère was honoured with the rank of a domestic prelate.[33] It was a greatly deserved tribute.

Bruyère continued to serve Walsh as vicar general, trusted advisor, and friend, and for the next decade remained at Walsh's side, until he was felled by a stroke in late January 1888. He died in mid-February. Sadly, Walsh was out of the country at that time.[34] On learning of Bruyère's death, he was greatly distressed: "The diocese has suffered an irreparable loss, and the Bishop has lost a devoted friend. A truer and better priest I never met." He also confessed his sadness at not being present for his friend's funeral. In response to the question of Bruyère's place of burial, in a touching gesture of appreciation, generosity, and friendship, Walsh ordered that Bruyère be buried in the crypt of the cathedral, in the very spot that had been designed for the bishop himself.[35] This thoughtful gesture demonstrated Walsh's sensitive appreciation for his friends; this was one of the qualities that made Walsh so endearing.

The "Bruyère affair," with its related issues of the role of clergy and the influence of politicians in the Church, gives a further insight into Walsh's character. John Walsh was very much aware of the prevalent fear that the Church would try to control the government. He lived in the wake of John Strachan, the first Anglican bishop of Toronto some twenty years earlier, who had pushed for an established church in Canada. Strachan had been beaten out, as it were, by Catholics and Methodists who rejected the notion.

Walsh certainly would have been hesitant even to give the impression he favoured such a place for the Catholic Church in society. He not only was restricted by the laws of the country in that area, but kept the balance in the many ways he worked behind the scenes to attain his goals. By nature, he worked more comfortably in that fashion, but also saw firsthand and understood the effects of the closeness of the bishops in Quebec with the government there. That was something Walsh wanted to avoid in Ontario, where Catholics were in the minority and where Protestants would surely have pushed back. Walsh and Macdonald instinctively knew this – they both said so in various letters – and they worked to avoid any such backlash. Finally, Walsh maintained the balance since he certainly did not want politicians mucking around in the affairs of the Church!

Canada's dealings with the Holy See had a great influence on how dioceses were structured and how bishops were chosen there.[36] By 1875, Rome began to fear that the bishops of Quebec were compromising the future of the Church in Canada, since they seemed more concerned about keeping good relations with the aggressively francophone provincial government than about caring for the needs of the many new immigrants flooding into the country. Rome had come to doubt the real importance of the French language – and, in a way, therefore, of the French-speaking clergy themselves – in North America, as governmental statistics pointed to the growing number of English-speaking immigrants: "For the Holy See, the political weight of Catholicism in Canada was in the process of shifting to Ontario. It was not surprising, then, that in 1897 [Rafaele] Merry del Val declared that the only hope for Canadian Catholicism resided with the Ontario bishops."[37]

As this change, ill-received in Quebec, was coming about, the Church in Ontario was gradually coming of age. Even as early as the late 1860s, the bishops there had agitated for an ecclesiastical province separate from Quebec. With the steady increase in the Catholic population throughout the province, and with the growing importance of Toronto as the civil provincial capital, the first consideration of the bishops was to have that city as the seat of the proposed ecclesiastical province. They presented that proposal to Rome, through Lynch, while the Vatican Council was in session. The road to a new province, however, was not smooth. The archdiocese of Quebec and the diocese of Kingston, for very different reasons, put up vigorous opposition. In one letter from Rome while attending the Council, Lynch informed Walsh, who had been unable to be there, of the developments: "The Archbishopric for Toronto is decided upon, and were it not for the opposition of Kingston backed by Quebec, the Apostolic letters would be expected. The matter was settled upon before we arrived. I can afford to have patience."[38]

Clearly, Propaganda Fide desired to reflect a new approach in Canada, one which favoured the English-speaking Church more than hitherto, a recognition of its distinctiveness and of the ability of the dioceses in Ontario to function fully on their own without relying on the "Mother Church" of Quebec, as Walsh had once referred to it. With opposition mounting in Quebec, however, against a new ecclesiastical province in Ontario, the officials at Propaganda Fide decided to delay for a time any formal decision in order to allow the Canadian bishops time to work out their problems. Nevertheless, in the end, the reorganization would go ahead. That fact, the administrator of Quebec, Vicar General C.F. Cazeau, communicated in a letter to Walsh on 17 February 1870. Archbishop Charles-François Baillargeon of Quebec had instructed Cazeau to inform Walsh of that new development: Toronto, Kingston, Hamilton, and London had been formed into a new ecclesiastical province. Its seat was not named. The archdiocese of Saint-Boniface, he added, would remain linked to Quebec until the next year when it too would be joined in a new province with the vicariate apostolic of British Columbia. No mention was made of the diocese of Ottawa.[39]

Though that much had been accomplished, there still was no decision about the seat of the ecclesiastical province by the end of February. In fact, a new wrinkle had developed which slowed any announcement. The bishops of Quebec, Rimouski, and Saint-Hyacinthe had joined their colleague, Edward Horan of Kingston, in requesting that, as the oldest diocese in Ontario and the second-oldest in Canada, Kingston should become the archdiocese, the seat of the new ecclesiastical province. Meanwhile, however, the bishops of Montreal, Trois-Rivières, Ottawa, and Hamilton had signed a document for Rome requesting the elevation of Toronto as the metropolitan see. Lynch had appended his signature to that document and, acting as Walsh's procurator, Walsh's name as well. Lynch assured Walsh that the cardinals had promised that the choice of Toronto would be maintained.[40]

Of course, Horan's argument for Kingston was historically well-founded. It was, after all, the first diocese to have been created in Canada after Quebec City, and therefore represented the earliest roots of the English-speaking Catholic Church in Canada beyond the earliest settlements of *La Nouvelle France*. Nonetheless, while Kingston may have had a pre-eminence in history, Toronto had a pre-eminence in size and civic importance. That was why it was eventually chosen over

Kingston, and thus raised, on 18 March 1870, to the status of the first ecclesiastical province in English-speaking Canada.

Walsh's role in the negotiations which brought about this success cannot be forgotten. Not only had he been involved from the very first in the discussions to found a new province; he also assisted in preparing the documents which went to Propaganda Fide. In his mind, too, he had supported what he knew would not only be a successful venture but would also advance the cause of the Catholic Church in Ontario. Not surprisingly, therefore, he was pleased with the outcome.

Although at first strongly opposed to Toronto being the metropolitan see instead of Kingston, and having advanced his arguments to that end, Baillargeon later came to accept the new ecclesiastical reality in Ontario. After the definitive decision was taken by Rome, on 17 May he sent congratulations to Walsh as senior bishop, expressing his happiness at the new establishment. He realized, he assured Walsh, that it would be good for the welfare of the Catholic religion in Canada, and that he had always enjoyed and appreciated the sincere friendship of his former suffragans, who were now suffragans of Toronto.[41]

Bishop Horan of Kingston was not so happy. It had not been easy for him. He had so wanted Kingston to become the metropolitan see, with himself as its first archbishop. Like a wound that would not heal, the exclusion of Kingston's metropolitan status festered in him. His diocese – and he along with it – had been slighted, he felt, and he had been forced into subservience, as he saw it, as a titular suffragan of the newly elevated archbishop of Toronto. That was especially galling. Reflecting the growing antagonism of many in Kingston towards the city of Toronto, the city of Kingston itself, he asserted, older and longer-settled than Toronto, likewise had been bypassed by an upstart. Therefore, most Catholics in his diocese considered Toronto unworthy. He did not mask his anger or moderate his words in any way. To the new metropolitan, Archbishop Lynch, he crossly expressed his determination to protect his own rights as bishop: "You will find in me an obedient and faithful suffragan, but understand well that I will always defend the rights of my see and I will refuse to submit to all encroachments upon these rights. If I must answer for my actions to the archbishop, then I will ask the Holy Father either to define the powers of the metropolitan or to accept my resignation ... Life will be intolerable if such rights of appeal are recognized."[42] However understandable it may have seemed to some at the time, Horan's unseemly outburst was more damaging to himself than anyone else. His "wound" continued to fester, and eventually led to grave illness. Soon his health began to fail. Three years later, when he was not yet sixty, his resignation was officially sought by the Holy See. He made a visit to Rome to safeguard his right to remain bishop of the diocese, but that visit only convinced Rome all the more that he had to resign. He did so officially on 16 June 1874, becoming in retirement the titular bishop of Chrysopolis in Arabia. He died the following year. Such battles as these, despite the sad outcome for Horan, endeared Walsh even more to the other bishops of Ontario.

As he grew in experience and wisdom in London, Walsh's greatest strengths, besides his intelligence and wit, included his affability, his likeable personality, and his sociability, all of which made relations and exchanges with people of every rank very easy for him. He especially came to know well those who were closely associated with him and, consequently, was able to promote harmony and good relations among them. To be sure, he was most effective in that regard with his episcopal colleagues, with few exceptions; fostering excellent rapport with them greatly mattered to him. He was good at it, and it said a great deal about his charm and reputation that he was able to nurture such close links.

Indications of his social skill were evident time and again in various reports of the *Catholic Record*, but especially in the personal visits to him from other bishops which reflected their close and appreciative ties of friendship. Noticeable too was how, when he was injured and hospitalized in New York in March 1888, so many bishops contacted him. Especially was he pleased to report to Lynch in Toronto that Michael Corrigan, the archbishop of New York, was "visiting frequently and [was] most kind." At that time, too, he easily convinced the bishop of Harbour Grace, Newfoundland, Ronald MacDonald, who also had visited him in New York, to spend Holy Week in London, to preside, in Walsh's stead, at the liturgical celebrations in the cathedral there. Such a very generous act on the part of the Newfoundland bishop was a sure sign of their friendship and mutual appreciation, given the great distance and the extreme difficulty of travel.[43]

Over time, Walsh himself received many invitations to visit other bishops, and was ever amenable to travelling extensively for special occasions to be with them. There were many invitations yearly, some of which he could accept, others that he regretfully had to turn down. One he was pleased to accept was for the celebrations in 1874 for the two hundredth anniversary of the establishment of the diocese of Quebec. To Taschereau he expressed his pleasure in attending: "It will give me great pleasure to go to Quebec for this interesting occasion and by my presence to testify my veneration for this ancient See, my profound respect for its present occupant, and my grateful acknowledgement of the religious benefits which for years flowed from this Mother-Church over so vast a frontier of North America."[44] Another occasion was the "Month Mind" Mass for his friend, Crinnon of Hamilton, following his untimely death in November 1882. It was customary at that time to have this special requiem Mass celebrated one month after a person's death. Walsh was among the several bishops invited to be in attendance in Hamilton in January 1883 for that Mass.[45] In like manner, he happily accepted an invitation from Joseph-Thomas Duhamel of Ottawa to be present at the "interesting and important ceremonies" planned for the city and the archdiocese on 9 and 10 October 1889.[46]

All these visits, and many more, evoke images of the fraternal and supportive companionship that Walsh had with his fellow bishops. Very frequently they expressed their profound admiration of the role he played amongst them. By his own admission, it was greatly disappointing to have to refuse any of the visits; he well understood the importance of maintaining close social ties and friendship among bishops in nurturing the Catholic Church, still an emerging body in Canada. Each regretted refusal of an episcopal invitation, however, provided him an opportunity to write, praising the host for the invitation, or affirming once again the friendly bonds between them. One such example was in the letter he wrote to the vicar general of Quebec in 1870, at the time Archbishop Baillargeon died. He could not assist at his friend's funeral, Walsh lamented, nor could he send his vicar general, who was himself ill. Instead, his personal condolences and the heartfelt expression of his own loss were conveyed by a delegate, Joseph Bayard, the pastor of Sarnia: "In the death of the good Archbishop Baillargeon," Walsh wrote, "I lose one of the best and most sincere friends I have ever had the happiness of making and, since the sad intelligence of his decease has arrived, I feel as deprived of a father. That God may bless your diocese with a successor equally good and holy is the fervent prayer of – Your faithful serv[an]t in [Christ]."[47] In turn, the succeeding archbishop, Taschereau, expressed his regrets by means of a letter and a gift when, for reasons of health, Walsh was unable to attend the archbishop's consecration on 19 March 1871. Taschereau assured Walsh that his esteem and friendship for him was no less as a result of his absence, and he firmly believed that Walsh's heart was nonetheless in their midst.[48] With that letter, Taschereau also included a second one in which he appointed Walsh vicar general of the archdiocese of Quebec.[49] Though that was a titular role, and usually given to a number of bishops, it was still a considerable honour and a mark of personal respect. Earlier, in 1867, Walsh had received a similar honorary gesture from Edward Horan of Kingston, within twelve days of Walsh's consecration as a bishop, and again afterwards in 1875 from Casper Borgess, bishop of Detroit, who had first accepted the title of vicar general of London before bestowing the same title upon Walsh for Detroit.[50]

There were other acts of collegial respect and friendship offered Walsh by bishops from across the country. It was, above all, his many humane qualities that most endeared him to them. The support he gave to Lynch over the friction with the school trustees was one such example;[51] another was that given to Borgess when scandal arose in his diocese after an Austrian-Polish priest was charged with having "carnal intercourse" with two married women as well as three single women in his parish. It was a sordid affair and very distressing for Borgess. Yet, as if that were not enough, equally unsavoury was that the priest's "sister," who lived with him as his housekeeper, turned out to be a common prostitute. Borgess wrote a letter of warm gratitude to Walsh for his kind and sympathetic support and helpful advice.[52]

Among Walsh's many long-term episcopal friends was, above all, John Lynch of Toronto. Despite their differences in personality, policies, and politics, their friendship endured, extending all the way back to 1859 when Lynch had first arrived in Toronto while Walsh was yet a young priest there. Walsh appreciated the advice and help Lynch many times offered him, and as a gesture of appreciation, one of Walsh's first acts after he was installed as bishop was to appoint Lynch as a vicar general for the diocese.[53] That signalled the beginning of an even stronger relationship; from their respective sees, they would work in close harmony for the next twenty years for the betterment and prosperity of the Catholic Church throughout the vast area of southern Ontario which encompassed their dioceses.

In his diaries over the years, Lynch recorded many personal visits made by the two bishops to each other, including special visits to see Walsh in London, at which times Lynch also visited schools there and in Windsor and Chatham. The social occasions were numerous: in 1877, a visit with Walsh and other bishops and senior priests at the archiepiscopal palace in Toronto; in 1881, a visit by Lynch to Walsh's country house thirty-five kilometres south of London, at the lovely setting of Port Stanley on Lake Erie; in 1884, a visit by Walsh to Toronto to see Lynch, which also included seeing Carberry of Hamilton; and in 1885, a visit by Lynch to London, during which he participated in "the bishop's festival," at the time of the consecration of the new cathedral.[54] Their correspondence also indicates a number of official visits between them.[55] There were, however, at least two major events which Walsh could not attend, the anniversary celebrations in late 1882 for James Cleary in Kingston and John Lynch in Toronto. Regretfully he wrote that he had made prior arrangements to visit parishes in his diocese which were distant and most inaccessible: "There are urgent and special reasons for not postponing these visitations which will occupy the remaining portion of this month and the beginning of next. Under the circumstances I am compelled to make the sacrifice of the pleasure and gratification it would give me to assist in the coming anniversaries but I will be with you in mind and heart and holy prayer."[56]

A further way the two friends maintained their personal relationship was by exchanges of cordial greetings for Christmas, Easter, and the celebrations of their feast days, in the forms of telegrams or short written notes.[57] They also corresponded when either one was out of the country, as illustrated by the letters from Lynch during the Vatican Council in Rome, and Walsh's letters to Lynch from Rome when he made his *ad limina* visits, or whenever he took his holidays.[58] Correspondence clearly was a pleasure for them, and they seemed anxious to share with one another whatever news and experiences came their way.

Though they came from a similar ethnic and social class, and they shared convictions about the direction for the Catholic Church in Canada (and more specifically in Ontario), their personalities and outlooks were far from alike. In fact, they disagreed, however civilly, over many things: the use of Protestant Bibles and prayers in public schools with Catholic students, their respective political dealings, and their divergent political views, among others. Yet, notwithstanding those differences, and any others not immediately reconciled, their friendship was solid, strengthened each time that it was tested. In the course of things, they actually tended to complement each other, and their passionate interest in the welfare and growth of the Catholic Church in Canada would creep into their discussions, plans, and decisions – even when relaxing and socializing together – which, in turn, commonly led them to act in close harmony. In that way, too, together they were able to give leadership to their episcopal colleagues in the province and across the nation.

One complex issued developed in 1876, however, which placed Walsh in a particularly uncomfortable position, and which he feared might damage his good relationship with Lynch. That was when the archbishop, due to his increasing poor health, asked Alessandro Cardinal

Barnabò at Propaganda Fide to appoint a coadjutor bishop for Toronto. The strain placed on his health was especially due to the uncompromising attacks from Catholic members of the Toronto Separate School Board over the use of secret ballots in board elections. In his letter to Barnabò, Lynch proposed a *terna* made up of the names proposed to him by other bishops in the ecclesiastical province, including Walsh, Jean-François Jamot (the vicar apostolic for Northern Canada), Peter Crinnon of Hamilton, and John O'Brien of Kingston. This *terna* consisted of Michael Joseph O'Farrell of New York; Patrick Dowd, ss, of Montreal; and William Fortune. O'Farrell was designated *dignissimus*.[59] No answer was forthcoming from Rome, however. A year later, and still without a reply from Propaganda Fide, Lynch learned that the reason for the delay was that Bishop George Conroy, the newly appointed apostolic delegate to Canada, had been secretly interfering in the matter; he was promoting Walsh for the position of coadjutor.[60]

Lynch was not pleased; neither was Walsh. On 11 June 1877, Lynch, Walsh, Crinnon, and Jamot – all the Ontario bishops but one, O'Brien of Kingston – met again, with Conroy presiding, to discuss the candidates for the coadjutorship; they confirmed the choice of O'Farrell and then submitted the *terna* to Rome a second time. Within days, and still favouring Walsh, Conroy travelled to London and Hamilton, to consult the bishops there; he was insisting that Lynch give up the whole administration of the archdiocese to a coadjutor.[61]

Greatly frustrated and defiant, Lynch wrote Conroy, angrily stating he was not pleased with Conroy's meddling, and preferred that Conroy instead respect his wishes that O'Farrell be appointed his coadjutor.[62] Conroy was not about to give in, however. Two days later he wrote to the new prefect at Propaganda Fide, Alessandro Cardinal Franchi, again proposing Walsh for the office. He emphasized the importance of that choice for Toronto: it was a capital city and needed someone of Walsh's political acumen and pastoral outlook, and besides, he noted,there were problems with the archbishop's candidate, O'Farrell. Unrelentingly, the next month, in July, Conroy again wrote Rome, demanding haste in naming the coadjutor. As well, in that letter he discredited O'Farrell by placing into question his abilities as a bishop.[63] Events then took a strange turn. Because of the pressure put on him by the apostolic delegate, and possibly feeling weary from his battles with the school trustees and with Rome itself, Lynch wrote a letter on 11 August 1877 resigning the administration of his archdiocese, and asking that a coadjutor be appointed at once.[64] It must have seemed the only way out of the quagmire. Two days later, though, and before Lynch's letter could possibly have reached the offices in Rome, Propaganda Fide proposed to name no-one for the position. Rather, it would seek further consultation, a decision which Pius IX approved in audience on 19 August.[65]

Meantime, and still presuming that his ploy to manoeuvre Walsh into Toronto had been successful, the persistent delegate wrote confidently to him on 16 September 1877: "You will probably have already received Cardinal Franchi's letter announcing that the Sacred Congregation of the Propaganda [Fide], with the approval of His Holiness, has designated you as Coadjutor for Toronto."[66] Walsh had received no such notice. He reacted negatively to Conroy's renewed overture, and urged him to cease pushing his nomination. He had never received any official notification, Walsh insisted, nor did he even want the position. The fact of the matter was that, though a friend of Lynch, and therefore loath to hurt him, Walsh could not imagine himself working happily under Lynch's authority, or under any other bishop for that matter, for an indeterminate length of time. He was, therefore, quite unappreciative of the delegate's proposal.

In the meantime, Lynch finally received a response, a letter from the secretary of Propaganda Fide stating that the Congregation and the Holy Father wanted to name a coadjutor for Toronto, and that they were recommending Walsh instead of his candidate, O'Farrell.[67] Having reached the limit of his patience, Lynch wasted no time pressing his case again with the officials in Rome.[68] He stated pointedly that Walsh was not the choice of the bishops of Ontario, but that O'Farrell was. The Ontario bishops, he insisted, had followed the approved procedures, but some persons – unnamed – were writing to Rome promoting Walsh. The bishop of London himself, Lynch added, was certainly not among those writing; he made it very clear he was fully aware what had been going on secretly behind his back. In a manner which belied the displeasure of the archbishop over his treatment by the apostolic delegate, he further questioned why he should hand over the administration to a coadjutor. Certainly, he had always intended to name the coadjutor a vicar general, and confide to him a part of the administration of the diocese, but never would he hand it over completely to a stranger, leaving himself in a humiliated and powerless position. Without ordinary jurisdiction, Lynch warned, he would no longer have the authority to negotiate with civil authorities, to purchase or dispose of properties as he saw fit, or to care for other matters with ecclesiastical authority. "It would be most imprudent to make any changes whatsoever in these present circumstances." With that in mind, he formally retracted his resignation of the administration of the archdiocese on 11 August and reiterated to Franchi that the bishops of Ontario, in presenting their *terna,* had followed the approved procedures, especially those prescribed for bishops in Canada and the United States.[69]

A month earlier, in fact, Lynch had asked Conroy to telegraph that same message to Rome, even if the archbishop had to pay the expense himself. Conroy claimed to take offence at Lynch's suggestion, and thus refused to telegraph the message. He would write it instead, and that would have the same effect. It was nothing but a new ploy by Conroy, however, to obtain his own candidate's appointment. He well knew a letter would take weeks to arrive in Rome – sufficient time, he assumed, for the Congregation to have made the appointment already.

In his letter of 17 September, Lynch noted further that when Walsh's name had been raised at one of their earlier meetings as a possible candidate, "Bishop Walsh refused absolutely, saying that he [had] come to this determination, after mature reflection, that it would be too odious for him to come to Toronto and to await my death or my retirement."[70] Other circumstances had arisen, he continued, which made the move even more odious: that is, the newspapers had come out with the story and made public the matter. In response, forty secular priests of the archdiocese had written a petition supporting Lynch, and begging him not to retire. The nine who had not signed, he noted, were malcontents with whom he earlier had had difficulties. Yet, Lynch added, being a man of the Church, and always obedient to the Holy See, notwithstanding all that he had said in the letter, if it were the will of the Holy Father that Walsh should be appointed the coadjutor archbishop of Toronto, then he would accept him: "I will do all I can to receive him well. I will give him the powers of Vicar General, while, however, reserving the right to be consulted on the transferal of priests and other important matters, as well as promising to do nothing of importance without consulting him beforehand."[71]

Meantime, and not one to accept defeat easily, Conroy again wrote Walsh in December, after learning of his tenth anniversary celebration and of the tributes his priests had paid him. He still mistakenly presumed that Walsh was indeed Lynch's coadjutor: "I congratulate you on the interesting meeting of the other day, in which your Clergy paid you so splendid and so well merited a compliment. I do not wonder that you shrink from exchanging the diocese which, through you, has been blessed with such men, for the difficult honor of being Coadjutor to an Archbishop."[72] Where he might have received his information, inaccurate as it was, was mystifying. In truth, he should have been receiving the same dispatches from Rome – or copies thereof – that Lynch had received. Certainly, too, Conroy should have known that the appointment had been deferred in August. Eventually, two years later and after Conroy was dead, Lynch got a definitive answer on 14 November 1879; Thomas Timothy O'Mahony was named auxiliary bishop of Toronto.[73]

All the while that the correspondence was passing between Lynch and Propaganda Fide, until the resolution of the matter in 1879, he and Walsh met on numerous occasions over the appointment, and likewise discussed it frequently with other bishops. Both men desired what was best for the Catholic Church in Toronto. Certainly, from the outset, they were in agreement on who should be appointed, and had appealed to Rome, through the delegate, for their preferred choice of O'Farrell. Nevertheless, they also must have been profoundly irritated at Conroy; unquestionably, neither of them would have easily allowed him, a meddling outsider and an ill-informed one at that, to dictate the outcome of Lynch's request.[74]

Propaganda Fide offered Walsh at least one other archdiocese, but not officially: Halifax. When Archbishop Michael Hannan died there in 1882, Propaganda Fide received a *terna* naming three priests, with Cornelius O'Brien listed as *dignissimus*. Before a decision was reached, however, the bishop of Arichat, John Cameron, independently suggested Walsh's name for the vacant see.[75] Not surprisingly, the other bishops of the maritime provinces were not pleased by their colleague, and privately wrote to the prefect in Rome demanding that he block Walsh's nomination. He was not, they complained, from the Maritimes. Those writing included Peter McIntyre, bishop of Charlottetown, who insisted that the bishops, priests, and laity would all prefer to have "a priest from the island," and John Sweeney, bishop of St John of New Brunswick, who made it clear that London was too far from Nova Scotia, and that therefore Walsh could not know the local situation well enough. Furthermore, Sweeney reminded Simeoni, the bishops of the ecclesiastical province had already sent in two *ternae* with suitable names, and they wanted particular attention paid to their first choice, a Maritimer.[76]

By means of his several contacts across the country, Walsh was able to react quickly to have his name withdrawn. He wrote directly to Simeoni. Succinctly, he gave three reasons for his request: first, his health was feeble and precarious at that moment because he had worked hard in his diocese and his strength had suffered, and he would therefore be unable to fulfil the role of archbishop of Halifax; second, since he was in the middle of building a new cathedral, his departure at that time would be "a source of irreparable confusion" for the diocese because it would slow for a long time the completion of the building, and furthermore, due to the diverse population of his diocese, it would be harder to find someone for London than for Halifax; finally, and more to the point, clearly the suffragans of the Halifax see, with one exception, did not wish to have him as archbishop.

> In consideration of all these things, I implore the Sacred Congregation of the Propaganda not to remove me from my present position. The Diocese of London, in its present state, is the fruit of hard labors and of many worries and sacrifices on my part, and at my age, and in the feeble state of my health, it would be totally unwillingly that I would consent to leave it, in order to be transferred to a see a thousand miles away from here, and to begin life all over again, in the midst of an unknown people and clergy, and among suffragan Bishops who would accept me as their Metropolitan only with the greatest repugnance.[77]

Without doubt, Walsh discussed the matter with Cameron and with his colleagues in Ontario, including Lynch. The fact was, given his uncertain health, he had enough reason not to move to Halifax. Yet, more importantly, for a man to whom the support of the local community was important, it was essential to have the backing of the bishops of the ecclesiastical province of Halifax along with that of the priests and laity in Halifax and its environs. Without that, he would have an uphill struggle. Of course, even if his health should rebound, as it had many times before, unquestionably the construction of the cathedral was a further and very important consideration. Although the cathedral could have been finished by another (admittedly with difficulty), nonetheless, for Walsh, the support of the local Church was indispensable in order to assume any episcopal position.

Whether or not, in the final analysis, Cameron's recommendation or Walsh's own letter carried any weight is hard to judge. The fact was Walsh did not receive the nomination for Halifax; Cornelius O'Brien was named archbishop on 1 December 1882. Immediately prior to O'Brien's consecration on 21 January 1883, in a letter to Lynch, Walsh penned a few sensitive and encouraging words about the new archbishop: "He has a hard task before him, but he is healthy and strong, has piety and talents, and will doubtless be unanimously upheld by his clergy."[78]

Though he had been the youngest bishop in Canada at the time of his consecration, John Walsh had soon risen to a position of prestige and influence among his fellow bishops and the priests and Catholics of Ontario. In every way he was a natural leader, willing to fulfil his responsibilities and make considerable personal sacrifices whenever required. By his attention to detail and his patient handling of problems, he quickly assumed responsibility as a leading bishop throughout the province, and thus helped forge a strong Catholic Church in Ontario. Still, in fact, the position of the "senior bishop of the ecclesiastical province of Toronto" was granted him principally by precedence of his episcopal consecration. After the ecclesiastical province had been formed on 18 March 1870, Lynch, as archbishop of Toronto, *ex officio* became the highest-ranking prelate in Ontario. Next to him at that time, as "senior," was Edward Horan of Kingston, who had been a bishop longer than any other in the province. Walsh was third in order of precedence. Thus, upon Horan's retirement in 1874, Walsh became the "senior bishop," a title and influence he maintained until 1889 when he was appointed the archbishop of Toronto.

As bishop of London and senior bishop, he was called upon to play a major role at the First Provincial Council of Toronto, held in 1875 at St Michael's episcopal palace. Meeting under the presidency of Lynch, the council included the bishops Walsh, Crinnon, Jamot, and Joseph-Thomas Duhamel of Ottawa, along with a number of theologians, all of whom were priests from the participating dioceses. Though not a member of the ecclesiastical province of Toronto, Duhamel was there as an observer.

The council began on 26 September, with an opening ceremony at St Michael's Cathedral. That included a procession, which wound its way through the streets of the city until it reached the cathedral. Walsh preached the sermon.[79] There, too, in the cathedral, discussions were held on matters of faith and doctrine, education, and discipline. The bishops paid great attention to the decrees of the Vatican Council, seeking ways to implement them in their dioceses. One pressing issue for the bishops was that of Catholic schools and governmental funding for them. As well, because they were bishops of a new ecclesiastical province, they had either to accept, as norms for their new province, all of the decrees of the earlier councils of Quebec, or to amend them accordingly. The council closed on 10 October, again with a ceremony at the cathedral, at which Lynch preached. In 1883 – a full eight years later – only after the decrees were approved by Propaganda Fide, Walsh wrote a pastoral letter promulgating, for the diocese of London, the decrees of that first provincial council.[80]

One year later, as senior bishop, Walsh was one of six bishops chosen to represent the Canadian hierarchy at the Third Plenary Council of Baltimore held that autumn. There, his knowledge of theology, his experience of parochial life, and his familiarity with administration were of great value to the council delegates. Along with the decrees of the Vatican Council, the Baltimore Council also considered such matters as Catholic education of youth, parochial schools, Christian doctrine, and the sacraments.[81]

Walsh's role as senior bishop also meant that he was often called upon to arbitrate between priests and their bishops. In one notorious case, John Gribbon, a priest of the archdiocese of Toronto, had been suspended by Lynch on charges of seduction, fornication, and failure to fulfil parochial responsibilities. Gribbon, on the other hand, claimed that he was being unfairly treated by the archbishop. Walsh granted Gribbon an interview, during which he encouraged him to seek recourse to an ecclesiastical tribunal, something which Gribbon had not yet attempted to do. The bishop did not judge the case; he only indicated to Gribbon that, if everything he said was true, then in fact he would have a good case for himself. Walsh, however, was sceptical. He found it hard to believe everything with which Gribbon charged the archbishop, and doubted that Lynch had wronged him. Meantime, Walsh also urged the archbishop not to take seriously the charges of calumny brought by Gribbon, and assured Lynch that he still continued to enjoy a good reputation among those who knew him.[82] Other than that, Walsh never gave his judgment on the case or took sides.

A second incident also involved Lynch. Another one of his priests, John J. Shea, was likewise caught in acts of moral turpitude. Shea had made recourse to an ecclesiastical tribunal but, having received no redress, asked Walsh, as the senior bishop, to arbitrate in a new tribunal process. At first Walsh handled him in like fashion as with Gribbon. After having received information about the case, and with the knowledge of Shea's petition to Propaganda Fide, Walsh judged it prudent to place the whole matter in the hands of the Congregation; he simply forwarded the petition anew to the prefect without embellishments, offering no judgment or even a comment of any kind.[83]

Three years later, Lynch became mixed up in a different kind of case concerning a priest, this time not of Toronto but of the diocese of Kingston. Once more, he turned to Walsh to act as the arbitrator. The case centred on a dispute over the will of a priest who had died in 1886. Writing to Cardinal Simeoni, Lynch pointed out that as the senior bishop, Walsh was therefore the one most fitting to arbitrate the case, which he did.[84]

Other cases involving the bishop of Kingston called for Bishop Walsh's attention, wisdom, and insight. In the early 1880s, James Cleary of Kingston had suspended a priest, Thomas C. McMahon, for unspecified priestly failures. After a time, and having left the country, McMahon had exhausted all his resources; he sought to re-enter the diocese and be re-instated in ministry. With no ecclesiastical appointment forthcoming from Cleary, however, McMahon insisted that he had to be given some form of compensation. He turned to Walsh, asking him to arbitrate the matter. In this case, Walsh unhesitatingly took a side in the dispute, by giving his unqualified support to Cleary in a letter to Propaganda Fide: "I hope, therefore, that Your Eminence would excuse me, in the interests of justice and of religion, being the senior Bishop of this Province, to give testimony to the merits and fruitful labor of the devoted, zealous and knowledgeable bishop of Kingston."[85]

Again, another priest of Kingston, John J. Brennan, found himself at loggerheads with Cleary. He too appealed to Walsh. His complaint concerned a decision made by Cleary in the late 1880s. Writing to Brennan, Walsh, as senior bishop, informed him of the process for such an appeal, and pointed out that he was unable to act in the case as presented, since Brennan had failed to make prior recourse to an ecclesiastical tribunal. Brennan first had to make a case before Lynch as the metropolitan. If he was unhappy with the results of that case, he then could turn to Walsh for further arbitration in an appeal. Only then could Walsh act. At the same time, however, Walsh judged Brennan's case unworthy of appeal, and advised him not to pursue the issue any further.[86]

The role of senior bishop had other ramifications for Walsh. On two occasions, with the death of Peter Crinnon in 1882 and that of James Carberry in 1887, Walsh was named administrator of their diocese, Hamilton. The naming of an administrator in such circumstances was a common practice. Likewise, one was named even when a bishop was on an extended absence from the diocese, which might occur frequently enough during the regular *ad limina* visits to Rome or during holidays abroad. At such times, the vicar general of the diocese in question, or another senior priest, would have assumed the respon-

sibility of the day-to-day administration of the diocese, only calling
on the bishop-administrator for extraordinary matters, such as those
which required the attention of someone with episcopal rank. During a *sede vacante*, however, the role of bishop-administrator took on
a greater significance. Then he would have to attend to the diocesan
affairs more closely in order to ensure that the needs of the people and
the good of the Church were being maintained. It was precisely this
role that Walsh was called upon to fulfill in the diocese of Hamilton
on the deaths of its two bishops.[87]

During his years in London, there were eight bishops appointed
in the dioceses of Ontario; of those, Walsh influenced the choice of
six. The selection of Crinnon for Hamilton in 1874 was greatly due to
Walsh. He had known Crinnon well, for not only had Crinnon been a
priest of the London diocese, but Walsh had also named him a vicar
general the year after he came to the diocese, in December 1868. Walsh
grew to have considerable respect for Crinnon's capabilities, and successfully urged his promotion to Hamilton. As a sign of his esteem
for his former bishop, Crinnon asked Walsh to be a co-consecrator at
the ceremony in Stratford on 19 April 1874. The two remained lifelong
friends.[88]

When Edward Horan of Kingston was forced to retire due to ill
health in 1874, the Ontario bishops met to take up the matter of his successor.[89] Crinnon was going to Rome, and therefore would present the
terna to Propaganda Fide personally. Walsh, as expected, was present
at the meeting. Unusually, though, he had not consulted beforehand
with Horan himself, since his forced retirement had created such a
delicate situation. Walsh obviously would have felt considerable strain
speaking with Horan, especially since he preferred to deal with matters – including personal relations – in a harmonious way without risk
of tension arising. Lynch thought otherwise, and was not pleased that
Walsh had not met Horan to discuss the matter. He, therefore, invited
Horan himself, as was his right as metropolitan, to join the bishops at
their upcoming meeting.[90]

While all that was going on, the bishops of the Toronto province
had meanwhile consulted Paul Cardinal Cullen, the archbishop of
Dublin, for suggested names for the vacant see of Kingston. Although
it was not a usual procedure at that time in Canada to appoint bishops from Europe who had not already served as priests in Canada,
still it happened from time to time. James V. Cleary, a priest from the
diocese of Ossory in Ireland, whom Walsh had met during one of
his visits there, was presented as a candidate. The prefect of Propa-

ganda Fide, Franchi, however, reacted vigorously against it. In a stiffly worded reply, he observed: "This measure does not please this Sacred Congregation ... If there is among you qualified priests to govern the diocese of Kingston, it is not fitting that you ignore them and give greater importance to priests strange to your ecclesiastical province." Lynch and the others, therefore, would have to wait for another opportunity to propose Cleary for the Canadian episcopacy. Horan's proffered candidates to fill the see were not taken seriously either; his first choice was too young while, bizarrely, his other two were solely French-speaking.[91]

The choice for Kingston eventually fell to John O'Brien, a priest of that diocese.[92] Lynch, Crinnon, and Walsh consecrated him on 18 April 1875. Yet, in less than five years, the new bishop was dead, a victim "des faiblesses sérieuses," that is, alcoholism. Another bishop for Kingston was sought. James Cleary was again deemed *dignissimus* on the *terna* prepared by Lynch, Jamot, Crinnon, and Walsh. They also included two Sulpicians, James Hogan, ss, and Patrick Dowd, ss, of Montreal, as well as a fourth candidate (a departure from the norm), Edward Heenan, a vicar general of Hamilton. This time Cleary was successful. On 5 January 1881, he was consecrated in Rome with the prefect of Propaganda Fide, Cardinal Simeoni, acting as the principal consecrator.[93]

Within a year, Crinnon of Hamilton died suddenly in Florida, while at the same time, the bishops in the Maritimes were seeking a new archbishop for Halifax. Several candidates were being discussed for the two sees. Because the Toronto ecclesiastical province was unable to settle quickly on a candidate for Hamilton, the bishops there appointed a vicar capitular instead for the short term to act as administrator. That was Lynch's doing; Walsh was in agreement. In a revealing remark, he wrote the archbishop that such an appointment "will prevent gossip and intrigue and even dissensions and bitterness between the clergy."[94] Previously, Lynch had sent him a document from Pope Benedict XIV which had instructions concerning the proper procedure at the unexpected death of a bishop, of which Walsh wrote: "This document of Benedict XIV is not as well known as it should be, as the mode of procedure it authorizes in the event of a sudden death of a bishop would save a great deal of confusion and trouble."[95] As with the choice for Kingston in 1880, once again a priest from Ireland was chosen for the vacant see of Hamilton: a Dominican, James J. Carberry. He too was consecrated in Rome, on 11 November 1883, with Cleary of Kingston representing the Canadian bishops as a co-consecrator.

Again, within a very short space of time, other new episcopal appointments were required. Jean-François Jamot, the first bishop of
Peterborough, died in 1886. Within seven months his Irish-born successor, Thomas J. Dowling, was chosen and consecrated. Because he
had been a priest of the diocese of Hamilton, Dowling was consecrated there on 1 May 1887; Walsh acted as a co-consecrator. Later that
year, while visiting Ireland, Carberry of Hamilton died suddenly on 17
December 1887 after only four years in office. Soon afterwards, while
in Paris the following January, Walsh wrote to Lynch concerning the
needed *terna* for Hamilton. Walsh was on his way home from Rome
and informed Lynch that, while there, he had spoken to Cleary about
the vacancy. He urged Lynch to take no action until all the bishops
of the province could meet and deliberate together on the names to
be submitted. He added, in a tongue-in-cheek fashion, "there is much
more reason for this delay since the Diocese of Hamilton has the good
fortune of having a Bishop as its administrator during the vacancy."
He was referring to himself.[96] Before the bishops could gather, however, Lynch himself died unexpectedly on 12 May following.

In their discussions in July, then, the three bishops – Walsh, Cleary,
and Dowling – drew up a master plan to be presented to Rome, which
they presumed would be accepted. They first agreed on Dowling moving from Peterborough to fill the vacancy of his home diocese of Hamilton. The *terna* for Hamilton included, as *dignissimus,* Dowling; as
dignior, Richard A. O'Connor, a priest and one of the vicars forane of
Hamilton; and as *dignus*, a Jesuit, William Doherty. The three prelates
next drew up a list of candidates for the soon-to-be vacant Peterborough, listing the same Richard A. O'Connor as *dignissimus*, Doherty
as *dignior*, and Denis O'Connor, the Basilian superior and president of
Assumption College, Sandwich, as *dignus*. The triumvirate of bishops
was successful on both counts: Dowling was named fourth bishop of
Hamilton and Richard O'Connor was named third bishop of Peterborough, both on 11 January 1889.[97] Cleary was the principal consecrator for Richard O'Connor and Walsh preached the sermon.

Most often the deliberations for drawing up a *terna* were held under
the presidency of the archbishop of Toronto. He, then, would be the
principal consecrator for any episcopal consecration taking place
within his province. Walsh always played a leading role at such times,
and his opinions carried even more weight after he became senior
bishop. That was evident from the number of times he was asked to
be either a co-consecrator or the preacher at episcopal consecrations,
privileges that came at the invitation of the one being consecrated. He
had promoted candidates well known to himself, and they in turn sig-

nalled their respect and appreciation with requests for his assistance in the sacred ceremonies.

Of all selections of successors in a bishopric, the diocese of Ottawa was especially complex. Although located mostly within the province of Ontario, the diocese was almost wholly French-speaking. After the formation of the ecclesiastical province of Toronto in 1870, which had incorporated all the other Ontario dioceses, Ottawa had remained a suffragan bishopric of Quebec and, for that reason, the selection of its bishops had remained the privilege of the bishops of the province of Quebec rather than of those of Ontario.

The diocese of Ottawa had not been included in the new Ontario ecclesiastical province, largely due to the growing French-English rivalry that had begun during the debate about the raising of Toronto to a metropolitan see. The first bishop of Ottawa, Joseph-Eugène-Bruno Guigues, OMI, and the archbishops of Quebec – first Baillargeon and then Taschereau – were adamantly opposed to such an inclusion. Nor, when writing to Walsh on other matters, did they make any reference to the glaring omission of Ottawa, even though attention was already being focused on that diocese in the early 1870s. When Ottawa became vacant in 1874 at the death of Guigues, the attention of Quebec's bishops, therefore, quickly turned to seeking a replacement.[98] They were successful. The Quebec episcopate secured the nomination of Joseph-Thomas Duhamel, who was then consecrated at Ottawa on 28 October 1874, by the archbishop of Quebec himself, assisted by the bishop of Trois-Rivières and the coadjutor bishop of Montreal. The Ontario bishops were not even invited. They had been isolated from the decision and from the liturgical ceremony.

Despite the attitude of the new bishop of Ottawa – "The diocese that I inherited from Bishop Guigues is becoming more and more French-Canadian" – the bishops of Ontario did not give up so easily; they continued to press Rome for the juridical inclusion of Ottawa in the ecclesiastical province of Toronto instead of in Quebec. The bishops of Quebec, on the other hand, moved to ensure their "coveted objective" (that the diocese of Ottawa would not become part of the English-speaking Catholic Church in Ontario) and the struggle for jurisdiction between the Ontario and Quebec hierarchies intensified in the following years.[99] Strangely enough, as many Ontario bishops recognized, while most of the Catholic dioceses in Ontario had bishops whose first language was English, the reality was that a large portion of the population of the province was still French-speaking. That was notably true throughout southwestern Ontario, with nearly one-quarter of Walsh's diocese and the northern parts of Ontario being French-speaking. In the minds of many, therefore, if the Quebec bishops had really followed their compatriots beyond the borders of the province of Quebec, they would have acknowledged as well that "French fact" outside of Ottawa. They did not do so.

In the end, that was one of the chief arguments raised by Walsh against the Quebec bishops when, during the late 1870s, they made overtures to Propaganda Fide to establish Ottawa as an archdiocese. The fact that they had done so without ever consulting the bishops of Ontario concerning Ottawa's status, only exacerbated the situation in the minds of Walsh and the other Ontario bishops. Their blatantly untrue allegation that the English-speaking bishops were not properly caring for their French-speaking people only increased the frustration in Ontario. In his letter to Lynch, 12 June 1880, Walsh pointedly criticized the Quebec bishops for their failure to know and understand Ontario: "The objection that French Canadian Catholics would not be well attended by us is not founded on truth. There are fourteen thousand French Canadians in this diocese and their religious interests are as well cared for to say the least, as if they were situated in the centre of Lower Canada."[100]

Walsh was especially annoyed at the unnecessarily aggressive behaviour of the Quebec episcopate. For him, because their attitudes and actions tended to ignore juridical boundaries (however undefined these may have been in Ontario at the time), they were dangerously undermining the Catholic Church in general. In the end, though, Walsh saved his strongest words for his assessment of the situation in Quebec itself. Weighing in with indicting invectives, and showing not a little of his own deep Irish nationalism, Walsh lashed out at the narrow nationalism of the Quebec episcopate itself, and at the damage this was bringing to the Catholic Church:

Is not the Church which the present Lower Canadian Episcopate received from their predecessors in a thoroughly well-organized state, distracted and torn asunder by their mismanagement and, instead of making any impression on the aggressive Protestantism that confronts it, is instead truly invaded, and numbers of its children seduced from it into heresy? These, as we know, are the facts of the case. This is also true of Manitoba. Wherever the weaker race meets the stronger, the former necessarily go to the wall. It is only the Irish race with their descendants that can present a bold unyielding front to Protestantism in this country and experience, sad experience teaches that Irish Catholic interests invariably suffer and are utterly neglected under French Canadian management.[101]

Even if he were exaggerating the condition of the Church in Quebec somewhat, for Walsh the timing was important. He strongly urged Lynch to join him immediately in "solemnly and emphatically" protesting against the Quebec scheme, which he saw would "work perniciously for the interest of the Church in the future ... [F]or if we do not do our utmost to prevent them, the future will judge us pretty severely." He was willing, however, to submit to the judgment of the archbishop and of his episcopal *confrères*, Crinnon and Jamot, even if that were to mean taking no further action.[102]

Without much hesitation, though, further action was taken. The bishops of Ontario began to press their case vigorously in Rome for the inclusion of Ottawa in their ecclesiastical province. When it seemed, however, that they were unlikely to win out, and moreover that Ottawa would achieve the new status desired by the Quebec episcopate, Walsh and his colleagues began a campaign in Rome to establish Kingston as an archdiocese. That, they believed, would keep the balance in Ontario, and would ensure worthy recognition for the oldest Ontario diocese. Although by then long dead, Bishop Horan would have been delighted: his arguments were formulated in new ways and given new prominence.

Nonetheless, the bishops of Quebec won the day. On 8 June 1886, Ottawa was elevated to the status of an archdiocese with Duhamel its archbishop. As before, the boundaries of the diocese continued to straddle the provincial borders, firmly planted in the two civil provinces. The vicariate apostolic of Pontiac was given as Ottawa's only suffragan see.[103]

Not at all pleased at what had happened, the Ontario bishops set out to plan anew, and three years later, by 1889, had formulated their scheme for a new ecclesiastical province of Kingston, which they forwarded to Propaganda Fide. Rome concurred, and Kingston's pre-eminence as the first diocese in Ontario and the first outside of Quebec, was recognized with the title "archdiocese." Peterborough would be its first suffragan see but, since only one suffragan seemed inconvenient, the eastern region of Kingston was hived off and established as a separate diocese, made up of the counties of Glengarry, Cornwall, and Stormont. This area, which now made up the new diocese, was historically the cradle of the Catholic faith in eastern Ontario, due largely to the Scots and United Empire Loyalist Catholic settlements in the St Raphael's area established in the eighteenth and early nineteenth centuries. The new diocese was to be called Alexandria, with its seat in that city. The archdiocese of Kingston was canonically erected on 28 December 1889, along with Peterborough; Alexandria was erected in January of the next year. James Cleary, Kingston's sixth bishop, became the first archbishop of the new archdiocese.[104] With Lynch of Toronto already dead by that time, as the senior ecclesiastic in Ontario, leadership of the Catholic Church in English-speaking Canada still rested with Walsh.

As with those sometimes vociferous divisions between Ontario and Quebec within the Catholic hierarchy, there could at times be dangerous divisions and even deadly hatreds among the Irish Catholics themselves. That was eminently so in one of the most celebrated, if not thoroughly notorious, murder cases in nineteenth-century Ontario, the Donnelly massacres. Theirs was a sordid tale. This Catholic family from Ireland – headed by James and Johannah Donnelly – which had settled in 1847 in Biddulph Township, close by the small village of Lucan, were "largely victims of a very complicated social convention imported from Tipperary [Ireland]."[105]

James Donnelly began operating a stagecoach service between Lucan and London. From the beginning, there were acrimonious relations with the family's Irish Catholic neighbours, which intensified when the Donnellys were evicted from half of their property because they could not afford to make further payments on it. In a drunken brawl, Donnelly killed his neighbour Patrick Farrell and, after one year of avoiding arrest, surrendered and was convicted of his death. Donnelly spent seven years in the Kingston penitentiary. No doubt due to the absence of their father for such an extended period, James and Johannah's seven sons began to gain a bad reputation as rowdies and bullies. To add to the tension, the second son, Will, attempted to marry a local woman, angering her family. After being rebuffed by them on two occasions, he eloped with another woman, Nora Kennedy, in 1876, and so angered her family as well. Also, given the local entrenched loyalties towards political parties, the Donnellys were castigated by their Catholic neighbours for voting against the local Catholic Conservative candidate in the general federal election of 1878. In addition, there were unproven charges of arson and some petty crimes, which would not have been totally unimaginable, given the rowdy nature of the seven sons.[106] The backdrop to this unfolding tragedy was the drama of the imported "Tipperary problem." Protestants loyal to the British Crown had been settled on land in Tipperary, Ireland, that had been forcibly taken from Catholics. The government of England thereby caused great unrest and injustices in Ireland that would lead to centuries of fighting. As a result, there grew up in Tipperary an organized movement of resistance, known as the Whiteboys, which in effect was a Catholic faction fighting the Protestants.[107] The Catholics in Tipperary, however, were divided, since many were willing to live in peace with their new "neighbours," and so, complicating matters further, fighting also developed among Catholics, with the Whiteboys on one side and those Catholics who desired peace on the other.

By a terrible twist of fate, members of all three factions, on coming to the New World, ended up settling in the same area, Biddulph Township. The Donnellys were part of the latter Catholic group who generally desired to live in peace with their neighbours. On coming to Canada, therefore, they especially wanted to leave behind in Ireland the feuds of past generations. Yet it was not to be. Their lawlessness and troubles with their neighbours, therefore, were greatly aggravated further by the "Tipperary problem."[108]

Those troubles among the Catholic neighbours in Biddulph Township took on greater seriousness with the arrival of a new pastor at St Patrick's at Lucan, John Connolly, on 4 February 1879, his first appointment in the diocese of London. Walsh appointed him there because of his Irish background. The previous pastors, both German, had never been able to bring peace to the troubled parish, so it was the bishop's hope that Connolly could accomplish what had eluded his predecessors.[109] Connolly was considered a man of strong convictions, as well as eager and zealous to promote the Catholic faith. He was "prideful of his cloth and at times intransigent in the defence of his Church against those he considered his enemies. He was often dangerously uncritical of those of his flock whose profession of Christian virtues blinded his eyes to their secular activities."[110] This last characteristic might have been his greatest fault.

Yet just as serious was what seemed to be his habit of believing whoever spoke to him first on a particular issue. That would in the end lead to tragic consequences, especially when he listened to those in his congregation who were opposed to the Donnellys. In his zeal to establish peace, he foolishly gave his blessing to a group of parishioners who promised, in the absence of a regular or effective constabulary, to root out and put down crime in the parish. They formed themselves into a group calling itself the Vigilance Committee, whose members all took an oath:

> We the undersigned Roman Catholics of St Patrick's of Biddulph solemnly pledge ourselves to aid our spiritual director and Parish priest, in the discovery & putting down of crime in our mission. While we at the same time protest as Irishmen and as Catholics against any interference with him in the legitimate discharge of his spiritual duties.[111]

Their very names and their oath should have been a warning to Connolly that serious trouble was in store. Instead, he allowed that a book with the oath be left in the church for anyone who wished to join. Ninety-four men appended their signatures to the oath; no member of the Donnelly family joined.

Walsh knew of the family and the associated troubles, since word about the whole affair had made its way to London. In addition, Will Donnelly indicated at the later trial that he had written a letter to the bishop in October 1879 asking him to intervene. Will felt that Connolly was treating the family badly. He complained bitterly in the letter about Connolly's prejudice, feeling strongly that that was chiefly responsible for the continuing antagonism. Eerily, Will foretold a dismal end: "if something is not done I am sure it will end in bloodshed."[112] Walsh turned over the letter to Connolly, according to the report from Will. In his turn, Connolly publicly berated Will for having the impudence to write the bishop, and then castigated all those who were named as character witnesses by Donnelly.[113]

The Vigilance Committee quickly became a vigilante committee. During the early hours of 4 February 1880, several committee members, under the leadership of the local constable, James Carroll (himself a member), took the law into their own hands. Seeking reprisal against what they perceived to be the evils of the Donnelly family, they entered the home of James and Johannah Donnelly and beat them to death with shillelaghs and farm implements. At the same time, they killed one of the young sons, Tom, and a visiting niece, Bridget Donnelly, whom they also raped before murdering her. The vigilantes then set the house on fire. A second group of the committee simultaneously went to the home of Will and Nora Donnelly, determined to kill Will. When they approached the house, it was Will's younger brother John who opened the door to the murderers and received the brunt of their attack, two fatal gun shots.[114] The township woke up that morning to the horror of the murders, as the news quickly spread.

Within seven days, an inquest began with thirty-three accused persons. The verdict of this inquest on 2 March stated that the Donnellys were murdered by "parties unknown." A preliminary hearing was subsequently held, and on 13 March, formal charges were laid against only six persons. The trial opened on 12 April in London's court house. The first order of business in the trial was a request by the defence for a change of venue, and herein is found the first recorded instance of Bishop Walsh's involvement in the case: his letter to the Catholic parish priest of Lindsay, Ontario, Michael Stafford, asking him to speak to a Mr Wood to argue against a change of venue. Walsh indicated that enough impartial jurors could be found in Middlesex County to provide the prisoners with a fair trial based on strict and impartial justice.[115] Eventually, the change of venue was ruled out.

The trial began in earnest during the last week of September. The charges were read, and innocent pleas were entered by all those charged. The judge, John Douglas Armour, then decided to hold the trials separately, so James Carroll, the Lucan constable, against whom the strongest case existed, was tried first. After two weeks of proceedings, which included little of the testimony heard at the inquest, the jury was unable to reach a verdict.[116]

A second trial, slated to begin during the last week of January 1881, got underway after two judges, in an unusual move by the attorney general for Ontario, were appointed to hear the case. Once again Carroll was tried, but that time was found not guilty and released. When the Crown prosecutor asked for a stay of proceedings, so he could prepare a better case against the others, all of the accused were released on bail, on the condition they would appear for a trial when summoned. They never were called.[117]

On 14 May 1881, as the Crown prosecutor was preparing his new case, Walsh held a secret meeting at his palace with Adam Crooks, the minister of Education, who was also the acting premier for Oliver Mowat, and Charles Hutchinson, the Crown attorney for Middlesex County. It is certain that, during the meeting, Walsh was able to convince Crooks and Hutchinson not to prosecute Connolly for aiding and abetting the murderers. A compromise had been reached: if Connolly was not to be prosecuted, then no one else would be either. In consequence, no one stood trial again for the murders of the five members of the Donnelly family, nor has the case ever been resolved, nor has anyone ever made restitution for the crime.[118]

A reason for the meeting, as suggested by one historian, may have been Walsh's concern for Connolly and for his own episcopal career. Certainly Connolly was at risk of being implicated in the whole murderous affair as an accessory; foolishly and reprehensibly he had given approbation to the Vigilance Committee, and had also allowed their taking of oaths in his church. Charges were made, which Connolly denied vehemently, that he had actually singled out the Donnelly family for action by the committee. There is no evidence that he ever did so. Yet, nevertheless, as pastor, he certainly would have known about the blood feud in his parish, and his responsibility for the committee was undeniable, attested by the oath taken in his very church. In that view, Walsh was seen as putting "a lid on a potential scandal that could have ruined his episcopate."[119] On the other hand, although Walsh's career may have been a personal concern, the matter existed in a much larger context: that is, Walsh's concern for the Catholic Church in its struggle with Orangeism. At the time the case was proceeding in London, the cities of Montreal, Kingston, and Toronto were all caught in the grip of anti-Catholic riots, often attributed to Orangeism. Sporadic outbreaks of violence occurred in all three cities from time to time, with Montreal experiencing the worst of the trouble. In Walsh's mind, therefore, there had already been enough violence in Biddulph. Putting Connolly on trial might have led to further outbreaks in the township, and possibly in London as well, but most assuredly in the three larger centres, which were "simmering pots of hatred."[120]

Walsh knew of the old troubles in Toronto firsthand, of course. Though written eight years later, in 1889, a letter to the archbishop of Montreal, Édouard-Charles Fabre, indicated the precarious nature of the situation and the ease with which a riot could have broken out in any one of those cities. When Walsh wrote, Fabre had just returned from a trip to Rome:

> Your Grace has safely escaped from the storms of the sea but you will come in for a share in the storm of Protestant fanaticism that is now raging in Ontario and that doubtless is felt in Montreal with more or less violence, the occasion of it all being the restitution made to the Jesuits by the Mercier Government. Our consolation is that all the violence will not endure and that the calm will come, sooner or later, when it pleases God to command it.[121]

The bishop was as familiar as anyone in London with the peaceful relations between most Catholics and Protestants, despite outbreaks of anti-Catholicism by Orangemen elsewhere in Ontario. He himself had done much to encourage, maintain, and strengthen those peaceful relations. In fact, London had been an island of tranquillity compared to elsewhere, with Protestants and Catholics there having enjoyed excellent relations for over a century. At times Protestants had even helped Catholics build some of their churches, and they worked together in such organizations as the Irish Benevolent Society.[122] Yet despite this amity, Walsh was also aware that three-quarters of the population of the city of London was Protestant, and probably half of those were members of the Orange Lodge. For this reason, he was careful not to disturb the delicate balance of peace.

Certainly, that was the concern of the premier and the Crown attorney at the time of the secret meeting with Walsh. Not only did Walsh want to prevent any riots in London, but the government's representatives as well would have been anxious that peace should be maintained there between the Catholic "Whiteboys" and the Catholics seeking peace, and between Orangemen and Catholics in general. In foreswearing the further prosecution of the Donnellys' murderers, Walsh and the officials might have let the guilty go free, but the avoidance of large-scale riots would, they hoped, save many more lives.

It was, arguably, for that reason that Walsh had intervened at the very beginning through the parish priest of Lindsay in order to prevent a change of venue for the trial. While moving the trial might have better assured an impartial jury, it definitely would have brought more attention to the case, and thus dangerously fanned any flames of Orangeism latent in London's population. Ever mindful of his role in maintaining peace, Walsh therefore intervened in the case. Walsh was determined to settle the long-simmering feud and to bring peace to the region.[123]

Along with the attention Walsh paid to developing parishes and schools, hospitals and orphanages, and to supporting the priests and Religious who worked in all those institutions, as bishop, he also demonstrated a careful attention to detail in his continuing administration of his diocese. As did all bishops, he found visitations to parishes to be excellent opportunities to meet large numbers of Catholics, as well to gain accurate information about his priests and people. Visitations also allowed Catholics to see their bishop on occasion. While Walsh held his visitations on a regular basis, he also celebrated in the parishes the sacrament of Confirmation, or assisted at special parochial occasions such as the blessing of a church. It was his way, too, of praying with his people, teaching them the truths of the faith, and preaching the gospel. By those means, he was also able to keep abreast of the diocesan needs, both spiritual and temporal.[124]

He never seemed to waver in these responsibilities, even in his later years, despite his precarious health and the difficulties of travelling over poorly maintained roads or during the winter months. A letter to the archbishop of Toronto, written in 1886, indicated that he had just finished another series of visits, but that he had three or four left before he could "settle down for the winter's work at home."[125] Nonetheless, he still put the needs of the diocese ahead of any personal matter.[126]

Concern for the spiritual welfare of his people was ever present. He continued to promote retreats in parishes throughout the diocese on a systematic basis. A circular letter to his priests, issued 12 August 1883, brought to their attention that he had secured the services of two Redemptorists who would give retreats in all the French parishes of the diocese, throughout that coming autumn: "The missionaries will give you due notice of the time in which they will be ready to begin their holy work in your mission so that you may have ample time to announce the retreat to your people and to make all prerequisite arrangements for it. You would do well to explain to your flock the nature and object of a retreat and to point out the many graces and spiritual favours it is calculated to bestow."[127] Ever practical in an administrative sense, the bishop informed the parish priests that they could take up a collection during the mission "to defray expenses and for the just remuneration of the missionaries." Many parishes in the diocese welcomed the Redemptorists' retreat that year. As well, other parishes were visited by Jesuits or by Carmelites. By far, though, the Redemptorists attended to the largest number of parishes.[128] In such wise, it was evident Walsh was a pastor not only for the people, but for the priests as well; he prayed that the retreats would be "a great help and consolation" to them as pastors of souls.

His care of souls was evident even in the way he requested and received annual reports on the financial and spiritual health of each parish. Such reports were usually collected at the time of the priests' annual retreat: "Please be so good as to give written answers to the questions contained in the accompanying sheet, and hand them to Rev. M. Tiernan, at the Retreat, as we wish to have a full and accurate knowledge of the spiritual and financial condition of each mission."[129] That accounting would not only give Walsh a picture of the growth and spiritual and financial health of the diocese, but would also aid him in planning its general direction. In many cases, the reports probably only confirmed what he already knew from his visits, so thorough was he in his powers of observation.

On another practical note, to bring consistency throughout the diocese, he published from time to time a table for fees which indicated what stipends were to be collected by priests and what amounts were to be paid to the Chancery. At one time, he even considered establishing a *caisse ecclésiastique* – a church-run credit union – in the diocese. It might well have provided a valuable service, but in the end he was unable to conclude this project satisfactorily.[130]

Good administration of his diocese also depended on the dissemination of other types of information: Walsh regularly published circular letters meant not only for the priests but for the benefit of all within the diocese. These included his proclamation of the jubilee connected with Pope Leo XIII's anniversary, the promulgation of the decrees of the First Provincial Council of Toronto, his institution of the collection for the shrines in the Holy Land, and even his personal greetings to everyone in the diocese, one year – 1887 – even sent from Rome.[131] In these he not only used the postal system and pulpits, but the local Catholic newspaper as well, reaching as many people as possible, in order to preserve and enhance the growth of the Catholic Church throughout his diocese. He wanted it to be kept healthy, balanced, well insured, and steadily moving forward. While he had to rely greatly on his priests, he had to make timely decisions, communicate them, and see them through to their conclusions. Walsh's vision and way of proceeding, and his evident care for even the smallest detail, garnered much goodwill, affection, and cooperation from priests and parishioners alike.

Of his very many accomplishments in London, perhaps the most remarkable was, without doubt, his construction of a new cathedral. As well as the obvious need for a new building to accommodate the ever-growing congregation, there was also a desire for new churches and related institutions as expressions of faith and the newfound prominence of religion in the latter part of the nineteenth century. A "profusion of church spires" began to dominate the Ontario landscape: "At the end of the nineteenth century Toronto's tallest structure was not a bank headquarters or a communications tower but the spire of St James's [Anglican] Cathedral ... While they were intended primarily for the worship of God, the churches of the era also reflected the activist and optimistic temper of the time."[132] Indeed, by the 1870s, almost every village and town in the province had several churches of all major denominations, either built or under construction, while even in rural areas, a lone church, Protestant or Catholic, would be seen along roadways. Larger centres, too, saw large churches built, cathedrals or at least imposing parochial churches. Walsh was certainly a man of his time in this respect, and, reflecting the perceived need to give a public face to the growing prominence of the Catholic Church as a public institution, he wanted a Catholic cathedral that would send a strong message to the world. It was to be not only an imposing house of God, but architecturally pleasing as well.

In the pastoral letter to his clergy and people which announced the building of the new cathedral (though it was published after the foundation had already been laid), Walsh expressed his consciousness of the formidable nature of the undertaking. To support his proposal, he called on the examples of the former builders of the great churches of Europe and North America, often built on the pennies and hard-earned silver of the poor:

> The building of a suitable Cathedral is a most serious undertaking and will tax to the utmost limits your generosity and means, but it is an unavoidable necessity ... Faith can remove mountains and your Faith in God and your love for His Holy Church will enable you to remove the mountains of difficulties that may beset this work and will urge you to accomplish wonders of labor and self-sacrifice in erecting in this city a splendid Cathedral which will be in some measure not unworthy of the Divine Majesty and will be to future generations a noble and enduring monument of your Faith and piety.[133]

He had been careful in the matter of timing; the project would not have been financially possible when he first arrived in the diocese. Only after dealing with the enormous debt which the diocese carried, only after building numerous parish churches, schools, hospitals, and presbyteries, and only after establishing on solid ground the college at Sandwich, did Walsh see fit to begin the cathedral project.

The first official announcement of his plans was actually made on 15 February 1880, and by March, the most famous architect of the day, Joseph Connolly of Toronto, had been chosen to design the cathedral church. In his letter to Connolly, Walsh clearly outlined the desired specifications for the building, and set his estimated cost, less furnishings, at $60,000. Connolly was encouraged to calculate "nicely and exactly" so as not to involve the diocese in a crushing debt: "It is in this case most important to cut the cloth according to the measure."[134]

It was at the same time determined that St Peter would be the heavenly patron of the new cathedral, as he had been of the first cathedral since the time of Bishop Pinsoneault. St Lawrence, who had been the original patron of the London parish and who had been secondary patron since Pinsoneault's time, was replaced by Walsh's own patron saint, John the Evangelist. Walsh turned the first sod in an official ceremony in July 1880, and the new foundations were dug by March 1881, with the cornerstone put in place on 22 May 1881.[135] There then began a burst of activity to raise funds for the building.

Walsh had, in fact, been planning this project for a long time. James Wagner had written, on behalf of Walsh, to Propaganda Fide late in 1876 to ask for the donation of an object blessed by the pope, to be sold in an effort to raise funds for a new cathedral. The next year he received a favourable reply in the form of a cameo from Pius IX, accompanied by his best wishes.[136] Many bazaars, lasting more than a week at a time, were held by the cathedral parishioners for the purpose of fundraising. As well, the Grand Opera House was the venue for benefit concerts.[137] For one such concert, the Protestants of London showed a great interest in the project by purchasing tickets for large blocks of seats. Specifically cited were members of the United St Andrew's and Caledonian Society: "It would appear from this generous offer of those outside our faith that already the efforts put forth by the Bishop and the diocese of London is [sic] receiving recognition from them, and this concert is a fitting recognition from our citizens that our New Cathedral is a work in the construction of which they take a deep interest."[138] Near the end of construction, Protestants in the area surpassed all previous examples of their generosity by putting forth a magnanimous offer. Due to a paucity of funds, as the building was reaching completion, a decision had to be made to leave the front towers unfinished. Eager to see the building finished, a group of non-Catholics offered to pay for the finishing of one tower if the Catholics would pay for the other. Unfortunately, Walsh felt he had already asked for as much as he could from the people, and this friendly gesture was never carried out.[139]

Musical concerts were also held by individual Catholic schools, with the proceeds given to the bishop for the cathedral. Interestingly, Walsh himself also called in some loans during that period, so the money could be directed accordingly. In a letter to Hugh McMahon, a lawyer who had formerly lived in the diocese, but who was by that time practising law in Winnipeg, Walsh reminded him it was time to repay the $1,100 loan taken from the diocesan fund for infirm priests:

Considering the uncertainty of life and the accidents of business, I cannot in conscience consent to leave any longer in your hands such an amount of church money in the unsettled and unbusiness-like manner which it has been thus far ... You will excuse me for calling your immediate attention to these matters with a view to their adjustment, for it is an imperative duty and a strict obligation on conscience for me to do so. These things are matters of business and even amongst friends should be treated and conducted in a business-like manner.[140]

Undoubtedly, the most ambitious project launched to raise funds for the cathedral was a land-settlement deal. Walsh had heard of various prospectors who had received grants of land in Canada's western provinces. The stipulation was that prospectors were to settle the lands by first clearing them, and then selling them at reasonable prices to the newcomers in the region. As early as February 1882, Walsh had sent one of his priests, Edmund Kilroy, as his "confidential agent," to have an audience with Prime Minister Macdonald. In a cover letter Walsh asked for a township or two in the west. He made it clear that he was requesting this as a personal favour of Macdonald, but that it was for a good cause, the new cathedral. Furthermore, his understanding was that both Lynch of Toronto and Taché of Saint-Boniface had received similar grants from the prime minister. Macdonald corrected that misunderstanding – it was the British Government that was handling the deal – and indicated that he thought "their two Graces" should take care of the settlers.[141]

Macdonald, however, signalled by May that grants would be available. Yet the fact was, Walsh had trouble finding the funds to purchase the lands. At one point, in May 1883, Kilroy wrote to James Patterson, his local member of Parliament, to ask that Macdonald ensure that the land would be held for six months or a year. That would give Walsh time to put into place all the prerequisites for the deal. Kilroy also indicated the need for a clear deed for the land.[142] In the end, recognizing all the pitfalls involved, Walsh acted no further on the land deal. Funds for the cathedral had to come from other sources, mainly donations from the various parishes across the diocese.[143]

Everything had been prepared for an unofficial opening by April 1885. The *Catholic Record* reported on "Bishop Walsh's Pathetic Parting Sermon" in the old cathedral, which had taken place 19 April 1885. The following Sunday, the congregation worshipped in their new cathedral even though its official dedication would not take place until two months later, on Sunday, 28 June, the eve of the feast of St Peter and St Paul. The *Catholic Record* also carried extensive coverage of that event, colourfully hailing it as the "Grandest Pageant Ever Witnessed in the Forest City," and vividly describing the cathedral itself, with all its furnishings and artistic appointments. Grandly it heralded the opening of the cathedral as "the most signal event in the long and useful career of Bishop Walsh," a fitting testimony to the building and to the bishop who had overseen its construction:

> The greatest day in the ecclesiastical history of this city, diocese and province was Sunday last. It had been for many months looked forward to with most eager anticipation by the Catholics of the whole western peninsula. But no anticipation, however sanguine, could equal the splendor of the demonstration of that day. Well indeed might one of our city contemporaries declare that there has been no event in this Province at all comparable to it in importance, magnitude and splendor. Every portion of the Dominion, from far-off Prince Edward's Island to distant Algoma, was represented in this splendid pageant and ceremony. There was [sic] also present illustrious bishops, distinguished prelates and representative laymen from various American dioceses.[144]

The day began with the solemn High Mass of dedication, at which Walsh himself presided. The sermon was preached by Bernard McQuaid, the bishop of Rochester, New York, and the music was taken from Mozart's Twelfth Mass.[145] Following the High Mass, a grand banquet was given by the bishop at Mount Hope orphanage. In the introductory remarks of his speech there, Walsh warmly thanked all present as well as all those who had contributed to the project. He then singled out the bishops present, one after another, and most especially Lynch, along with those bishops from the United States. Equally deserving attention in his mind were the non-Catholics in the audience. He glowingly paid particular reference to them: "There is no city with which I am acquainted whose citizens are more distinguished for tolerance, liberality, good-neighbourliness, and for the precious kindnesses and sweet charities of life than are the citizens of London, and I am glad of this opportunity to bear my public testimony to this fact so creditable to this city and its people, irrespective of creed or race."[146]

Walsh then went on to describe the devotion and dedication of his beloved people of London diocese:

The Cathedral is the expression in stone of the great zeal and love for religion of the noble clergy and generous laity of the whole diocese; and of their cordial union and cooperation with their Bishop, and it will stand for ages an eloquent and enduring monument of their faith, hope and charity; and of their unswerving and loyal devotion to their religious connections, and to that faith made sacred and dear to them by its blessed ordinances and by the memory of their fathers.[147]

Reflecting the age's proliferation of churches, he spoke of the new cathedral in contrast with secular buildings: "I am satisfied that Christian men will admit that in a material age, when great and colossal structures are raised for the purposes of commerce and the worship of mammon, the clergy and laity of this diocese have deserved well of religion, and have done a noble Christian work by building this beautiful and stately temple for the glory of God and of His Christ, the honor of Holy Church and the sanctification of immortal souls."[148]

Following that, he took care to offer special thanks for the architect, Joseph Connolly, "under whose creative genius the unconscious stones of our Cathedral have grown into shape and beauty, and the symmetry and perfection of life," and for all the contractors, artisans, and workmen. Finally, as he ended his speech, he summed up the entire event with an age-old comparison: "May we all be one day members of heavenly Jerusalem, the blessed vision of peace, which, of living stones upbuilded, towers aloft majestically above the stars – a temple not made with hands, eternal in the heavens." The day then fittingly concluded with Solemn Vespers in the cathedral, accompanied by a full orchestra and choir. Walsh presided, and Michael O'Farrell, the bishop of Trenton, New Jersey, preached the sermon at Vespers.[149]

Over the following years, up to his last days in the diocese, Walsh continued to augment the decorations and furnishings of the cathedral. In the following November of 1885, a new organ made by the Casavant Frères of Saint-Hyacinthe, Quebec, was installed; Bishop Carberry of Hamilton was in attendance and preached for that occasion. Late in Walsh's time in London, in October 1889, magnificent stained glass windows were installed in the sanctuary, Stations of the Cross in oil paintings were hung, and a new Marian altar was unveiled, each in appropriate ceremonies.[150]

The windows, however, caused some consternation for Walsh, who had to turn again to his old friend, Macdonald in Ottawa, for assistance. In an effort to tidy up loose ends before transferring to Toronto, he wished to oversee the installation of the windows. They had been imported from Innsbruck, Austria, but were being held up by Customs over a matter of excise and duty taxes. In typical fashion, Walsh devised a compromise plan, one which he hoped would please all parties: have the windows released from Customs so they could be installed, on his promise to pay any duties required whenever the matter was settled. He implored Macdonald to get the minister of Customs, the Honourable Mackenzie Bowell, to agree to that proposal. He pleaded his case: "Now, my Dear Sir John, please do not fail me on this occasion, and like the guilty boy I promise that 'I will not do it anymore.'" Ever grateful to his long-time friend, Macdonald did not fail; he scribbled a note on the back of Walsh's letter: "stained glass, see Bowell."[151] He replied affirmatively to Walsh within three months. At the same time, however, there was always politics involved. Macdonald made reference to the same compromise having been made for Cleary of Kingston over the stained glass windows for his beautiful cathedral. Bowell, however, Macdonald noted, was afraid that the matter would come up in the House of Commons, and that the government would be accused of favouritism, an accusation made frequently against Macdonald. Ten days after Macdonald sent his letter, Walsh's member of Parliament, Patterson, pressed the prime minister to resolve the issue quickly; Patterson was afraid that Walsh would be annoyed because Cleary had already had his windows installed: "You led me to expect that this would be arranged and surely as much might be done for our friend at London as was done for the Laodicean at Kingston ... Matters are sufficiently hard for us in this part of the country without alienating anybody and if a distinction is made in favour of Kingston, London and his friends will never forgive it. Please get this matter arranged before it is too late."[152] Patterson was exaggerating Walsh's dismay at the delay, and no doubt Macdonald knew that. Nonetheless, he obliged. The windows were released by Customs and then installed in London's cathedral in October shortly before Walsh's departure for Toronto, a parting gift to his diocese from his own personal funds.[153]

By then and in every way, Walsh had proven himself a most capable administrator in London. His abilities were proven not only in the many projects which he had overseen throughout his diocese and in the general growth of the Catholic Church there, but also in the way that he had engaged so very many in the use of their talents alongside him for the good of the diocese, proving himself an "administrator of rare ability and personal charm":

The most glowing tribute for any administrator is to know that he has been able to steer a project to its completion and at the same time to have left in its wake a contented group of collaborators ... Only a man sensitive to existing differences and feelings of [others] with whom he must work is able to leave such an aura of calm behind him."[154]

That described Walsh: he was that type of man. The priests of the diocese agreed; they made that quite clear in their tribute to him as he prepared to leave London to take up his new archiepiscopal responsibilities in Toronto. In the flowery language of the Victorian era, their farewell address to him, given at the official ceremony at the cathedral, captured heartfelt sentiments of gratitude and respect:

When, by the will of Divine Providence and appointment of the Holy See, you first came among us, you found a heavy diocesan debt, few church edifices and yet fewer priests. The heavy encumbrance of debt soon disappeared as if by magic. Churches, schools, academies seemed to grow like the palm tree by the running waters and blossom into fruit at your approach. The waste places became populous with pious congregations of Christian men and women. The solitudes were made vocal with the clarion voice of the parish bell and the merry romp and laughter of children wending their cheery way to the Catholic separate school.[155]

Though the prose was embroidered, certainly Walsh's accomplishments over twenty-two years of episcopal service in the diocese of London left an entirely favourable impression. While there, he truly sought the spiritual and temporal progress of his people, and it showed. His was an impressive legacy: the eradication of the diocese's crippling debt, the many parishes he had founded, the churches and schools he had built, the hospitals and orphanages he had constructed, the congregations of Religious men and women he had established and supported in the diocese, and his beloved cathedral. Yet most of all, his legacy remained in the hearts and minds of the Catholics of London diocese. He was their beloved bishop, the one who had served them so well. They would never forget him.

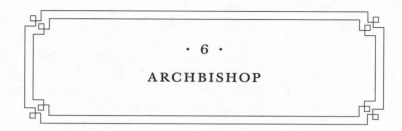

· 6 ·

ARCHBISHOP

I left you in the Summer of my life, I return in the advanced Autumn.
I come back to you changed in appearance, it is true, for time and cares
and labors have left their marks upon me, but unchanged, I am sure,
in my heart's best wishes for you. I trust, therefore, that we will labor
together in harmony, good will and zeal for the furtherance
of the great interests of our holy religion.

ARCHBISHOP JOHN WALSH, 27 NOVEMBER 1889

JOHN JOSEPH LYNCH WAS DEAD! THE NEWS WAS AS MUCH OF A surprise to Bishop John Walsh as to most everyone else. Lynch had been in good health in recent times, even though he had suffered from occasional "fevers" ever since his youth. Yet he seemed vigorous enough, certainly able to travel to St Catharines for a conference of clergy on Tuesday, 8 May 1888, then on to Merritton to confer the sacrament of Confirmation the next day. In fact, however, he was not well when he left for St Catharines, but he did not want to disappoint either the priests or the young people. He returned as quickly as possible to Toronto, to his beloved summer home at St John's Grove, on the outskirts of Toronto, which had become his principal residence in recent years.[1]

Hardly had he returned home than Lynch was attended by his doctors, who diagnosed a congestion of the lungs that had progressed to the point of no recovery. Fully conscious of his situation, he made provisions for the administration of his archdiocese, added a codicil to his will, and then asked for the last sacraments. His auxiliary, Bishop Timothy O'Mahony, anointed him while the archbishop's closest assistants stood at his bedside. Lynch died peacefully, shortly after midnight on Saturday, 12 May, at the age of seventy-two.

Francis Rooney and Joseph Laurent, the newly appointed administrators of the archdiocese, immediately began preparations for the funeral.[2] The solemn Requiem Mass was held at St Michael's Cathedral on 16 May. In great numbers they gathered, from all over the archdiocese and from as far away as Quebec City and Philadelphia, the largest crowd ever to assemble for a Catholic funeral in Ontario: some 5,000 people, Catholic and Protestant alike. Seven archbishops and bishops, including Lynch's longtime friend John Walsh, and two hundred priests led the coffin in procession through the nave of the cathedral to the altar railing, and soon filled the cathedral's sanctuary, while what seemed to be countless lay people crowded together in the cathedral's nave, with the majority in the surrounding streets to watch the funeral cortege arrive and depart.

The primate of Canada, Elzéar-Alexandre Cardinal Taschereau of Quebec City, himself advanced in years, officiated, while Stephen Ryan, the bishop of Buffalo and Lynch's dear friend, gave the sermon. Both had known Lynch for decades. Present also, in the nave of the cathedral, were Sir Alexander Campbell, the lieutenant governor of Ontario, resplendent in viceregal attire; representatives of the federal and provincial parliaments; Edward F. Clarke, mayor of Toronto; and the city's councillors and other dignitaries. All wished to show their respect for the man who had guided the archdiocese for twenty-eight years. According to his wishes, Lynch was buried on the grounds on the north side of the cathedral, rather than in its crypt. Rooney and Laurent informed Propaganda Fide that the archbishop had died, asked for faculties as the administrators, and gave some account of the funeral rites. O'Mahony sent his own report.[3]

The archbishop's death created a critical vacancy in the hierarchy of Ontario. Thanks to Lynch's dynamic spiritual leadership of the large, developing archdiocese, Toronto was a stable city, with growing parishes and institutions and, for the most part, an educated and energetic clergy and devoted Religious and lay people eager to support the Church and help its continued growth. The choice of a successor to build on this legacy, therefore, was crucial. The hope of the Church in English-speaking Canada rested in the strength of leadership that Lynch had provided in Toronto. "[Its] metropolitan influence was felt throughout Ontario, the prairies and even the Maritimes."[4] His successor would inherit that mantle. There was, inevitably, considerable speculation as to whom that would be.

As the senior bishop of the ecclesiastical province, Walsh had the official task of informing Propaganda Fide of Lynch's death, which he did in a letter to Cardinal Simeoni. He also had the task of consulting the bishops of the province, and of putting together a *terna* for submission to Propaganda Fide. In his letter, therefore, he informed the prefect that he would gather with bishops James Cleary of Kingston and Thomas Dowling of Peterborough to choose names for Toronto and for Hamilton, which was also vacant since the death of Bishop Carberry the previous December.[5]

On the same day that Walsh wrote to Propaganda Fide, John A. Macdonald wrote to the governor general of Canada, Henry Charles Keith Petty-Fitzmaurice, the fifth marquess of Lansdowne, regarding the same subject. Macdonald had a candidate in mind for Toronto: none other than his longtime friend, John Walsh. He had "direct and indirect" knowledge, he wrote, that many of the priests and laity of Toronto were in dread that Cleary would succeed Lynch. "Some are much afraid of Bishop Cleary's being named." Macdonald then went on to point out that, in fact, there was a consensus among Catholics that Walsh would be "the right man" for Toronto. Walsh was "a gentleman, an Irishman by birth, [who] from long residence in Canada has laid aside all the prejudices that a newcomer would bring from Ireland – I can vouch for Bishop Walsh's loyalty to the Throne and to British connections." Macdonald concluded his letter with a plea for the governor general's help "in getting the information conveyed in some way to the Vatican that Bishop Walsh would be persona grata with the loyal Catholics of Ontario."[6]

Lord Lansdowne did not waste any time with this request, communicating with those in England he thought could help, including the Duke of Norfolk, Henry Fitzalan-Howard. On 15 June, Norfolk, the pre-eminent Catholic peer in the House of Lords, wrote to Monsignor Domenico Jacobini, secretary of Propaganda Fide, suggesting Walsh for Toronto. Norfolk not only supported Walsh but also repeated Macdonald's concern about how many feared that Cleary would get the see instead. "It has been strongly represented to me that great anxiety on the subject exists among both Clergy and Laity and this anxiety is very fully shared by the Government." He then went on to stress the great hope that "the choice of the Holy See will fall upon Dr. Walsh." Walsh was, Norfolk assured Rome, "much admired by the loyal Catholics of Canada and that it is sincerely hoped that he may be appointed ... May I then very earnestly plead for the consideration of this communication which I make to you most seriously."[7]

Soon afterwards, Macdonald took care to write to Walsh himself "confessing" to having proposed him for the vacancy. He had written to Lansdowne, he admitted, "suggesting that some means might be found – as before – of having a word said at the Vatican." That would be, he confided, "in the highest degree satisfactory to the Government

& people of Canada. I felt that I had some right to speak of the feel-ings of Catholics for I have been overwhelmed with others first – the clergy as well as the laity on the subject ... the importance of having Your Lordship selected." Macdonald also made reference to the earlier discussion of Walsh becoming coadjutor to Lynch: "I hope history to be able to support myself."[8]

In the meantime, during July 1888, the three bishops of the metro-politan province of Toronto, Walsh, Dowling, and Cleary, met and then submitted three *ternae* to Rome: first for Hamilton, with Thomas Dowling listed as *dignissimus*; second, a replacement for Dowling in Peterborough, suggesting Richard O'Connor as *dignissimus*; and third, John Walsh was listed as *dignissimus* for Toronto. The name of William Doherty, a Jesuit, appeared on all three *ternae* as *dignior*. In the *terna* for Toronto, Francis Rooney, the administrator, was *dignus*.[9] It should be noted that at the same time, Walsh, Cleary, and Dowling also had been pressing the Holy See to promote Kingston to the status of an archdiocese. That meant that everyone at the meeting was proposing himself and each other for some sort of promotion. In January of the following year, 1889, Dowling was named bishop of Hamilton and O'Connor bishop of Peterborough. Kingston was raised to an arch-diocese in December, making Cleary its first archbishop.

Macdonald had not left much to chance in the appointment of Walsh to Toronto, and continued to press his case now through Sir Charles Tupper, who was High Commissioner for Canada to the Court of St James's since May 1883, and could use his position and influence to monitor the situation. What Tupper discovered from Norfolk, and what he reported to Macdonald, was that Jacobini was concerned about a negative reaction from Cardinal Manning regarding John Walsh's appointment, since Walsh was known to favour Home Rule for Ireland. A strong British nationalist, Manning was not wholly sym-pathetic to the cause of Irish independence. Jacobini feared that Man-ning would interfere and block the nomination. In view of that infor-mation, Tupper emphasized in his reply to Macdonald that he would proceed carefully in his attempt to influence the decision and keep the Dominion government "entirely out of it" as Macdonald wished. The prime minister responded within a short time, and expressed his hope once again to Tupper that Walsh would get the nomination. Even rec-ognizing that the bishop was "a Home Ruler," Macdonald did not believe that Walsh's political views should play a role in the appoint-ment. In his opinion, Walsh would be acceptable to Canadians and especially to Irish clergymen in Toronto.[10]

Propaganda Fide agreed. At its General Congregation in July, it recommended Walsh for the vacancy. Besides noting the relevant correspondence, including the letter from Norfolk, the secretary at the Congregation gave an apt description of Walsh's tenure in London. He emphasized the bishop's zeal, orthodoxy, and illustrious prudence, and recognized all he had done for the spiritual life of his diocese. It was noted, as well, that he was very respected among Catholics and Protestants alike, and that the clergy of Toronto had written in his favour.[11] All was confirmed in an audience with Pope Leo XIII.[12] Walsh was officially raised to the archbishopric of Toronto on 13 August 1889. With that, the entire list of nominations sent the previous year to Propaganda Fide was fulfilled.

Even before the official announcement was made in Rome, the news reached London, and the Catholic press promptly trumpeted it across the country. The *Catholic Record* underscored the sadness Walsh's departure would mean for the people of London diocese. It also emphasized the impact of his twenty-two years in London: "The name of Bishop Walsh is indelibly engraved on every monument of religion or charity in this diocese, nor can it ever be dissociated from the history of any church or religious or educational establishment whose foundation stone he blessed and whose completion he heralded in eloquence rarely surpassed."[13]

Other tributes and letters of congratulation began to pour in to the episcopal palace before the official announcement had arrived. Among those congratulatory letters was one from Macdonald himself. He recognized that, for Walsh, leaving London would not be easy, but emphasized that he was "glad to believe that 'the back [was] equal to the burden.'"[14] A month later, in a letter of gratitude to Archbishop Duhamel of Ottawa for his warm congratulations, Walsh expressed his own unease about having to leave London. "The change, should it take place, will not be for my ease or happiness, but I trust I shall live and die the obedient and willing Servant of the Holy See."[15]

In fact, however, the official announcement of the appointment did not reach London until 9 September, along with a letter of congratulations from Simeoni. The prefect indicated that Walsh's pallium (a sign of his office: a circular band of white woollen material with two hanging strips and six black crosses, worn on the shoulders) would be requested at the next consistory and sent as soon as it was granted.[16] Walsh replied on 1 October that he accepted the nomination, and asked that Cardinal Taschereau, archbishop of Quebec and primate of Canada, be delegated to give him the pallium on 27 November, the date set for his installation. The pallium was not sent at that time, for reasons unknown, so Walsh requested it again the following February.[17] It arrived later that year.

The archbishop-elect began to prepare for his departure from London, at the same time continuing a flurry of activity to oversee the completion of the interior decoration of the new cathedral. He named Denis O'Connor, the Basilian superior of Assumption College in Sandwich, to be the administrator of the diocese during the *inter regnum*, and conferred upon him the appropriate faculties for the task.[18] Later that autumn, Walsh issued a pastoral letter, poignantly expressing his gratitude and farewell to the "laborious, devoted clergy ... [the] fervent religious communities ... [and the] united, generous and loyal people." The ties that bound them, he emphasized, were close and intimate:

> For twenty-two years we have labored together – Bishop, priests
> and people – in our respective spheres for the glory of God and
> the progress of our holy religion. We have worked together in
> mutual confidence, in unity of purpose, and with disinterested
> and magnanimous cooperation; and God has blessed and fructi-
> fied, as with the dews of heaven, our united labors, our arduous
> undertakings for the honor and weal of the Church within the
> diocese and the spiritual welfare of its people.[19]

Before leaving, Walsh celebrated his last Mass and preached his final sermon in London's cathedral on 27 November 1889, on a cold day with overcast skies and a mixture of snow and heavy rain. At the end of the Mass, the archbishop-elect received several congratulatory addresses and farewell tributes from his clergy and people, along with a generous gift of $2,000 for the purchase of new archiepiscopal robes. The priests were effusive in their praise, as offered by their spokesman:

> So far have we shared in your joys and your sorrows, and we
> make bold to say that we were at times willing to accept our
> measure of whatever burden fell upon you, and to participate
> in the toils and difficulties that are inseparable from the life of
> an earnest and zealous overseer of souls. But it is not in human
> nature that our felicitations on your elevation to so exalted a pos-
> ition to that of Metropolitan could be free from pain and anxious
> concern. What is a matter for rejoicing in other places, and for
> the priests over whom you are called to preside, is for us a source

of sadness and deep regret. Your career in the diocese of London
has been one of successful labors, of unwearied solicitude and of
continued triumph ... For all these meritorious works brought to
so happy a consummation, for these and many other blessings
conferred on the clergy and laity of your diocese, we can but
give feeble expression to our unbounded gratitude. The recol-
lection of all that has been accomplished by Your Grace for this
diocese can never be obliterated from the grateful, affectionate,
and, to-day, alas! stricken hearts of the priests you are leaving in
obedience to the voice of Leo, the supreme shepherd of the flock.

Your life and labors as priest and Bishop for thirty-five long
years are before the country, and form a bright chapter in the
ecclesiastical history of Ontario wherein your honored name has
long since been a household word.[20]

Similar warm sentiments were expressed by the laity on that occasion:

You have been approached by representatives of your ever-zeal-
ous, ever-watchful and ever-faithful priests. The warmest feelings
of attachment for your person and your sacred office have been
proclaimed in their behalf in a manner and in terms evincing
a depth of sincerity seldom called forth on similar occasions.
We, too, Your Grace, Your obedient children in the faith, crave
permission to approach you to bear testimony of the deep and
warm admiration and love we entertain for you. This admiration
and this love are not sentiments born of yesterday. Twenty-two
years – a long span in a lifetime – have you labored with us and
for us ... Looking back over the past, and taking note of what
has been accomplished – calling to mind the blessed peace that
has prevailed in every portion of the Diocese – no dissensions,
no heart-burnings, no scandals – your administration has truly
been blessed, and it would appear indeed as though the smile of
God had shone on our favored Diocese; for where can be found
greater progress, greater love of Holy Church, and greater anxiety to extend her domain – where can be found a larger measure
of God-given tranquillity, a greater love of priest for people and
people for priest, and a greater love of all for a Bishop whose
life and whose works have been the admiration of the people of
Ontario for nearly a quarter of a century.[21]

At half past noon, Walsh hosted a farewell luncheon for the priests of London, imparting words of gratitude and paternal love to them. Then at half past one, accompanied by Cleary of Kingston and Dowling of Hamilton, along with two thousand priests and lay people, Walsh made his way to the train station in a great procession consisting of more than a dozen carriages. These were lined up in front of the palace on Dufferin Avenue. The Seventh Band, along with members of the Catholic Mutual Benefit Association and the school board, were joined by numerous boys and girls at the head of the carriages, all ready to march through the snow and mud, while the rain continued to pour down. The procession with the carriages headed north on Richmond Street to the Canadian Pacific Railway station. From there, Walsh began his journey to his new see and home.[22]

His train left the station at two o'clock. The three-hour trip took until half past seven that evening to reach Toronto, as unusually long stops were made at certain stations so that people could meet the archbishop-elect *en route*. This included Hamilton, where there was a reception on the platform amidst loud cheering from the crowd which had gathered to see him. The Honourable Frank Smith, a senator and chairman of Toronto's reception committee, boarded the train there in company with other prominent people from various parishes in Toronto.[23] Upon arrival in Toronto's Union Station, the crowd was so great that it spilled out onto the surrounding streets. When the train pulled into the station, "a mighty shout of welcome went up from the crowd." Fifty or more carriages formed up in a procession, ready to accompany the archbishop-elect the short distance from the station to St Michael's Cathedral. Due to the continuing heavy rain, however, the procession was cancelled. Instead, a detail of police officers on horseback escorted Walsh.[24]

Sadly, this hearty and warm welcome was marred by a demonstration by members of the Orange Lodge, who followed the carriages from near the station to the cathedral. It must have seemed like déja vû for Walsh, recalling the battles of his former days in Toronto against the Orange Lodge at the time of the visit of the Prince of Wales nearly thirty years earlier. In this instance, a band of rowdy youths hurled brickbats and stones at the passing carriages, shouting vulgar insults while bellowing out the Lodge's popular song, "We'll Hang the Pope on a Sour Apple Tree." One stone struck the coachman of Senator Smith, while another made its mark on Walsh's carriage, smashing the window next to him and giving him a very bad bruise on his arm. At

the door of the cathedral, the "ruffians" and "hoodlums," as one jour-
nalist called them, tried to force their way in, but they were rebuffed
by a priest who managed to close the great doors against them. After
being routed by the police, they turned their hatred toward the nearby
Loretto convent, smashing its front windows.[25]

Despite the hooligans, the enthusiastic welcome continued inside
the cathedral, aglow with lights and candles. People packed the pews
past which filed the long line of dignitaries, clergy, and prelates.
Among these latter were two archbishops and three bishops: Édouard-
Charles Fabre of Montreal, Duhamel of Ottawa, Cleary of Kingston,
Dowling of Hamilton, and Richard O'Connor of Peterborough. The
many priests present included some from the archdiocese of Toronto
and the diocese of London, and from Religious communities. Among
the priests were James Walsh, the archbishop-elect's nephew, who had
transferred with his uncle to Toronto in order to assist him, and Denis
O'Connor, who would succeed Walsh in London, and later in Toronto.

Walsh stood outside the main door, which was closed, awaiting
the beginning of the ceremony. After everyone was in place, a loud
knocking was heard at the door. The priest-in-charge in the cathedral
inquired who was knocking, to which the archbishop-elect replied,
"John Walsh." At that, the great doors were opened, and Walsh pro-
ceeded through the immense crowd to the sanctuary of the cathedral,
while the choir sang the traditional *Ecce Sacerdos Magnus* from the loft,
accompanied by the great organ. As he was led by the senior clergy to
his new archiepiscopal throne, the symbol of his office, the choir sang
the *Te Deum* in thanksgiving.

When the ceremony of installation was completed, to the enthusiastic congratulations and welcome of laity and clergy alike, the new
archbishop gave a typically gracious and deferential reply. He began
with a description of the role and authority of a bishop, which, as he
said, "Jesus Christ possessed as the teacher ... and the sanctifier of
His people ... I come, therefore, with the authority of Christ to lead
you in the way of salvation. The task is beyond human strength and
the burden too great for angels' shoulders ... The work of the Church
is God's work, carried out not infrequently through weak and feeble
human agencies. This fact is for me a ground of hope and encouragement in accepting the very responsible position that has been assigned
to me." He then paid tribute to his predecessors, the priests, Religious,
and faithful of the archdiocese, and recalled that he had begun his
priesthood among them. With his gifts of eloquent speech and poetic
expression, he pledged to work with all his heart and soul:

I left you in the Summer of my life, I return in the advanced
Autumn. I come back to you changed in appearance, it is true,
for time and cares and labors have left their marks upon me, but
unchanged, I am sure, in my heart's best wishes for you. I trust,
therefore, that we will labor together in harmony, good will and
zeal for the furtherance of the great interests of our holy religion ... I have come amongst you to promote this cause according to my opportunities and the measure of my capacity. This is
my mission, this is my only policy, to promote to the best of my
ability and with the Divine assistance, glory to God in the highest and on earth peace to men of good will.[26]

One chronicler described the archbishop's appearance that evening
as he gave the final blessing: "The hand which gave it still wore its
strength and vigor of old. Time had dealt gently with Dr. Walsh. The
form was erect; the voice full and rich as erst it rang through those
vaulted walls. The silver hair showing beneath the mitre alone told the
story that years had passed and age was coming on."[27] Despite the earlier demonstration by members of the Orange Lodge, Walsh's return
to Toronto was a triumph. Lieutenant Governor Campbell and other
distinguished citizens were received by Walsh in the throne room of
his palace, where they paid their respects. They also voiced "their
indignation and shame at the horrible conduct of the Toronto hoodlums."[28] The overwhelmingly favourable reception that he received
indicated that Walsh had once again won the hearts of Catholics and
most Protestants alike in the city and the archdiocese.
    Almost at once, however, Walsh must have sensed that the city and
the archdiocese had changed during his twenty-two-year absence. To
preside over such an immense archdiocese would call upon the depth
of his spirituality and all his teaching, pastoral, and administrative
skills, which he himself recognized in his address during his installation. He must also have realized that the challenges before him in
Toronto were different from those he had faced in London. While statistics differ from source to source about the city and the archdiocese,
they do give an indication of the task facing him. By the most conservative estimate, Toronto itself had a population of approximately
60,000, of which 12,000 were Catholic; there were another 30,000
Catholics across the archdiocese. Later statistics, based on the 1891
census, indicated that there were already 21,830 Catholics in the city
alone. That figure represented more than fifteen per cent of the population, a tenfold increase over the last fifty years.[29]

Walsh set to work. In response to the rapidly increasing population during the 1890s, he would have to oversee the building of sixteen churches and three chapels, would ordain twelve men for the archdiocese, and would work tirelessly to promote a native-born clergy to serve his growing parishes. He visited many of the new churches and residences for the laying of the cornerstones. As far as possible, too, he encouraged Religious life, ordaining three men for Religious communities, and granting permission for a new Basilian residence and three convents for women Religious. On one such occasion, in 1892, at the new novitiate of the Basilian Fathers, he mentioned that he was using the same trowel that Bishop Michael Power had used nearly fifty years earlier when he laid the cathedral's cornerstone.[30] In early May 1890, within a year of his arrival in Toronto, Walsh announced that he had hired the renowned architect Joseph Connolly to undertake improvements in Toronto's cathedral. Built in the late 1840s under the direction of Bishop Power and the architect William Thomas, the cathedral needed major renovations and changes. Connolly had designed St Peter's cathedral in London during the 1880s, as well as the parish church in Kinkora; Walsh now turned to him again. He not only knew firsthand of Connolly's talent, but also had a good working relationship with him and favoured his neo-gothic architectural style.

Typical of his administrative acumen, Walsh established a committee to oversee the renovations, which included Frank Smith as its chairman, Eugene O'Keefe (of the famed brewing family) as treasurer, and several members of the clergy. Connolly's renovations were to include a new chapel to be named in honour of St John, clerestory windows and dormers to provide additional light, and decoration throughout in colours common to the era. The work was completed in 1891, and Walsh re-dedicated the cathedral on 7 June.[31]

Equally valuable was Walsh's foresight in purchasing fifty-two acres of land for a new Catholic cemetery on nearby Yonge Street, eight kilometres north of town. In that endeavour, he was assisted again by his trusted advisors, Smith and O'Keefe. Interestingly enough, Walsh was not allowed to purchase the parcel of land that was his first choice, such was still the antagonism toward Catholics in Toronto. In the end, Smith and O'Keefe had to purchase the property, in order to hide the identity of the real purchaser and the property's intended use. They paid $5,000 to C.D. Warren, and then turned it over to the archbishop for the same sum. He blessed the new cemetery on 9 July 1898, and gave it the name "Mount Hope Cemetery." As it turned out, that event would be the last public appearance of John Walsh. He died three weeks later.[32]

As a seminarian and young priest, Walsh had enjoyed a good relationship with his bishop. It was Toronto's second bishop, Armand-
François-Marie le Comte de Charbonnel, who had recruited him from
Ireland to study for Toronto and, in 1854, had ordained him a priest
for Toronto. Two years later, de Charbonnel oversaw the creation of
Hamilton and London dioceses by a severance of the vast diocese of
Toronto. Now, returning as Toronto's archbishop and de Charbonnel's
successor, Walsh ironically had the sad responsibility, among his first
duties, to announce the death at Crest, France, of his much-beloved
predecessor and mentor. Walsh's missive to the priests of the archdiocese conveyed what were probably the tender feelings of all who knew
de Charbonnel: "His name shall be held in benediction in this diocese
for the great works he accomplished herein for God's glory and the
salvation of souls. We earnestly recommend his departed soul to the
prayers of yourself and your faithful people." That was accompanied
by a notice for a Requiem Mass to be held the following week in St
Michael's.[33]

The experience of a good relationship with his own bishop during
his younger years had taught Walsh how to nurture similar warm relations with his priests as well as with men and women Religious. While
in London, he had greatly relied on their collaboration for carrying
out his work; in Toronto it would be no different. His felicitous connections with the Basilian Fathers, built up through his association
with them at Assumption College in Sandwich, especially continued in
Toronto at St Michael's College. The Carmelites, at their retreat house
in Niagara, and the Redemptorist Fathers and Brothers in various parishes, were encouraged to continue their work in the archdiocese, as
were visiting Jesuit priests who from time to time conducted parish
missions. Ever interested in attracting new Religious orders, Walsh
contacted some Dominican Friars in Ireland, to enquire whether they
would establish a priory in Toronto. They had to decline.[34]

Not surprisingly, Walsh also corresponded with women Religious,
including a Sister of the Sacred Heart, Mary Archer, who lived in a
convent in Saint John. He had known her over the years. She was a
Lay Sister who worked in the convent's refectory. Walsh received several letters from her, all signed "Little Mary, R.S.H." Their extant
correspondence spanned a two-year period, from early 1890 until late
1891.[35] "Little Mary" included personal news of her family, of the Sisters that Walsh knew, and of the local church, along with occasional
questions and concerns about mutual acquaintances. She wrote about
the archbishop's family and expressed seasonal greetings at times such
as Christmas. She responded in one letter to his report of how his car-

riage had been stoned upon his arrival in Toronto, and paraphrased the insightful reaction of her superior, Reverend Mother Schulten: the superior "chimed in that it was the best thing that could have happened to you. She added that the bad reception your enemies gave you did you a great deal of good instead of harm & that you are already much loved in Toronto."[36]

Later, in one of Walsh's letters to Archer, he included a copy of his recent pastoral letter on devotion to the Blessed Virgin Mary. Her reply to that was particularly interesting. She summarized the reaction of one local priest, a Redemptorist by the name of Hayden. He "pronounced it a very fine thing; 'but', he added, 'everything is good that comes from [Walsh's] pen'!!!" In addition, she reflected on their friendship, making reference to "jokes [he] used to crack at [their] expense in by-gone days."[37]

The writings of another correspondent from London, Mother Ignatia Campbell, CSJ, superior of the Sisters of St Joseph, were also illustrative of the warm relations Walsh generally had with women Religious. They had met some fifty years previously, while he was pastor of the Brock mission. At that time, he had encouraged her vocation to Religious life, and they had corresponded over the years. In early 1893, she wrote him about the illness of her brother Kenneth, at the time pastor of the Orillia parish, and thanked the archbishop for his letter which had been forwarded to Montreal where her brother was convalescing. She was anxious that Walsh knew that her brother had been taken out of the hospice, where he had received good care from the Sisters and the doctors, and had been removed to London: "Your Grace's letter did much to cheer and encourage him and he will reply as soon as he feels strong enough to write. Thanking Your Grace from the depth of my heart for all your kindness to Father Campbell and myself, during our time of trial, and with best wishes for your own health, I beg to remain, Your Grace's most devoted child, Mother Ignatia."[38]

Since the priests of Toronto were in the habit of annual retreats and conferences for continuing education, Walsh followed the example of his predecessor in Toronto and his own experience of having held retreats for priests in London. The priests would be summoned by the archbishop when such events approached. Attendance was not optional! Retreats were often held at St Michael's College during the summer months, while the educational conferences took place earlier in the year, during Lent.[39]

Walsh faced difficulties in Toronto with some of his priests as he had in London, and was even consulted by O'Connor of London concerning at least three priests with serious problems in that diocese. Among those were the notorious Joseph Molphy and Bartholomew Boubat, and William Dillon, who had served at LaSalette and had borrowed money without authorization.[40] Such priests were also in Toronto, Walsh would discover. Within the first year of his archiepiscopate, he was forced to take action against a Peter McCabe who had given scandal at his mission in Apto. Walsh summoned him to the palace, and later removed his priestly faculties until he sought help at the St John's hospice. Walsh brooked no opposition when scandal was evident or even possible.[41]

Close to the heart of the archbishop were his seminarians. While he zealously promoted a native-born clergy and desired to build a seminary in Toronto, he helped educate his seminarians at Le Grand Séminaire in Montreal and at All Hallows in Dublin.[42] His support for them included an annual collection throughout the archdiocese. In his pastoral letter of August 1890, which he wrote for that purpose, he exhorted parents to encourage their sons to consider a vocation to the priesthood. Pastors too, he emphasized, were to take special care to promote priestly vocations among young boys. He requested a donation of one dollar from every family, which was to be collected during October. Yet, despite his support of his seminarians and his desire and need for vocations, he willingly dismissed those who were deemed unsuitable candidates by the seminaries' faculties.[43]

A very happy event during his Toronto years was the approval by the Holy See in 1896 of a community of cloistered women, the Institute of the Sisters of the Precious Blood. Founded earlier as a diocesan community in 1861 at Saint-Hyacinthe, Quebec, by Catherine Aurélia Caouette, the Sisters had been established in Toronto since 1869 at the invitation of Lynch. Hence they were known to Walsh, who was delighted to have such a community dedicated to prayer, especially for priests and for vocations. He had written in 1888, at the urging of Louis-Zéphirin Moreau, bishop of Saint-Hyacinthe, to support their first request for establishment as a community. Later, to gain final papal approval, Moreau, on 28 September 1895, forwarded to Rome the Sisters' petition to become a Religious institute. Walsh was pleased to include another letter of endorsement, written 8 September 1895, along with letters from other Canadian archbishops and bishops.[44]

As far as possible, in the pastoral administration of his archdiocese, Walsh was frequently involved with the sacraments of Confirmation and Marriage. As expected at that time, he would travel from parish to parish to confer the sacrament of Confirmation on young boys and

girls, often during his annual parochial visitations. In addition to celebrating Confirmation, a visitation was the occasion for him to meet
Catholics in each parish, and to support their faith. He would have a
private discussion with the parish priest about the parish and about
the priest's own personal life, and also would learn about the spiritual life as well as the financial status of a parish. At times, Walsh met
Catholic school board officials, and sometimes even local Protestant
neighbours paid him a courtesy call. One administrative detail always
included was his inspecting and signing of parochial registers. Such
inspections ensured that these sacramental records were being kept
up-to-date. All these were ways to affirm a parish's connection to the
local and universal Catholic Church.[45]

Concerning the sacrament of Marriage, Walsh, unlike his predecessor, accepted as a fact of life that many Catholics desired to marry Protestants rather than other Catholics. That was a reflection of the demo-
graphics of largely Protestant Toronto, where more and more Catholics commonly met and socialized with Protestants. Whereas Lynch
had been "stingy in granting dispensations" to Catholics to marry
Protestants, Walsh acknowledged the need to grant them in order to
keep Catholics "in the fold." His concern stemmed from the large
number of so-called "mixed" marriages, which had increased from
one-in-twenty to one-in-five.[46] He recognized that, failing to receive
a dispensation for a mixed marriage, a couple would marry before a
Protestant minister. For such an act, the Catholic party would be *ipso
facto* excommunicated, something the archbishop strongly wanted to
prevent. Rarely would an excommunicant ever return to the Catholic
Church. To help resolve this pastoral problem, Walsh found it necessary to petition Rome for one hundred dispensations for mixed marriages, rather than the normal fifty a bishop would receive. Because of
his sensitivity to people's economic situations, Walsh often went so far
as to waive the required fee for such dispensations.[47]

Among his many pastoral responsibilities, the most important for
Walsh was the promotion of Catholic lay spirituality. During the nineteenth century, considerable emphasis had been placed on adoration
of the Blessed Sacrament during the Forty Hours devotions.[48] Usually
a bishop did not attend such parochial devotions. Not so for Walsh. He
was present in many parishes for their devotions; he often preached,
but sometimes simply gave the Benediction at the end of a day.[49]

As he had done in London, he also encouraged another important
nineteenth-century devotional practice: parish missions. Often members of Religious orders, such as the Jesuits, the Redemptorists, or other
specially invited priests, would promote a parish mission at all the par-

ish's Sunday morning Masses prior to the event. Particular emphasis was often placed on reaching out to and gaining back "lapsed" Catholics. Usually the preachers began a mission on a Sunday evening, and it lasted for the next three days. Each evening a service with hymns, prayers, readings of Scripture, and a lengthy sermon aimed to teach the basics of the faith, encourage greater devotion, and give Catholics a better sense of belonging to the universal Church. "Going to Confession," as it was called, was stressed; it was the moment of conversion and reform of lives sought during the missions. Consequently, a parish mission was an essential vehicle for supporting and developing lay spirituality and, in Walsh's words, a "quickening in the Catholic spirit."[50]

Along with Forty Hours devotions and parish missions, Walsh also promoted lay spirituality through other forms of piety, notably to the Sacred Heart and to the Blessed Virgin Mary, as well as the Rosary. Other devotions of the day included scapulars, pictorial prayer cards, and medals of the saints, such as St Christopher, St Joseph, the Blessed Virgin Mary, and the Miraculous Medal. Devotions were, for the most part, in the vernacular, an attractive and necessary feature for uneducated Catholics. The Mass, however, was always celebrated in Latin, and remained very much a mystery, with the emphasis on the Mass as a sacrifice rather than on the Lord's Supper at which the consecrated bread was received. In practice, during the nineteenth century, frequent reception of Holy Communion was unknown, since people were made to feel unworthy. One attended as an observer rather than as a recipient of Holy Communion. Frequent Confession went hand in hand with that thinking, since for many, there was a hesitancy to receive Holy Communion at Mass or even to go to Confession. That was largely due to the heresy of Jansenism, still a strong influence among Catholics. Their main worry was that they might not be able to make reparation for what they perceived, or had been led to believe, was either venial or mortal sin. That attitude often led to unhealthy scrupulosity and a failure to receive Holy Communion.[51]

The immigration of so many Irish Catholics into the Toronto area led to the establishment of organizations dedicated to assisting them, since many came to the New World in an impoverished state. Coupled with the widespread economic depression of the last decade of the nineteenth century, that meant much hardship for many Catholics throughout the archdiocese. Consequently, there was a great strain on charitable resources. Earlier, while in London, Walsh had known the Irish Benevolent Society, which was established in 1877, ten years after his arrival in that diocese. The Society was dedicated to serving new

Irish immigrants, Catholics and Protestants alike, especially those in need of housing, food, clothing, work, and social contacts. Toronto had four similar charitable organizations: the Emerald Benevolent Association, the Irish Catholic Benevolent Union, the Knights of St John – officially welcomed to the city in 1892 by city council – and the Ancient Order of Hibernians, all of which Walsh had a keen interest in supporting because of the tremendous assistance they offered to new Irish immigrants in his archdiocese.[52]

One charitable organization to which he was especially devoted was the Catholic Mutual Benefit Association (CMBA). It had been organized by Bishop Stephen Ryan of Buffalo, New York, in 1876, and quickly spread across the continent, reaching Toronto in 1882. Earlier, the first Canadian branch had been established in 1878 in Windsor; Walsh became the first Canadian bishop to acquire membership. After his move to Toronto, where the CMBA had been firmly supported by his predecessor, he enthusiastically encouraged it. By 1888, the CMBA had 3,220 members nationwide – phenomenal growth at the time – and within seven more years, with the intent to be truly national, it began a bilingual monthly newsletter. Weekly reports of its holdings and financial transactions were published in the *Catholic Record*. Walsh was happy to give support to the work of his longtime friend, Stephen Ryan.[53]

In Toronto, Walsh continued to be a remarkable preacher and teacher of Catholic doctrine, a man who expressed himself with "accustomed eloquence and power," as he had been since the earliest days of his priesthood and throughout his episcopate in London. In fact, that was among the principal reasons why he was chosen to be a bishop in the first place; it was also why he had been appointed to the Toronto see. Though the occasions to preach may have become noticeably fewer as he aged, nevertheless in Toronto, he took every opportunity that time and health permitted to preach and to explain the Catholic faith. Ever faithful himself to the gospel and to the teachings of the Catholic Church, he deeply believed it was his responsibility as chief pastor to continue to fill the role of preacher and teacher of the Word of God with tenacity and determination.

St Michael's Cathedral was his regular venue for preaching, at which he covered a variety of topics about Catholicism. Indeed, too, even in the smallest parish churches, every parochial visit he made, every

Confirmation or Forty Hours at which he officiated, each gave him a receptive audience willing to listen to his learned expositions of the Catholic faith. The opportunities were many; one such was at the cathedral, when he delivered a series of talks during Lent in 1890. Usually, the archbishop would deliver the first talk, with the remainder being given during the subsequent weeks by learned priests. That Lent, Walsh addressed the assembly with "Christ, the Saviour of Human Society."[54] A later talk, delivered at Our Lady of Lourdes parish at St John's Grove, drew great but typical praise, reflecting upon his style of delivery: "His Grace was in fine form, and delivered himself with his accustomed eloquence and power ... The beautiful ideas he expressed clothed in the choicest language, and delivered with an irresistible force of oratory, afforded indeed great pleasure as well as instruction and made one feel sorry when the end came."[55] He seemed willing to use his oratorical skills at every chance which was offered him.

On another occasion, in fact, he went into the very heart of Protestant Ontario, Orangeville, in order to explain Catholicism there. Walsh thoroughly understood the Protestant antipathy there, even the entrenched hostility towards the Catholic Church. He wanted to explain Catholicism so that his listeners would have a clearer understanding of what Catholics actually believed and practised. By that gesture, intended in the friendliest fashion, he hoped to break down some of the prejudices and misunderstandings which were the source of so many of the Catholic-Protestant conflicts in nineteenth-century Ontario. His speech was, therefore, no attack on Protestantism. Rather, he sought only an opportunity for dialogue. Cleverly titling his speech "What Catholics Do Not Believe," Walsh carefully traced the history of the times and the way that, as he saw it, Catholics had been persecuted and maligned over the centuries. He did not blame Protestants for that, he emphasized; they believed, however mistakenly, what they had been told for centuries. He hoped to help clarify some of the misunderstandings, and so among the several themes devoted to Catholic doctrines and devotions, he spoke about the Scriptures, the divinity of Christ, the Virgin Mary, the sacrament of Confession and indulgences, and Catholics' support of the civil society. His lecture was a tour de force.[56]

Throughout, he also highlighted the need for tolerance and civility among Christians on both sides, without any sense of symbolic syncretism or of compromising the Creed. He pointed out that Protestants were on the same road to heaven as Catholics, and that both Catholics and Protestants, however much they might differ in matters of faith, were living and acting in good conscience. That reflected his long-standing respect for and good relations with Protestants. Orangeville was a very special challenge, given its profoundly embedded suspicion of Catholics. Walsh was quite aware of that, and aware too that his audience that evening was peppered with interested Protestants, many of whom nonetheless felt that they had very good reason for their suspicions. Still, he gave them new grounds for rethinking and reflecting.

Such an approach, of course, was rare in the nineteenth century, and would scarcely ever, if at all, have been expressed by a prominent churchman of the day. It was the common thinking of the time that "outside the Church there is no salvation," but to most of Walsh's audience that evening, he must have seemed a most exceptional Catholic bishop.[57] One reporter described his concluding comments:

> The Archbishop's peroration was eloquent. He referred to the grand heritage which Canadians enjoyed – a country of untold resources, and the inestimable boon of civil and religious liberty. Christians were all striving in different ways to reach the same goal, and in doing this they should be neighborly and forbearing towards each other, and though they might differ in matters of religious belief they should do so in a spirit of kindness and friendship, and work earnestly and harmoniously together in making the land of their birth or adoption happy, contented and prosperous.[58]

While often fully engaged in Toronto, given his renown as an orator, Walsh was much sought after outside the archdiocese. Some of those invitations he accepted, such as when Thomas Dowling, bishop of Hamilton, invited him there for the consecration of the new church of St Lawrence in November 1890. Denis O'Connor of London officiated while Walsh preached. Once again, by his eloquent sermon, he showed his knack of taking every opportunity to promote the Catholic faith. He reminded his listeners that they lived in a time when the Church's teachings were being "assailed" and "undermined" so that the faithful were encouraged

> to substitute cold, barren philosophy for the doctrines of the Christian Church … If we are assembled here today it is because here the Son of God continues and will continue the office of redeemer. Here He will continue to preach, to offer Himself upon the altar and to labor for the poor, sick and bereaved.

Come to the church, dear children, come to the ordinances and sacraments, that having lived as good members of the Church militant, you may deserve to become members of the Church triumphant.[59]

On 16 December 1894, he was also invited to preach at a memorial Mass for Sir John S.D. Thompson, Canada's first Catholic prime minister from 1892 to 1894, who had died in London, England, immediately after being sworn into the Privy Council by Queen Victoria. It was surely a sign of Walsh's acceptance by the general public that he was invited to take on such a role.[60]

The archbishop also exercised his teaching authority through his many pastoral letters, in which he was able to focus on specific teachings of the Catholic Church and highlight particular aspects that were being questioned at the time, as he had previously done in London. His themes ranged from "Devotion to the Blessed Virgin" – in a pastoral letter he promulgated and distributed in April 1891 – to various Lenten pastoral letters issued throughout his years in Toronto, and to letters which accompanied the distribution of papal encyclicals. Other letters raised various matters of Catholic interest, and after the mid-1890s, in conjunction with the other bishops of the ecclesiastical province, he wrote about the hotly debated Manitoba Schools Question (discussed below).[61]

Noteworthy, too, was his pastoral letter regarding papal financial support. That dealt with what was known as "Peter's Pence." That letter made evident Walsh's great sensitivity to the financial plight of his people. Shortly after his arrival in Toronto, he had written to the prefect of Propaganda Fide, Giovanni Cardinal Simeoni, indicating that he could not at that time order a collection for Peter's Pence, because of the impoverished state of Catholic workers in Toronto.[62] Yet in no way did his concern signal any less respect for the pope; rather, Walsh was simply being pragmatic and pastoral. Later, by the mid-1890s, when the recession had lessened, Walsh called for the people of the archdiocese to give generously to Peter's Pence, as a sign of filial love for the pope. He reminded them that no such collection had been taken in the archdiocese for eight years and that it was once again time "to contribute of our means and in accordance with our capacity towards the support and maintenance of our Holy Father the Pope." In a somewhat forceful way, he went on to stress the historical reasons for the pope's needs; it was the result of the unification of Italy and of Giuseppe Garibaldi seizing the Papal States which deprived the Church and the papacy of its income: "The Vicar of Christ has been robbed of his independence and liberty as head of the Church; he has been deprived of his civil princedom secured to him for centuries by the action of Divine Providence; and he has been made dependent on the contributions of the faithful for the means that are necessary to enable him to exercise his Divine and world-wide ministry." Walsh also placed considerable emphasis on the history of the papacy itself, and on the meaning of papal supremacy, something *au courant* in the wake of the Vatican Council.[63] He concluded with accolades for Leo XIII, along with specific directions for promoting and collecting Peter's Pence.[64]

Mindful of how valuable a Catholic newspaper had been in London for explaining Catholic teachings as well as forging a sense of community throughout the diocese, Walsh decided to create a new Catholic paper in Toronto, the *Catholic Register*, by amalgamating, in January 1893, the *Catholic Weekly Review* with the *Irish Canadian*. The latter newspaper had its roots in the early 1800s, and served the Catholics of the archdiocese with news of Ireland and Canada. The former, established in 1887, had decidedly more religious content than the *Irish Canadian* had. Given the small Catholic population, by the early 1890s both these newspapers were in serious financial difficulties. Walsh arranged for their merger, and the resultant *Catholic Register*, an "offspring of the shotgun wedding ... bore a similarity to both its parents without being identical to either one. [It] ... was obedient to the hierarchy, particularly Archbishop John Walsh." In effect, it became a valuable medium for advancing the teachings of the archbishop, as well as promoting the Catholic faith. It also strove to reflect the principles of modern Canadian journalism.[65]

During the nineteenth century, one especially important responsibility for every Canadian bishop was to oversee Catholic education throughout his diocese. Those bishops fortunate enough to have Catholic schools were expected by Rome to ensure their orthodoxy in Catholic teaching, while also demonstrating strict compliance with provincial governmental regulations. That was not always easy to maintain, especially in Ontario with its longstanding hostility towards Catholic schools. Yet, Walsh was able to maintain that balance as well in Toronto as he had in London. He often made it clear to Catholics where he stood on the matter of education. On one occasion, while addressing the members of the Catholic school board in Toronto, he stressed how much he considered Catholic education to be "a subject of great importance, and one well worthy of their best attention and labors."[66] He made sure that the Catholic schools were current with provincial requirements and directions. To that end, kindergarten was established in 1890, and the St John's Industrial School for boys was opened in 1897, under the direction of the Christian Brothers. That school provided a tremendous opportunity for boys from every background, but especially for those from immigrant families and troubled homes, giving them "an open and community-styled environment where they could learn agricultural skills, floriculture, baking, tailoring, carpentry, typewriting and printing." At the same time, there were other Catholic high schools which offered typewriting, bookkeeping, business, photography, and sewing classes in addition to the usual academic subjects.[67] In Walsh's mind, all these educational opportunities would help to ensure that young Catholic students could learn all the requisite skills for either joining the work force or continuing their education at the university level.[68]

In addition, Walsh was ever conscious of the need for Catholics to integrate into, and take leadership in, civil society. "Catholic schools in Toronto," he maintained, "were committed to produce virtuous Christians and good citizens of Canada and the Empire." When addressing groups of teachers, Walsh would remind them of their onerous duties to uphold the twin pillars of piety and patriotism, and "to fit [the children] as far as possible for their future duties, and at the same time deposit in their young minds the seeds of virtue."[69] It was a tall order, but one which he believed was attainable.

One issue gave him considerable concern. As in London, Walsh had to confront the question of the secret ballot for the election of members of Catholic school boards. It was the same battle that had been fought by Archbishop Lynch. The use of secret ballots, after all, was introduced only in 1874, and therefore was something relatively new on the Canadian political landscape; secret ballots had not yet been adopted at all levels of voting in the various provinces.

Believing that voters should be prepared to literally stand behind their candidates and let their choices be known publicly by a show of hands, Walsh continued to raise the objections about the new voting methods, despite being very democratic in his thinking. However, he came to realize that the Ontario government was moving toward this change, and, as in most things, he "preferred the quiet diplomacy of the back room to the showy bombasts of Archbishop Lynch."[70] Eventually, therefore, when the Ontario government introduced in 1894 a bill to establish secret balloting throughout the province, Walsh clearly "sensed the times were too inflammatory for the bishops to oppose the will of the government, and he went out of his way to persuade several of his colleagues to join him in silent submission to the inevitable."[71]

During the later decades of the century, an issue developed which seemed at the time to be one of the greatest threats to Catholic education in Canada: the Manitoba Schools Question. Manitoba joined Confederation as a province in 1870, with, among other minority rights, guarantees for Catholics to establish their own schools and to receive a pro-rated share of government funding collected through taxation. By 1890, in the face of a sparse Catholic population, the Liberal government of Manitoba under Thomas Greenway no longer found it viable to maintain separate schools, nor to keep French as an official language in the province. It was no surprise, then, when the Manitoba legislature passed an act in March 1890 to abolish funding of separate schools. This act, according to the British North America Act of 1867, would automatically take effect if it were not challenged by the federal Parliament.[72]

Despite being centred in Manitoba, the question took on national significance and became a defining moment in relations between Catholics and Protestants in Canada, and equally importantly, between French-speaking and English-speaking Canadians. It was a time, also, when Catholic bishops discovered just how much power they had to sway public opinion, when local rights seemed more important to some than rights for all Catholics, and when the Vatican's own delegate tried to direct the Canadian bishops in their course of action. For Walsh, it was an occasion when his diplomatic skills were needed to bring about a compromise to save Catholic education.

The archbishop of Saint-Boniface, Alexandre-Antonin Taché, OMI, launched an appeal to the governor general within one month of the passage of the legislation in Manitoba, indicating that he had the support of several influential parties. By March 1891, Cardinal Taschereau of Quebec waded in with a petition addressed to the governor general, carrying the signatures of twenty-four other bishops, which called attention to the elimination of Catholic education and urged "that a remedy should be adopted to defeat the pernicious legislation."[73] Walsh kept his own counsel initially, making no public declarations while he determined what role he should play.

Buoyed by the inaction of the federal Parliament, the city of Winnipeg passed a by-law forcing Catholic ratepayers to be taxed for support of the public school system. The Supreme Court of Manitoba upheld the by-law, but in October that year, on appeal, the Supreme Court of Canada reversed the judgment, declaring that the city did not have jurisdiction to change the system of taxation. An appeal was then made by the city of Winnipeg to the Judicial Committee of the Privy Council in England. Ultimately, the Privy Council ruled that the province was within its rights, since Catholic education, though no longer publicly funded, was not denied in theory, and the Dominion government had the power to restore those minority education rights in Manitoba anyway. Catholics, Anglicans, and all other religious bodies in Manitoba were allowed to operate their own schools. Appeals were launched on behalf of the Catholics of Manitoba, including another petition in 1892 from Taschereau and his brother bishops.[74] Among these was Walsh, though he admitted that he had signed somewhat reluctantly. It would be the last petition of any kind that he would sign.[75]

Throughout the controversy, Walsh had taken a flexible but cautious stance on the issue. He would later encourage Louis-Philippe-Adélard Langevin, when he became archbishop of Saint-Boniface, to hold out for his rights on the Manitoba Schools Question, but, for the most part, Walsh and the bishops of Ontario believed that pushing for Catholic education rights in Manitoba would invite repression in other places, especially in Protestant Ontario. He also feared there could be problems for the governing federal Conservatives, as some suggested the controversy could lead to a federal-provincial clash, with possible harm to the stability of the federal government.[76] Nevertheless, Walsh repeatedly received appeals from various parties – Catholic and Protestant – to use his influence with the government. One such appeal came from the governor general's wife, writing in his name: Ishbel Aberdeen invited Walsh to come to Ottawa for a meeting with the governor general. A "Remedial Act" was being proposed by the federal Conservative government to restore Catholic schools in Manitoba, which, she believed, could lead to further problems for children in Catholic schools in the other English provinces. She hoped for Walsh's support to have the act defeated:

> We know pretty well your Grace's mind on the subject, how you feel that to press it to its extreme issue can do no good to any Church, or to any political party but can only rend the country & damage the cause of true religion ... We know that your Grace has discussed the question in all its bearings already with Archbishop Langevin, & we know too that your advice has great weight with him, coming as it does from one who has had so much experience & who knows too the people of Ontario.

But will you not write again & urge for another effort to be made towards conciliation without of course mentioning His Excellency?[77]

Lady Aberdeen even wondered if Leo XIII could be asked to express this opinion: "Could not a message come from Rome or through even Cardinal Satolli which would at least prevent the Church in Quebec from openly exercising political influence & thus from irritating the people elsewhere?"[78]

On the other side of the question, however, Langevin wrote seeking Walsh's support in favour of the remedial bill. Earlier, Langevin had realized it was not opportune to appeal to the federal government, but now he wanted to press ahead. He expressed regret that the Manitoba government had appealed "to the worst passions of the people in reference to this School Question, and now they would not even think of making any reasonable proposal."[79]

Soon afterwards, Walsh received a report on the schools question written by then-Senator Scott. Despite the complicated nature of the question, Scott did an impressive job of summarizing the issue, pointing out the strengths and weaknesses on both sides. His main concern echoed that of the governor general, that the remedial bill would pit Catholics against Protestants not only in Manitoba but throughout the country. Such a bill, he thought, might have been successful had it been introduced earlier, but sectarian division in the country now made its acceptance impossible. Even were it to be passed by the federal Parliament, he wrote, the Manitoba government would surely not be expected to enact it, leaving open the possibility of further hardship for Catholics and bad feelings across the board.[80]

During the summer months of 1896, the divided Conservative government was defeated on this hotly debated issue in a national general election. The new Liberal prime minister, Wilfrid Laurier, soon reached a compromise with the premier of Manitoba, Thomas Greenway. The Laurier-Greenway plan, as it was called, allowed for thirty minutes of religious instruction to take place at the end of each school day, which it was hoped would be the means for a renaissance of Catholic education in Manitoba. That compromise was studied carefully by the apostolic delegate to Canada, Monsignor Rafaele Merry del Val, who had been sent by Leo XIII in 1897 to examine the whole matter.[81]

As a result of the delegate's visit and his report to the pope, on 18 December 1897 Leo XIII issued an encyclical, *Affari Vos*. Papal encyclicals were still rare in the late nineteenth century, so for a Canadian issue to be the subject of one indicated the importance of the question for the pope. No doubt Walsh would have been delighted to have that letter issued from Rome. In the encyclical, Pope Leo praised the faith of Canadian Catholics, a faith which, he pointed out, had been cherished from the time of the first settlers and handed down from generation to generation. He emphasized the rights of parents to educate their children in Catholic schools, and the rights of the Catholic Church to establish and control such schools. Further, he described the laws eliminating these schools in Manitoba as "hardships," but more deplorable, he wrote, was that "Canadian Catholics themselves were unable to act in concert in the defence of interests which so closely touch the common good."[82] The pope also accepted the reality that "partial satisfaction" could be accepted in this case, with the hope of continuing to build on that foundation for greater freedoms in the future.[83]

That was precisely the position taken by Walsh and the other bishops of the Toronto ecclesiastical province, Dowling of Hamilton and O'Connor of London, as outlined in their joint pastoral letter which publicized the encyclical.[84] They echoed the thoughts of the pope on "partial satisfaction," which was in keeping with Walsh's belief that in securing Catholic rights in the country, sometimes it was necessary to accept compromises rather than lose all in rigid opposition. The hallmark of Walsh's political legacy would become evident again: to find the compromise that obtained the most good for the most people without sacrificing the Catholic faith and practices.

Within a month of the publication of the papal encyclical and the pastoral letter, Walsh wrote to Langevin to encourage him to accept the compromise. Laurier, he assured him, would support, if not the "letter," at least the "spirit" of the encyclical.[85] At the end of it all, Catholic education was restored to Manitoba schools in some limited fashion, and political peace for the sake of the common good was achieved through the efforts of Walsh and others.[86]

After arriving in Toronto, Walsh proved again and again his ability to mend the relations with various levels of government that Lynch's episcopate had strained. It was true that Lynch had been very open and had enjoyed a certain notoriety over his support of the Liberal party – at provincial and federal levels – but he had found more and more toward the end of his life that his influence among the Catholic laity and his fellow bishops had grown "seriously weakened" in many public matters. Cleary of Kingston, therefore, had begun taking the lead on major public issues with the support of Walsh and O'Mahony.[87]

Under John A. Macdonald's leadership, the Conservatives had generally aimed at consensus-building, while the Liberals often used a "divide and conquer" approach toward their opponents, something which often resulted in "Catholic-bashing." Thus, in Toronto, Walsh found himself still able to work with Macdonald as comfortably as before. In an 1890 letter to him, Walsh expressed his wariness about the Liberal party: "The result of the recent [1890] elections in Ontario should convince even the fanatics that the majority of Upper Canadians are utterly opposed to 'religious cries' raised for the purpose of factions, and not for the welfare of the country."[88]

For over three decades, Walsh had been a close friend and confidant of Macdonald throughout his long years in the federal Parliament. That relationship continued right up to Macdonald's death in 1891.[89] It was most obvious in Macdonald's intervention when Toronto was *sede vacante* in 1889. In fact, it was common knowledge that, although a strong Presbyterian, Macdonald had allowed a certain amount of patronage to flow to Catholics, something which, without proper attention, could have become a political minefield for him, especially in Protestant Ontario. Indications from the press of the day were that Catholics were satisfied with their share.[90] Not widely known, though, was the way Walsh's personal influence with Macdonald over the years had contributed to that flow of patronage.

Indeed, the flow of beneficiary requests from Toronto to Ottawa never ceased, as Walsh continued to plead the cause of various lay persons. One such request was made in 1889 on behalf of the widow of Mr Justice John O'Connor, Jr, originally from Essex County but by then living in Toronto. She needed a pension. The next year, Walsh proposed a candidate from the archdiocese, a Mr J. Gravely, to fill an opening for an officer at military headquarters. Walsh's concern also crossed the boundaries of other dioceses, where he knew many who would be suitable for government posts, including a barrister from Glengarry county, John MacDonell, whom he suggested for a seat in the Senate in 1891. Earlier, Walsh had written to suggest that the tender of his own brother-in-law, James McMahon, be considered for a federal project on the Rapide Plat canal. Nor did he hesitate to intervene in the same year for a man desiring a commission in the North West Mounted Police, Harold King, son of the nephew of the late lieutenant governor of Ontario, who had been a personal friend.[91]

As always in the matter of patronage, not all his requests were successful. Sometimes, in response, the prime minister would point out as before that his promises to others had to be kept first. At other times, he would assure Walsh that his suggestions would be considered at the earliest opportunity, or that they could not be considered at all, for one reason or another.[92] At the same time, on occasion, Macdonald continued to turn to Walsh to ask him to use – ever so discreetly, since Catholic bishops had to tread warily in political matters – his influence to assist the prime minister and his fellow Conservatives. Macdonald, as he had done before during Walsh's London episcopate, sometimes requested support for a particular candidate or issue, especially at election time. He even once used J.C. Patterson, a member of the Ontario legislature, as an intermediary with Walsh.[93] As important as their political manoeuvring, their correspondence also reflected the continuing warm personal relationship between Walsh and Macdonald, underlined by expressions of best wishes for holidays and eager anticipation of future visits.[94]

Overall, however much each may have sought from the other, be it personal gain or gain for friends, the key to their friendly relationship was their mutual desire to achieve the common good for the country. From the archbishop's perspective, that goal could be best served by establishing Catholic lay people in positions of influence. He wanted the Church to play a role in society and was certain that Catholics could "coexist comfortably with non-Catholic denominations in the city, and could even make valuable contributions to civic life without endangering the faith. From within the Catholic community itself there emerged a desire to put a Canadian face on the Church and to engage in the work of 'nation-building.'"[95] He had always thought so.

The tide of mutual support and patronage ended with Macdonald's death. Walsh was never able to transfer the kind of relationship that he had had with Macdonald to his successors in either the Conservative party or Laurier's Liberals.[96] Perhaps it was Walsh's advancing age, or perhaps his friendship with Macdonald was more widely known than he had thought, but after Macdonald's passing, Walsh's political influence was in decline. Yet despite that, in the mid-1890s, he was sought after by people on both sides of the political spectrum – even the officially politically neutral governor general – to weigh in on the Manitoba Schools Question. He was still a force to be dealt with. It had been that realization, and his keen political sense, that had led Walsh to support the Laurier-Greenway compromise.[97]

Where Walsh's influence did not waver, however, was on the national ecclesiastical level. Rather, it increased as metropolitan archbishop.

His advice was sought regularly, especially in the naming of bishops for vacant sees. When Taché of Saint-Boniface died in 1894, Walsh was consulted about the *terna* to be sent to Propaganda Fide. The candidate listed as *dignissimus* was Adélard Langevin, a priest of the Oblates of Mary Immaculate.[98] Two years later, in December 1896, Montreal became vacant following the death of Archbishop Fabre. Interestingly enough, the first consultations, held during the meeting of bishops of that ecclesiastical province, resulted in a split decision on the proposed *terna*: Narcisse-Zéphirin Lorrain, vicar apostolic of Pontiac, as *dignissimus*, followed by two priests of Montreal, Zotique Racicot and Louis-Joseph-Napoléon-Paul Bruchési, as *dignior* and *dignus* respectively. Some bishops from Quebec and elsewhere suggested that Lorrain, a pious bishop and good missionary, should be dropped, since he would not be suitable for Montreal. They had no opposition to the second or third candidates. Other bishops, including Walsh and the archbishop of Halifax, Cornelius O'Brien, suggested another candidate who was not on the *terna*, Paul-Stanislaus LaRocque, bishop of Sherbrooke. In the end, Bruchési, the *dignus* candidate, was appointed.[99]

The final ecclesiastical nomination that involved Walsh was for the archbishopric of Kingston. James Cleary died on 24 February 1898. Walsh met at the archiepiscopal palace with his suffragans, O'Connor of London and Dowling of Hamilton, on 25 March. There they drew up a *terna* and submitted it to Rome. Richard O'Connor, earlier named bishop of Peterborough in 1889, was listed as *dignissimus,* followed by two priests from Kingston, Charles-Hugues Gauthier as *dignior* and Thomas Kelly as *dignus.* Meanwhile, knowing that that *terna* had been submitted, O'Connor himself and Alexander MacDonell, the bishop of Alexandria, sent their own in which Gauthier was *dignissimus*, Kelly was *dignior*, and John Masterson, a third priest from Kingston, was *dignus*. O'Connor and MacDonell were acting on behalf of the priests of Kingston, who ardently supported the choice of Gauthier, as did Louis-Nazaire Bégin, the archbishop of Quebec and primate of Canada. They won out. Gauthier was nominated archbishop of Kingston by Propaganda Fide and subsequently was named by the pope on 5 July 1898.[100]

Interestingly, in this dossier of nomination for Kingston is found a letter from Walsh sent to the prefect of Propaganda Fide, nominating the same Thomas Kelly of Kingston as auxiliary bishop of Toronto. It was written in the time between Lynch's death and Walsh's own appointment there.[101] Nothing ever came of that nomination, however, and one is left to wonder about Walsh's timing. The see was vacant and besides, Toronto already had an auxiliary bishop, O'Mahony. Was Walsh preparing for his own – what many would believe – inevitable appointment to Toronto, and choosing his own auxiliary in advance? Perhaps he was simply convinced that Kelly was a suitable candidate and chose to promote this worthy priest. Certainly, too, others also thought highly of Kelly; his name appeared on two *ternae* within a short period of time.

During those same years, 1897 and 1898, MacDonell of Alexandria petitioned the prefect of Propaganda Fide for a change in boundaries to expand his see by hiving off the counties of Prescott and Russell from the archdiocese of Ottawa and attaching them to his. This matter of boundaries had been contentious ever since the Alexandria diocese had been established in 1890. The English-speaking bishops of Ontario were agitating to sever the English-speaking part of the archdiocese of Ottawa, itself a largely French-speaking diocese, in order to enlarge Alexandria, in the main an English-speaking diocese. At the heart of it, the matter reflected the long-festering tensions in Canadian English-French relations.[102]

On the other side, opposed to any change, stood Joseph-Thomas Duhamel of Ottawa, an ardent French-Canadian nationalist who was never much given to understanding the needs of English-speaking Catholics, even in his own diocese. Like any bishop, he wanted no changes to his boundaries. Of course, he also had history on his side, for traditionally Ottawa had been considered part of Quebec's hierarchy, and not of Ontario's. Quickly taking the matter in hand, on 8 February 1897, he fired off a letter to Propaganda Fide, bristling with indignation. "[T]he demand," he insisted, "that is made by the Irish bishops of Ontario is a new means employed by them in the incessant war they have waged for a quarter of a century against the diocese of Ottawa, given the French-Canadians forming the very great majority, and against the undersigned archbishop."[103]

It was an English plot, he went on, to have an Irish bishop in the capital of Canada. He complained that if the counties in question were annexed to Alexandria, then part of the city of Ottawa along with its Catholic cemetery would fall under the jurisdiction of the bishop of Alexandria, an intolerable situation if ever there was one. He asked that, before a decision was made, time might be given him to write a memorial and, as well, to consult the French-Canadian bishops (mainly in Quebec) regarding the matter. These latter were not about to support any diocesan enlargement in Ontario at the expense of a Quebec diocese.[104]

The whole matter became an unseemly tug-of-war between the two sides after Walsh and other English-speaking bishops signed a letter of support for MacDonell's request. Dowling of Hamilton, O'Connor of Peterborough, Cleary of Kingston, and O'Connor of London all signed. These were the principal bishops not only in Ontario, but also in English-speaking Canada. Along with that letter, Walsh provided testimony, in a memorandum dated 18 May 1896, stating that when Ottawa was erected as an ecclesiastical province, it was agreed that at the death of the incumbent, Eugène Guigues, "Ottawa and the counties forming a part of its diocese, but situate[d] in the Province of Ontario, should be brought under the jurisdiction of the Church in Ontario." That decision, he pointed out, had been made at the Fourth Provincial Council held at Quebec in May 1868, "in which all the Bishops of Lower and Upper Canada took part."[105]

Meantime, Duhamel's memorial reflected history differently. He emphasized the repeated attempts of the bishops of Ontario to claim Ottawa as an ecclesiastical province of Ontario and not of Quebec. To argue his point, he listed the various reasons why Ottawa was "the *true centre* and the *leading city* of Canada" and why such a division of his archdiocese would be a great evil for the French-Canadian population. Not surprisingly, the archbishops and all the auxiliary bishops of the archdioceses of Quebec and Montreal supported his side.[106] At the end of it all, the archdiocese was not divided, at least for that time.[107]

Even while concerned with national ecclesiastical matters, Walsh also faced another, totally different, but equally delicate matter, a protest by the priests of London against their bishop. Eight senior priests, including Michael Tiernan, the rector of the cathedral, signed a petition in February 1898 which they directed to Propaganda Fide. They detailed six grievances against Bishop O'Connor. These included his not having named a vicar general in the diocese, which, in effect, made it difficult to get dispensations in the bishop's absence. He did not pay attention to the age of priests and years of service when making appointments, seemingly favouring young priests with the best assignments. As well, the bishop made public statements that the majority of priests in the diocese were intemperate in drink. He would not receive priests who had been suspended or away from the diocese, leaving no hope for rehabilitation. Furthermore, the petitioners complained, the *cathedraticum* was far too high, giving O'Connor an annual income of $14,000, while the bishop of Detroit, for example, was content with $5,000. Finally, it was almost impossible, they said, to get dispensations for mixed marriages from the bishop, resulting in many Catholics leaving the Church to be married by Protestant ministers. They went on to speak of his cruel manner when reprimanding priests, his violent temper, his vindictive character, and his lack of honesty. They had made an appeal to the apostolic delegate, Merry del Val, while he was in Canada for the Manitoba Schools Question, they reported, but the delegate declined to become involved. It was not, he said to them, within his "sphere of action."[108]

The prefect, Ledóchowski, wrote to Walsh, and asked for his opinion on the matter. Walsh replied within a month with a lengthy summation, sympathetic to the priests of London. Later, in July of that year, Ledóchowski also wrote to O'Connor, who replied to the charges in August.[109] Nothing came of the protest, however. The man had enjoyed great success as superior of the Basilian Fathers and at Assumption school, for which he had been given the honorary title "Doctor of Divinity." Propaganda Fide was never gravely concerned, since O'Connor was named, within six months, to succeed Walsh in the see of Toronto.

In 1896, Propaganda Fide began consultation on the possibility of establishing a permanent apostolic delegation in Canada. By this time no longer an ultramontanist, Walsh did not favour that idea. On 2 May 1896, he wrote to O'Connor in London stating firmly where he stood. He would, he insisted, regard such an appointment "as a very disturbing element in our midst." Mindful of the delicate relations with the French-Canadian bishops, he also wondered about their reaction to such a proposal.[110] The federal Liberal government of the day strongly supported the idea, though. Walsh received copies of letters from both Prime Minister Laurier and Premier Félix-Gabriel Marchand of Quebec, which they had sent to the papal Secretary of State, Mariano Cardinal Rampolla del Tindaro, favouring the proposal. Merry del Val clearly was the favoured candidate of the Canadians.[111] Walsh, however, did not live to see the appointment; an apostolic delegation was established by Leo XIII on 3 August 1899, a year after Walsh's death.[112]

Although happy to be a Canadian, Walsh still felt strong ties to the land of his birth, especially to his family and to the cause of the civil rights of Irish Catholics. Catholic emancipation was a relatively new reality throughout his life – it had been declared only the year before he was born – and concern for Ireland and its people would perdure throughout his life in Canada. For that reason, as seen, he continually supported benevolent societies and other Irish organizations in Toronto, he attended the annual St Patrick's Day parade and festivities there, and he regularly preached at the Masses on those days. When and where he could, he gave words of encouragement to those helping the newest Irish immigrants into Canada, and he let his voice be heard on pertinent questions in Canada and in Ireland. He made a number of trips to Ireland over the years, and was featured as a guest speaker on grand occasions, such as in 1864 in Dublin, at the laying of the cornerstone of the monument to Daniel O'Connell.

Walsh continued to promote the cause of Home Rule, the desire of many in Ireland and of Irish descent throughout the world. Most of his priests and the majority of Canadian English-speaking Catholics were of Irish descent, and willingly supported the establishment of Home Rule there. Walsh sometimes instructed his priests in the archdiocese, as he had done in London, to take up collections for the people of Ireland.[113] When hopes for gaining Home Rule seemed to fade by the mid-1890s, he proposed to hold a convention of Irish people from across the world "as a means of effecting this desirable and necessary union ... of restoring unity to the Irish Parliamentary representatives ... and [as] an efficacious method of perpetuating that unity."[114] With these ideals in mind, the Irish Race Convention took place in Dublin in September 1896. Although Walsh was instrumental in getting it established and keenly wanted to attend, he could not, unfortunately, due to his frailty from advancing age. Instead, he appointed the rector of the cathedral, Francis Ryan, an ardent Home Ruler, to represent him at the convention.[115]

"Shepherding the flock" was an oft-used expression in the nineteenth century for a bishop's responsibilities. This "shepherding" included Walsh's duty to oversee the fiscal and physical needs of the archdiocese, especially during the depression of the 1890s. Besides approving the construction of sixteen churches and three chapels in the archdiocese, along with various houses for Religious women and men, and completing a major addition to and decoration of the cathedral, he also opened, in 1891, a girls' wing in the Sacred Heart orphanage as the children's numbers increased. As well, the St John's Industrial School was opened to train boys in various trades to aid them in finding employment. The St Vincent de Paul Society of Toronto was similarly established in 1894, to care for the needy in the difficult economic climate.

Earlier in 1892, the Sisters of St Joseph had founded St Michael's Hospital in central Toronto, which aimed to serve the Catholic population of the area. It brought much-needed relief to the sick, especially those of meagre means. Such medical care had been sorely lacking for them because most Catholics could not afford the costs at other hospitals in the city. Besides, those establishments were considered to be Protestant, and therefore Catholics were not especially welcome in them. Walsh was greatly pleased with the Sisters' charitable work in his diocese, and encouraged them considerably by his support. They were responsible for running the hospital, although the city helped with some of the finances. That financial assistance, however, was placed in jeopardy during the year following the hospital's founding, when the city's politicians announced they were withdrawing grants for "sectarian" hospitals. Walsh unleashed his fury on those he believed stood in the way of the grants. For the (mainly Protestant) politicians, the problem, which Walsh himself recognized, was that the Church was allowing some Sisters to work in the Catholic hospitals despite not being professionally trained. Yet Walsh had no patience for those who callously denied the needs of the poor. He was stinging in his broadside about the complaints:

> Can anyone for a moment deny that for the sick Catholic poor the ministrations of the Sisters ... their Christ like sympathy for the suffering, their life long consecration to the alleviation of human misery, their prayers and spiritual exhortations and instructions, the hopes and the trust in the merciful God, their presence and example as well as their words inspire, are of a value and an importance that are simply inestimable?[116]

Soon he was joined in his protest by testimonies from the medical staff of the hospital itself. Their reactions to the cutbacks appeared along with his open letter, and attested to the caring professionalism the Sisters showed at all times in their duties. In the end, Walsh was triumphant. The city council reversed its stand within the week, and St Michael's continued as before.

Throughout his long years in Toronto, by visiting far-flung parishes and communities, delivering countless lectures, and celebrating numerous special occasions, Walsh grew closer to the people of his archdiocese. Greatly admired, much loved, and in demand publicly and privately by those who sought his advice and company, despite his years and the occasional problems from ill health, Walsh still did his utmost to fulfil all his pastoral demands and social obligations. In every way, people wanted to be with him. Not only was he a renowned public figure, both ecclesial and secular, he was also a very warm person, with an engaging, witty, and outgoing personality, interested in people and their lives, a man who, despite his exalted office, truly attracted people. He had the good of all people at heart, and it showed. People responded enthusiastically to him wherever he went. Everywhere he was warmly welcomed, with people expressing their love and affection, esteem and loyalty towards him.

Two years after his arrival in Toronto, Walsh received a gift of "a magnificent carriage and span of horses" from friends there. Two years after that, in Walsh's twenty-fifth year as a bishop, Senator Frank Smith hosted a grand banquet in his honour, to which were invited bishops, clergymen of Toronto, and many prominent lay people, including judges and senior members of the military. Later again, in 1896, to celebrate his twenty-ninth anniversary of episcopal consecration, Walsh was the guest of honour at receptions held by the teachers and students at both the Loretto Abbey and St Joseph's Academy. At those celebratory events, the students sang, gave recitations, and delivered speeches of congratulations.[117]

In 1892, a severe influenza spread throughout the Toronto region, part of a world-wide epidemic. Concerned about the effects this would have on his people, Walsh penned a circular letter, dated the Feast of the Holy Name of Jesus, 17 January that year. It largely focused on asking people for prayers.[118] His letter also gave an interesting glimpse into his relationships. He expressed himself in three further and very different announcements. The first offered "heartfelt sympathy" to the Royal Family at the recent death of Prince Albert Victor, eldest son of the Prince and Princess of Wales (later Edward VII and Queen Alexandra). Prince Albert had died of influenza on 14 January. Despite his Irish roots, Walsh's affection for and loyalty to the Royal Family were well known. He saw no contradiction in that position, and clearly believed that one could be – indeed, must be – loyal to the Crown and to the Catholic Church at the same time. In the second announcement, he paid special tribute to Henry Edward Cardinal Manning, archbishop of Westminster, who had died after two years of failing health on the same day as the prince. Manning had been much beloved by Catholics and Protestants alike.[119] Walsh's third announcement paid tribute to Giovanni Cardinal Simeoni, former prefect of Propaganda Fide, who had also died around that time. Simeoni had played a major role in the development of the Church in Canada, particularly in its organization along diocesan lines and in the naming of its bishops. Walsh's tribute expressed what would have been the common sentiment of all the Canadian bishops: warm appreciation for his work and, through him, for their having had good relations with the Roman Curia.

During his declining years, death became ever-present for Walsh. His brother, Richard, died in Ireland, 23 September 1891. One can only imagine how difficult it must have been to preside at the Month's Mind Mass for this brother who had died so far away.[120] Vested in cope and mitre, Walsh sat in the sanctuary while Richard's son James – Walsh's long-time faithful secretary – celebrated the Mass in Toronto's cathedral. As a sign of respect and support for their archbishop and for those who had lost their loved one, many priests from London and Toronto were present, along with several lay people.

To add to Walsh's sorrow, one after another of his episcopal colleagues passed away during the 1890s: Cardinal Taschereau, Archbishop Fabre, Archbishop Taché, along with Walsh's closest episcopal friends, his auxiliary, Bishop O'Mahony, and Archbishop Cleary. O'Mahony had served the archdiocese of Toronto for thirteen years, first under Lynch and then Walsh, from 1879 until his death on 8 September 1892. Walsh, along with others, gave the eulogy, praising O'Mahony as a zealous pastor of souls and a faithful son of the Church. "He was beloved and revered in every part of his cure, and esteemed for his faithful labors and erudition throughout the city and Province."[121] Cleary preached at O'Mahony's funeral, but then, six years later, he himself succumbed to a stomach ailment on 24 February 1898. Walsh presided at the Pontifical High Mass of Requiem for Cleary on 1 March. Cleary's friend Bernard McQuaid, bishop of Rochester, New York, preached.

"A noble prelate gone to his reward" is how the *Catholic Record* announced John Walsh's final days, his death, funeral, and burial.[122] Death came suddenly and unexpectedly. He had gone to bless the new Mount Hope Cemetery on 9 July 1898, riding in the carriage of Eugene O'Keefe. Ironically, having chosen to walk part of the distance because the road was so bumpy, Walsh stumbled while stepping from the carriage. He severely sprained his knee and tore a ligament in his leg. O'Keefe saw that Walsh was driven home to his beloved St John's Grove, where his personal physician, Dr Robert Dwyer, the superintendent of St Michael's Hospital, cared for him. For a period of ten days, the archbishop was confined to his bed. After that, he began to move about his house, and appeared to be recovering nicely. For the next ten days he received many visitors on the veranda in the evenings.

It was greatly surprising, then, when a weakness overcame him on the evening of Sunday, 31 July 1898, while Thomas and John Long and Eugene O'Keefe were visiting him. He did not feel so well, he said, and his worried guests reluctantly departed so that he could take some rest. Fearing the worst, his nephew James, ever attentive to his uncle's needs, immediately called for Dwyer, who arrived at Walsh's bedside about half past nine.[123] Ellen McMahon, Walsh's niece, arrived shortly thereafter, and some other priests in the area, John Teefy, John Hand, James Treacy, Michael Cline, Michael Mungovan, and John McCann – his closest collaborators – were likewise summoned to St John's Grove.

The archbishop rested fitfully. Near half past ten, he roused himself, sitting up, saying, "I think I am going." He was. His nephew administered the last sacraments, and Walsh lay down once again. Ten minutes later, he "passed peacefully away." Dwyer sent for another physician, Barrington Nevitt, but there was no more to be done. The archbishop had died of heart failure, at the age of sixty-eight years.

The "sad and startling announcement" came as a great shock to people across the country. Most especially, the Catholics of the Toronto archdiocese were greatly surprised; few had known of his last illness. Everywhere his death "was genuinely lamented by all regardless of religious persuasion."[124] The bells of all the Catholic churches in the city tolled at eight o'clock that Monday morning, and many tributes to Walsh poured in during the days following his death. The sorrow was intense, as one scribe in the *Catholic Record* dramatically exclaimed, and "the words that fitted the occasion failed to come to the preachers. Hearts laden with sorrow [could not] give voice to their promptings. The wound was deep. The affliction was great – for Death had dealt a cruel blow."[125] Many letters of condolence were received at the palace from prelates and other dignitaries across Canada and America, including Canada's governor general, John Hamilton Gordon, the Earl of Aberdeen; and the leading American Catholic prelate, the great James Cardinal Gibbons of Baltimore. Toronto's City Council met in a special session to pass a resolution in praise of the city's beloved late archbishop.[126]

On Tuesday, 2 August, Walsh's remains were taken in formal procession from his home at "The Grove" to St Michael's Cathedral. Angus McDonald, a prominent lay Catholic, was the Grand Marshal of the procession. His assistants led groups of people representing no fewer than eleven societies and associations, including the Ancient Order of Hibernians, the Catholic Order of Foresters, and the St Vincent de Paul Society. These, in turn, were followed by a general throng of citizens, members of the Catholic school board, and Knights of St John, along with representatives of the clergy and the Christian Brothers. Then followed the hearse carrying the casket. Decorated with black bunting, it was drawn by four horses with black velvet covers, and driven by a coachman. Two footmen dressed in livery followed. Postilions, also in livery, guided the horses that pulled the hearse and the accompanying three carriages for family members, close friends, and senior clergymen. Surrounding the hearse was a uniformed honour guard made up of Knights of St John. The archbishop's family – his sister, Mrs James McMahon, her daughter Ellen, and his nephew James Walsh – came at the end of the long procession in their carriage, all of them dressed in formal black attire.

Upon arrival at the cathedral, while the great bells in the tower tolled, Walsh's casket was borne in and placed upon a catafalque for the lying-in-state. The casket itself was particularly stunning, with its wood finish, silver handles, and purple silk lining. As customary for an archbishop's funeral, his body was vested in the full robes of a bishop, with mitre and pectoral cross; his pallium was folded and placed beneath his head according to tradition. His archiepiscopal cross stood at the foot of the catafalque. Eight tall lighted candles in great candlesticks surrounded it, as did the Knights of St John, resplendent in their uniforms. They stood motionless on watch. Everywhere within, the cathedral was draped in black and white funeral bunting.

During that two-day period of mourning and lying-in-state, thousands upon thousands of people filed past his casket to gaze one last time upon their much-loved archbishop. During that first evening and on the next, the Office for the Dead was chanted in the sanctuary by the clergy, vested in cassock and surplice.

Thursday morning, 4 August, the day the Pontifical High Mass of Requiem was offered for the repose of Walsh's soul, was a pleasant summer's day. On the day of his funeral, as on the day he had been welcomed to Toronto to be their new archbishop, the cathedral was filled to capacity; throngs of people also stood in mournful silence on the grounds outside. Among the dignitaries present inside were Sir Oliver Mowat, the former premier of Ontario who was then lieutenant governor of Ontario and a personal friend of Walsh; representatives of the federal and provincial parliaments, including the premier of Ontario, Arthur S. Hardy, and several cabinet ministers; members of the Senate and the judiciary; and delegates from cities and towns across the region. Many former parishioners travelled from the London diocese to be there. The newly appointed governor general, the Earl of Minto, still in England, was represented by Major Septimus J.A. Denison.

Leading the procession into the cathedral to begin the solemn Requiem Mass, precisely at half past ten, were the uniformed Knights of St John; many of them also formed an honour guard at the doors. They were followed in order by the priest-servers, some Christian Brothers, along with the priests, bishops, and archbishops and their chaplains. All of those were attired in choir-dress, and filled the aisle with the black and white of the lower ranks, and the purple and white of the prelates.

The prelates in attendance were archbishops Paul Bruchési of Montreal and Joseph-Thomas Duhamel of Ottawa, and bishops Thomas Dowling of Hamilton, Denis O'Connor of London, Alexander MacDonell of Alexandria, Narcisse-Zéphirin Lorrain of Pembroke, James Quigley of Buffalo, and Bernard McQuaid of Rochester. Lionel Lindsay, a priest of the archdiocese of Quebec, represented the primate, Archbishop Louis-Nazaire Bégin. A great number of priests from Toronto, and from the dioceses of London, Hamilton, Kingston, Ottawa, and West Bay City in Michigan, crowded into the sanctuary. Among those also were an Anglican bishop, leaders of other Christian churches, and a rabbi.[127]

The presider, Bishop Dowling, the senior bishop of the ecclesiastical province of Toronto, with his assistants, came last in full pontifical vestments, including mitre and pectoral cross, and carrying his golden crozier. The sermon, based on Psalm 64, was preached by Bishop McQuaid at the end of the Mass.

The music for the Mass was sung by a combined choir composed of choristers from parishes across the city, and even from some Protestant churches. They were under the direction of Frederick Rohleder, a priest of Toronto, and J.L.R. Richardson. The organist, F.H. Torrington, accompanied the Requiem Mass, and interspersed throughout the ceremony selections from Haydn, Mendelssohn, Handel, Elsoldt, and Beethoven.

At the end of the sermon, Bruchési, Duhamel, O'Connor, MacDonell, and Dowling approached the casket for the final rites of commendation and farewell. They sprinkled it with holy water, incensed it, and then pronounced the final absolution. The lid, adorned with a silver crucifix and a silver plate bearing the archbishop's name, was then placed on the casket and sealed. The pallbearers, priests from London, Toronto, and Dollard in New Brunswick, took up their places to bear the archbishop's body to its resting place in the crypt beneath the altar of the Blessed Virgin in the north-east corner of the cathedral, according to his wishes. Once again, in florid language, the *Catholic Record* described the scene:

[T]o a great heart stilled in the silence of the tomb and placed ... beneath the altar of the Blessed Virgin ... a fitting receptacle for all that was mortal of him who many years ago received there at the hands of his Bishop the commission to preach the Word of God and labor in His vineyard. The priestly life began with the blessings of the Queen of Heaven around and about it – and now the priestly hands are folded and laid at rest, while the same heavenly smile seems to breathe the words, "Well done, faithful soul."[128]

The ceremony having ended, the great crowd departed.

For days after the funeral, tributes to the late archbishop continued to arrive from across Canada and the United States. One eulogist in the *Michigan Catholic* called him "one of the most active and influential churchmen in Canada. That he commanded the respect of all kinds of religionists in the commercial capital of Western Canada [sic] is the finest tribute to his genius as an administrator and his fidelity as priest and Bishop."[129] Another newspaper, the *Buffalo Catholic Union and Times,* wrote that the announcement of Walsh's death "[had] brought sorrow to many hearts in Canada and the United States, where the distinguished prelate was so well known ... [He] was long among the foremost ecclesiastics in Canada." It then went on to speak of his years in Toronto and of the occasions he visited Buffalo: "For upwards of ten years he governed the important See of Toronto with signal ability and broad charity that caused his name to be reverenced by all creeds and classes ... Archbishop Walsh was a prelate of commanding presence and engaging personality. As a public speaker he was both learned and eloquent. We well remember his magnificent speech at the dedication of our St Stephen's Hall. The last time we saw him was at the funeral of his friend, Bishop Ryan."[130] The chronicler concluded in his eulogy that "[t]he Master's summons came to him suddenly, but found him not unprepared. He goes to his eternal rest mourned by his bereaved priests and people, and amid the deepest respect of all Toronto."[131]

In due course, Archbishop Walsh's last will and testament was read. He made bequests to Agnes Morris, his housemaid,[132] to the diocese of London for the cathedral debt, to the Hôtel-Dieu Hospital in Windsor, and to Mount Hope, the new cemetery, which he had been instrumental in establishing. As customary, too, he also left monies for Masses to be celebrated for himself. In the end, however, his generosity exceeded the bounds of his estate: on probating the will, the executors discovered that Walsh's estate was $462.17 short of the total amount of the bequests. He had died with less than $6,500 to his name. Generous to the end, he left himself with nothing to spare, not even enough to have the Masses said. Later, as a mark of affection for his longtime friend, mentor, and colleague, Walsh's successor, Archbishop Denis O'Connor, ensured that all the bequests would be honoured by making up for the outstanding money for Masses.[133]

Thus passed into history one of the great ecclesiastics of the Catholic Church in Canada of the nineteenth century: John Walsh.

AFTERWORD

Oportet illum crescere, me autem minui. Quoting these words from the gospel of John, "he must increase, and I must decrease (3:30)," in a pastoral letter of 18 December 1866, Bishop Pierre-Adolphe Pinsoneault announced that his resignation as bishop of Sandwich/London had been accepted by the Holy See for reasons of advanced age and poor health. His every effort to establish the young diocese on a good footing had been in vain, since almost all his decisions had met with resistence and caused more trouble for those he came to serve. One disaster after another, from financial issues, to personnel, to public relations, to planning and building, finally led to the day when Pope Pius IX relieved Pinsoneault of the burden of office he could no longer carry. Into this troubled diocese came John Walsh.

With a bow to William Shakespeare, John Walsh was "neither born great nor had greatness thrust on him," but had to work his way out of obscurity in Ireland, and later in Montreal and Toronto as a young priest, by his own talents and deeply rooted desire to serve fully the Catholic faith he so greatly loved. He soon proved his capabilities as a leader. Thus, on 4 June 1867, he was chosen to be the bishop of Sandwich/London. There, until 1889, Walsh truly "increased" while Pinsoneault and his influence "decreased"; there, too, Walsh's influence was and still remains durable, whereas in Toronto, where his years were considerably shorter as he himself grew old, his time was effective but less noted. That had much to do with the historical context in which he lived and worked, and most particularly with the individual needs of the two sees which he inherited. London diocese was, in 1867, at its lowest point, so ridden with near-insoluble problems of morale and finances – even on the verge of bankruptcy – that the Canadian hierarchy, deeply concerned, actually pondered whether Rome would allow further establishment of new dioceses. Toronto archdiocese, on the other hand, was by 1889 a flourishing and well-ordered ecclesiastical organization, rich in resources and effortlessly administered by a staff which had learned its ways under the lengthy archiepiscopal governance of the highly competent John Lynch. To some degree, London had to adapt to Walsh's administrative and personal skills or perish, while Toronto subsumed him into its already smoothly running structures and continued on its way.

While in London, Walsh not only reversed the tide of misfortune in the young diocese but set it on a solid basis in terms of parochial life, priest-personnel, and invigorated Religious communities, along with new parishes, churches, schools, and hospitals, so that it became one of the greatest centres of Catholic Church life in Ontario, if not in Canada. Meantime, Walsh became one of Canada's leading churchmen, which eventually led to his promotion to Toronto. As the highly regarded archbishop of Toronto, he wielded great influence and, despite his advancing years, continued to be a pastoral presence to the people of Toronto. His teachings in sermons and letters, by then well-refined, were for the most part on the same basic themes he had developed in London. His administrative and building programs, though beneficial, were small in comparison to his many accomplishments in London, especially his crowning jewel there, St Peter's Cathedral.

All in all, John Walsh's life could be an example for bishops of every age. His personal gifts and talents notwithstanding, he demonstrated a great desire to continue learning throughout his life. He worked collaboratively with his priests, laity, and Religious alike to further the work of the Catholic Church. He taught them with care so they, in turn, could teach others. He unashamedly took a place in public life to promote the common good of all and the rights of Catholics. His political instincts guided him to bring this about as much as he possibly could, and while doing so, he proved himself a loyal friend and helpful colleague to any and all – regardless of class, race, or religion – who held the same goals. Walsh held those of other faiths in high respect, for he recognized that all were on their own paths towards God, even if they did not possess the fullness of the truth as the Catholic Church taught it. As well, he had a great awareness of his own authority as a bishop, without in any way compromising his personal respect for and devotion to the Holy Father, or his faithful submission to the Magisterium of the Church. In a truly extraordinary way, his work and ministry anticipated the role of bishops in the twentieth century. Such was the life and work of Archbishop John Walsh.

in laudem gloriae ipsius

AD EPH 1:14B

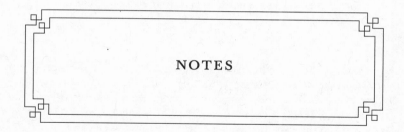

NOTES

Abbreviations

AAK	Archives of the Archdiocese of Kingston
AAL	Archives of the Archdiocese of Lyons
AAQ	Archives de l'Archidiocèse de Québec
ACAM	Archives de la Chancellerie de l'Archevêché de Montréal
AOA	Archdiocese of Ottawa Archives
APF	Archives of Propaganda Fide (Sacred Congregation for the Evangelization of Peoples)
ARCAT	Archives of the Roman Catholic Archdiocese of Toronto
ARSHJ	Archives of the Religious of the Sacred Heart of Jesus
ASSJ	Archives of the Sisters of St Joseph
CAS	Congressi America Settentrionale (part of APF)
CM	Congrégation de Marie (Marianists)
DCB	Dictionary of Canadian Biography
DLA	Diocese of London Archives
IBVM	Institute of the Blessed Virgin Mary
JAMLB	John A. Macdonald Letter Books (part of LAC)
JAMP	John A. Macdonald Papers (part of LAC)
LAC	Library and Archives Canada (formerly the National Archives of Canada)
LB	letter book
OMI	Oblates of Mary Immaculate
OSU	Order of St Ursula (Ursulines)
PSS	Prêtres de Saint-Sulpice (see "SS" below)
ROD	Record of Official Documents (part of DLA)
RSH	Religious of the Sacred Heart (RHSJ)
SJ	Society of Jesus (Jesuits)
SS	Society of St Sulpice (see "PSS" above)

SNJM   Sisters of the Holy Names of Jesus and Mary
SOCG   Scritture Originali Riferite nelle Congregazioni Generali
       (part of APF)

Chapter One

1 The account of the Silver Jubilee of John Walsh is based on the reports from
   the *Catholic Record*, 19 November 1892. The account of the Mass reported the
   singing of Haydn's *16th Mass*, but Haydn composed no work so titled.

   Begun 4 October 1878, and published weekly in London, the *Catholic Record*
   was owned and published by Walter Locke. It contained local, national, and
   international news, including special events in Ireland. Parochial events
   from across the country were reported along with summaries of items from
   other Catholic papers as well as columns for housewives, humour, teachings
   about the Catholic faith, Canadian history, and the writings of some of the
   Catholic bishops of Ireland, England, and the United States of America. For
   further treatment of the *Catholic Record*, see chapter 4.

2 *Catholic Record*, 19 November 1892.

3 This date is taken from a baptismal certificate issued by the parish priest
   at Mooncoin for the author. Other sources differ on the date of birth. John
   Coffey states Walsh was born 24 May 1830 (*City and Diocese*, 25), and John
   Teefy gives the date as 23 May (*Jubilee Volume*, iii). Michael Power, in
   "Walsh" in *DCB*, XII, 1083, says he was born 23 or 24 May.

4 This information comes from correspondence between the pastor of Mooncoin parish and the author. F. Grace to J.P. Comiskey, 22 April 1998.

5 Teefy, *Jubilee Volume*, iv.

6 Ibid. The last living relative of Walsh was probably a great-great-grandniece,
   Maura Malone Phelan, a one-time resident of Mooncoin. She was childless.
   The bishop's parents are buried in the parish cemetery. Grace to Comiskey,
   22 April 1998.

7 Coffey, *City and Diocese*, 25; Grace to Comiskey, 22 April 1998. The dates
   regarding his early education are not found in any of the sources.

8 Teefy, *Jubilee Volume*, iv.

9 Grace to Comiskey, 22 April 1998.

10 There is no indication in any early biography of John Walsh that he was
   related to the bishop of Ossory. Ossory is an ancient see, erected in 549,
   within fifty years of the death of St Patrick.

11 Power, "Walsh," in *DCB*, XII, 1083. There is no reference to John Walsh being
   related to the archbishop.

12 Farrell, *Church in London*, 52. ARCAT has records of these two priests, John
   Francis Synnott, born 29 May 1827 at Mooncoin, and James Hobin, born
   in 1833 in County Kilkenny. Both were educated at Le Grand Séminaire in
   Montreal with Walsh, and both served in the diocese of Toronto.

13 Teefy, *Jubilee Volume*, 25.

14 Perkins Bull, *Macdonell to McGuigan*, 278.

15 The Congregation for the Propagation of the Faith, often called by its Latin name, *Propaganda Fide*, was established by Pope Gregory XV by the Constitution *Inscrutabili Divinae*, on 22 June 1622. It was entrusted with overseeing the work of the Church in mission countries throughout the world, and was responsible for bishops and missionaries in those countries, and for training seminarians for future missionary work. See *Bullarum Diplomatum et Privilegiorum*, 690–3. Hereinafter, the Congregation will be referred to as "Propaganda Fide."

16 Farrell, *Church in London*, 52.

17 Teefy, *Jubilee Volume*, iv. See also APSS, Registre no 1 du Grand Séminaire de Montréal, 1840 à 1900; and Cahier 1: notes d'examens, 1852–85.

18 ACAM, Registre de la Chancellerie de Montréal, 11 juillet 1852 à 27 février 1855, 78r. The Registre indicates that tonsure was conferred by LaRocque. Some of the biographies say Walsh received tonsure "at Trinity, 1853," which could mean on Trinity Sunday, in that year 22 May, but the actual celebration was held the day before.

19 Cadotte, "Epidemic," *Canadian Encyclopedia*, 587.

20 Dignan, *London Diocese*, 383.

21 Teefy, *Jubilee Volume*, v.

22 Ibid.

23 Ibid.

24 The parish of St Joseph in Beaverton was established in 1854. It is now the main parish in the area, from which the pastor serves the missions of St Malachy at Brock and St Anthony at Virginia.

25 Power, "Walsh," in *DCB*, XII, 1083.

26 Dignan, *London Diocese*, 312–13. De Charbonnel requested and received the support of the other bishops who were part of the ecclesiastical province of Quebec. See "Letter from the Provincial Council of Quebec to Pope Pius IX," 3 June 1854, ARCAT, CLB 03.059; and "Letter from the Provincial Council of Quebec to Pope Pius IX," 4 June 1854, AAQ, 320 CN 6. The complete list of signatories to the petition included the archbishop of Quebec, Pierre-Flavien Turgeon; Ignace Bourget of Montreal; Jean-Charles Prince of Saint-Hyacinthe; Joseph-Eugène-Bruno Guigues, OMI, of Bytown, or present-day Ottawa; Thomas Cooke of Trois-Rivières; and Patrick Phelan, SS, the coadjutor bishop of Kingston. It is presumed that the bishop of Kingston, Rémi Gaulin, and Quebec's coadjutor bishop, Charles-François Baillargeon, though not present for the signing, would have given their approval.

27 Provincial Council of Quebec to Pius IX, 4 June 1854. Translation from the Latin by Farrell. See *Church in London*, 26.

28 Provincial Council of Quebec to Pius IX, 4 June 1854. The *terna* (a list of three possible candidates) for the diocese of London included Pierre-Adolphe Pinsoneault, a canon of the cathedral of Montreal; Jean-Mathieu Soulerin, a Basilian Father and superior of St Michael's College in Toronto; and Jean-Marie Bruyère, rector of the cathedral of Toronto. Bruyère would

come to play a crucial role in the life of Pierre-Adolphe Pinsoneault and later of John Walsh. Born in 1808 at Chazelles, France, Bruyère was ordained a priest in 1830. At the invitation of Benoit-Joseph Flaget, PSS, first bishop of Bardstown, Bruyère went to Bardstown where he taught at the college. The rector of the college, Martin J. Spalding, became bishop of Louisville in 1848 and invited Bruyère to become the rector of the cathedral there. In 1854, at the request of de Charbonnel, Bruyère began to work in the diocese of Toronto as rector of the cathedral. He was named vicar general in 1857. In 1860, Bruyère moved to Sandwich at Pinsoneault's invitation, where he became rector of the cathedral and vicar general of that diocese.

29 Sandwich was in the southwestern-most part of the diocese. It had begun as a mission served by the Jesuits from the fort at Detroit, and was later established as the first parish west of Montreal in 1767, the parish of the Assumption. Sandwich was eventually incorporated with other border cities into the municipality of Windsor.

30 P. Point to J. Roothaan, 31 December 1847, as cited in *Histoire*, 69.

31 See DLA, Roman Documents; also see APF, *Registro dei Brevi e Bolle*, vol. 6, 16v–18v; Circular Letter of his Lordship the Bishop of Toronto to his Clergy on the Subdivision of the Diocess [sic], 23 April 1856, ARCAT, AA 0417; and Giacomo Filippo Cardinal Fransoni to A.-F.-M. de Charbonnel, 8 March 1856, ARCAT, AA 0416. De Charbonnel resigned the see in 1860, and went to live in a monastery in France. Soon afterwards, however, he began pastoral work in the archdiocese of Lyons, and travelled widely for twenty-three years preaching, organizing and giving retreats, ordaining priests, and assisting in the general administration of the archdiocese. During this time he was called, according to the archivist in Lyons, the "unofficial auxiliary bishop of Lyons." In 1880, in recognition of his achievements and work in Canada, the titular "bishop" of Sozopolis was named titular "archbishop" of that see *in partibus infidelium* at the request of the bishops of Canada. De Charbonnel relinquished all public duties in 1883, at which time he retired to the Capuchin monastery at Crest. When he died on 29 March 1891, he was eulogized as the "father and founder of the ecclesiastical province of Toronto." H. Hours to J.P. Comiskey, personal communication, 15 April 1997.

32 See *Mother Teresa Dease*, ANA-IBVM, 153–6.

33 Power, "Walsh," in *DCB*, XII, 1084.

34 Lynch succeeded de Charbonnel 26 April 1860.

35 The history of the Protestant Reformation formed a part of the "collective memory" of the Protestant people of Ontario: "Events that happened in the sixteenth and seventeenth centuries were as fresh in people's minds as if they had taken place only a few years before. People observed the rituals of the Reformation with devotion, and the division between Protestant and Catholic remained one of the primary facts of the religious and social life of the province [of Ontario] well beyond the nineteenth century." See Westfall, *Two Worlds*, 12.

36 Grant, *Profusion of Spires*, 127. The Orange Order was a Protestant fraternal society founded in Ireland in 1795, to commemorate the victory of Protestant forces under William of Orange over the Catholic population of Ireland at the Battle of Boyne, 1690. The Order became a principal link between the Protestants in Ireland and the British government. It lost much influence after Catholic Emancipation in 1829, but remained a powerful anti-Catholic movement in some areas, especially Ulster. In the face of that emancipation, the Order was established in Canada in 1830, and its lodges became bases for launching political and professional careers until well into the twentieth century. They continued with their anti-Catholic prejudice for the same length of time.

37 Westfall, *Two Worlds*, 22.

38 Creighton, *Macdonald*, 301–3.

39 Teefy, *Jubilee Volume*, vii–viii. See also Perkins Bull, *Macdonell to McGuigan*, 148.

40 Teefy, *Jubilee Volume*, ix.

41 Power, "Walsh," in *DCB*, XII, 1084.

42 John Walsh to J.J. Lynch, 8 November 1864, ARCAT, L AEO.04.

43 Ibid.

44 Teefy, *Jubilee Volume*, vi.

45 Power, "Walsh," in *DCB*, XII, 1084.

46 Teefy, *Jubilee Volume*, xii. Teefy also included that Walsh preached at the laying of the cornerstone of the Church of Our Lady Immaculate in Guelph. This did not occur, however, until 1876, when he was already bishop of London.

47 The family name was sometimes rendered "Pinsonnault," "Pinsonault," or "Pinsonneault," but Adolphe signed "Pinsoneault." For further information on Pinsoneault, see McMahon, *Pinsoneault*, especially 41–2; and Choquette, "Pinsoneault," in *DCB*, XI, 692. See also APSS, ASSSM, *dossiers biographiques*, "Pinsoneault." See Power et al., *Gather up the Fragments*, for a biography of Pinsoneault and a complete history of the diocese of London.

48 Pope Pius IX to P.-A. Pinsoneault, Papal Bull of Episcopal Election, 29 February 1856, DLA. De Charbonnel was assisted at the consecration by Joseph LaRocque, coadjutor bishop of Montreal, and David W. Bacon, bishop of Portland, Maine. That day Pinsoneault issued his first pastoral letter announcing the erection of the diocese and his appointment as the first bishop of London. In the last part of the letter, he issued five regulations for the diocese, including naming the boundaries of the new diocese and proclaiming the diocesan patrons: the Virgin Mary under the title of the Immaculate Conception would be the principal patron of the diocese, with St Patrick as a secondary patron. This was a clear recognition of the two founding nationalities that made up the majority of faithful of the infant diocese, French-speaking and Irish people. P.-A. Pinsoneault, Pastoral Letter of the First Bishop of London, C[anada]. W[est]., 18 May 1856, DLA.

49 St Lawrence was "demoted" to being secondary patron of the cathedral.

50 While McMahon refers to an attempt to appoint an English-speaking priest, Patrick Dowd, SS, as coadjutor in Toronto, it seemed, and the perception remained, that only French-speaking priests were getting the episcopal nod. Such feelings led to resentment in an area far wider than London. Because the English language was seen as the "Protestant" language in Quebec, the English-speaking Catholics in the London area felt isolated. As a result, the English-French tensions of Montreal were transferred to Canada West (Ontario), causing considerable concern in the English-speaking countryside. McMahon referred to the complaints of one priest, Joseph Chisholm of Kingston, who warned that Pinsoneault "would not be kindly received in London, or in a diocese where the number of French-speaking parishes were few in comparison to the total … To allow the administration of French-speaking bishops over four of Upper Canada's proposed five dioceses was, in [Chisholm's] opinion, unrealistic. He was obviously concerned with what seemed to be a concerted attempt by the Quebec hierarchy to appoint only French-Canadian bishops to the dioceses of [Canada West]." McMahon, *Pinsoneault*, 27.

51 Choquette, "Pinsoneault," in *DCB*, XI, 693. Interdict is a type of ecclesiastical censure which prevents any sacrament or other solemn ritual from being celebrated or received in the parish.

52 P.-A. Pinsoneault to A.-F.-M. de Charbonnel, 17 April 1856, DLA, LB I. See also Dignan, *London Diocese*, 462–3; and Farrell, *Church in London*, 33–4.

53 Dignan, *London Diocese*, 368. Choquette specifically says the writers denounced the "French influence" and the "French-Canadian bishop of London." Some leading Catholic laymen met to discuss this attack on the bishop. They repudiated and censured the authors of the letters and, in this way, attempted to lay to rest the calumny directed against the bishop. See Choquette, "Pinsoneault," in *DCB*, XI, 693.

54 P.-A. Pinsoneault to the Bishops of Quebec, Montreal, Trois-Rivières, Saint-Hyacinthe, Bytown, Kingston, Toronto, and Hamilton, 26 January 1858, DLA, LB III. The bishop's reasons included the poverty and smallness of the Catholic population in London, the necessity of paying the debt on the cathedral, and the ease with which he felt he would be able to carry out the functions of his episcopal office in Sandwich as opposed to London.

55 J.-C. Prince to P.-A. Pinsoneault, 4 February 1858, AAQ, 30 CP 1. Dignan incorrectly refers to this as the "Memorial of Bishop LaRocque," attributing it to Prince's successor, Joseph LaRocque. See Dignan for an English translation of the complete text, *London Diocese*, 369–72. See also McMahon, *Pinsoneault*, 59–62. Only Turgeon of Quebec gave his approval for the move at first.

56 Choquette, "Pinsoneault," in *DCB*, XI, 693; and Dignan, *London Diocese*, 369 and 373. See also C.-F. Baillargeon to P.-A. Pinsoneault, August 1858, as cited in Dignan, 372–3.

57 McMahon, *Pinsoneault*, 65–6. When the public press, which was Protestant, entered the fray, Pinsoneault was maligned, leading the same prominent Catholic citizens to rally behind him, and consequently peace was temporarily restored in London between them.

58 Ibid., 67.

59 P. Point to P. Beckx, 20 April 1859, as found in *Histoire*, 161.

60 In fact, Pinsoneault acquired the deeds to thirty-three pieces of property from the bishop of Toronto, some of which had churches completed or in various stages of construction. It was appropriate for the new diocese to share the burden of this debt with Toronto. Receipt for properties, entitled "Received from the Right Reverend Armand Francis Mary de Charbonnel, the following Deeds etc. belonging to the new Diocese of London Canada West," dated at Toronto, 26 June 1856, and signed "+Adolphe, Bishop of London," ARCAT, C TAO1.36.

61 McMahon, *Pinsoneault*, 88–9. See also Farrell, *Church in London*, 87; and Dignan, *London Diocese*, 373.

62 McMahon, *Pinsoneault*, 89. The palace was so poorly built it had to be torn down in 1896.

63 Ibid., 92.

64 McMahon points out the irony of this dilemma: while the bishop found travel throughout the diocese difficult – it upset his stomach – he risked similar unpleasantness to travel abroad and to Cuba, for example during the winter of 1862, battling seasickness *en route*. McMahon, *Pinsoneault*, 91–2. See also P.-A. Pinsoneault to Alessandro Cardinal Barnabò, 15 February 1862, APF, CAS, vol. 8, 204r–205v, from Havana, Cuba, in which Pinsoneault reports to the prefect that he is taking rest in Havana under doctor's orders.

65 See McMahon, *Pinsoneault*, 92; Farrell, *Church in London*, 38; and Dignan, *London Diocese*, 373–4 and 380–1. According to Farrell, the barge was also dubbed "Pinsoneault's Folly." Ironically enough, Pinsoneault had a depiction of a boat in the shield of his personal coat of arms.

66 Dignan, *London Diocese*, 374.

67 Point's plan was to build a college at Sandwich, but to have another Religious congregation operate it and staff it. De Charbonnel had agreed to this but he was concerned that it might compete with St Michael's College in Toronto and, for this reason, limited the Sandwich college to a high school. For the full story of the development of the College of the Assumption at Sandwich, see Point, *Histoire*, 131–3, 141–5, 150–6, 160–7; Dignan, *London Diocese*, 405–23; McMahon, *Pinsoneault*, 74–7; and especially Power, *Assumption College*, I, vii–xxxi.

68 In fact, the Basilian superior, Soulerin, had no intention of sending anyone to Sandwich at the time, since the opposition of de Charbonnel was so great and the needs of St Michael's College were pressing. See Power, *Assumption College*, I, xxiv–xxxi.

69 Power succinctly summarizes the problems of the college: "Pinsoneault's self-delusion and authoritarianism had much to do with the demise of Assumption College ... He was not the man to make the fledging College the grand success it eventually became under the determined and imaginative leadership of the Basilians. Instead, he preferred to place its direction into the hands of others, often chosen in moments of crisis and panic." Power, *Assumption University*, I, xxxi. See also Dignan, *London Diocese*, 363–4; and McMahon, *Pinsoneault*, 203–4.

70 See Dignan, *London Diocese*, 365–7; and McMahon, *Pinsoneault*, 215–20. See also St John Thomas, *Rooted in Hope*, 5–10, 19–20, 32. When Pinsoneault was forced to resign, the Holy Names Sisters would have been among the few to lament "the loss of a devoted friend and understanding prelate." See St John Thomas, *Rooted in Hope*, 49–50.
The Ursuline Sisters, founded in 1535 by St Angela Merici, arrived in Chatham, led by Mother Xavier LeBihan, who landed on the banks of the Thames River at Chatham on 9 May 1860. See St Paul (Mother), *From Desenzano to "The Pines."*

71 In 1856 there were twelve canonically erected parishes and twelve priests in the diocese. Within ten years, the bishop had doubled the number of parishes and tripled the number of priests. These numbers, however, did not reveal the complete picture because, in all, eighty priests served under Pinsoneault, but twenty-four left the diocese for one reason or another, frustrated and, in the case of the Jesuits, never to return. Similarly with women's Religious congregations; of the six, only three remained by the time Pinsoneault left. See McMahon, *Pinsoneault*, 140–1.

72 All of these problems and complaints were further detailed in a long memorial sent by Baillargeon to the prefect of Propaganda Fide in August 1865. The *Œuvre de la Propagation de la Foi* was the organization that oversaw the distribution of funds for Propaganda Fide. The president of the organization's Central Committee of Lyons and Paris wrote to Alessandro Cardinal Barnabò in November 1866 from Lyons to inform him of the situation: no further funds would be sent to Sandwich because of problems in the diocese. "Very frequent reports exist ... of the sad circumstances relative to the diocese of Sandwich." Martial de Praudière to Alessandro Cardinal Barnabò, 2 November 1866, APF, CAS, vol. 9, 242r–243v.

73 Pinsoneault resigned in a letter dated 9 September, made effective 18 December 1866. See DLA, Pinsoneault LB VI; and C.-F. Baillargeon to Alessandro Cardinal Barnabò, 15 December 1866, APF, CAS, vol. 9, 252r–253v. In his final pastoral letter issued that day, Pinsoneault thanked the people for their support and asked their prayers for his successor: "But the steadily increasing wants of this young Diocese, which require corresponding efforts, and the very precarious state of my health together with my gradually increasing deafness and other motives made known to His Holiness, have convinced me, for a long time past, that the welfare of the Diocese requires that younger

and abler hands than mine should hold the reins of administration. It has pleased His Holiness to grant me this favour and now with a most grateful heart do I say of him whom the Holy Father will soon send to replace me: *Oportet illum crescere, me autem mindi* [he must increase, but I must decrease]." P.-A. Pinsoneault, Circular Letter to the Clergy of the Diocese of Sandwich, 18 December 1866, DLA.

74 *Catholic Record*, 6 August 1898.

75 Stortz, "Lynch," 5–23.

76 Every five years, bishops are required to make an *ad limina* visit, from the Latin meaning "to the threshold." It means, effectively, a visit to the pope and to the various Congregations in Rome, during which time they present an extensive report on the affairs and progress of their dioceses. While there, they are also required to visit the tombs of Saints Peter and Paul and the other major basilicas in the city.

77 Teefy, *Jubilee Volume*, xi.

78 Ibid.; and Flynn, *London Episcopacy*, 3.

79 From the Latin for "vacant see," *sede vacante* is the term which describes a diocese upon the death, resignation, or removal of its bishop.

80 See for example, P. Schneider to Alessandro Cardinal Barnabò, 29 June 1867, APF, CAS, vol. 9, 806r–807v.

81 See APF, Acta, vol. 232, 275r–285r; and Pius IX to John Walsh, 4 June 1867, brief of nomination as bishop of Sandwich, DLA.

82 Coffey, *City and Diocese*, 26.

83 See C.-F. Baillargeon, circular letter announcing the reception of the bulls for John Walsh as bishop-elect of Sandwich, 25 September 1867, ARCAT, L ADO3.08.

84 John Walsh to E.J. Horan, 7 October 1867, AAK.

85 John Walsh to I. Bourget, 16 October 1867, ACAM, 255.113, 867-4.

86 C. LaRocque to John Walsh, 16 October 1867, AESH, LaRocque LB.

87 J.-M. Bruyère, Circular Letter to the Clergy and Faithful of the Diocese of Sandwich, 18 October 1867, ACAM, 255.113, 867-5.

Chapter Two

1 Farrell, *Church in London*, 54.

2 *Canadian Freeman*, 14 November 1867, as found in Coffey, *City and Diocese*, 26–9. The *Canadian Freeman* was an independent Irish Catholic newspaper launched by Thomas D'Arcy McGee on 16 July 1858. It promised to be patriotic, independent of party politics, against Orangeism, and centred on the family. It had been approved by Bishop de Charbonnel, who often published official communications on religious matters in its pages, especially following diocesan councils.

3 The other bishops present included Jean-Pierre-François Langevin from Rimouski; Louis-François Laflèche, coadjutor of Trois-Rivières; John J. Conroy

from Albany, New York; Edward Horan of Kingston; John Farrell of Hamilton; and Joseph-Eugène-Bruno Guigues of Ottawa. Of these, Farrell, Guigues, Langevin, and Laflèche signed the decree of consecration on the back of the papal brief of nomination along with the consecrator and co-consecrators.

4   Cited in Coffey, *City and Diocese*, 26–7.

5   Baillargeon had been the coadjutor of Quebec but, by then, was the newly acclaimed archbishop since Archbishop Turgeon had died the previous August.

6   Patrick Dowd, SS, was born in Ireland on 24 November 1813, and studied in Paris where he was ordained a priest in 1837. He joined the society of priests of St Sulpice in 1847, after which time he began work in Montreal, serving the English-speaking community. He later founded St Patrick's Orphanage. He was considered for several episcopal appointments which he declined. He was subsequently named pastor of the newly created St Patrick parish. He became renowned for his charitable works, and died in Montreal on 19 December 1891. See Harel, "Dowd," in *DCB*, XII, 266–7.

7   Cited in Coffey, *City and Diocese*, 28.

8   Francis (Frank) Smith was an alderman from 1866 to 1871 and also the mayor of London (1867), the first Roman Catholic to hold the position. He was a successful wholesale merchant in London and was appointed to the Senate in 1871. In 1891, he was appointed the federal minister of Public Works in the government of Alexander McKenzie. Smith was later knighted by Queen Victoria. He boldly promoted Catholics for positions in government, and was a lifelong collaborator with Walsh. He died 17 January 1901.

9   Cited in Coffey, *City and Diocese*, 30.

10 Ibid., 31.

11 DLA, ROD II, 1, in which is noted the installation of Walsh as bishop of Sandwich by Baillargeon. The notation is signed by "all present," including priests of the diocese and visiting prelates. Interestingly, Coffey did not record who performed the installation ceremony but merely that Horan and Farrell were present. See Coffey, *City and Diocese*, 31.

12 Bruyère was appointed as vicar general on 14 October 1867, within days of Walsh receiving his nomination as bishop. See the letter cited by Dignan, *London Diocese*, 384–5.

13 Pastoral Letter of His Lordship the Right Rev. John Walsh, D.D., Bishop of Sandwich, 11 November 1867, *Canadian Freeman*, 19 December 1867.

14 Walsh, Pastoral Letter, 11 November 1867. St Peter actually led the Church at Antioch (Syria) before going to Rome.

15 Ibid.

16 Ibid.

17 Ibid.

18 See APF, CAS, vol. 9, 877r–879v; and Alessandro Cardinal Barnabò to C.-F. Baillargeon, 21 May 1867, AAQ, 10 CM, V:183.

19 See Coffey, *City and Diocese*, 31.

20 C.-F. Baillargeon to Alessandro Cardinal Barnabò, 14 November 1867, APF, Acta, vol. 235, 635r.

21 John Walsh to Alessandro Cardinal Barnabò, 29 December 1867, APF, Acta, vol. 235, 634rv.

22 The letter was dated 22 November 1868 and is cited in Flynn, *London Episcopacy*, 47.

23 Farrell, *Church in London*, 59.

24 It is ironic that Pinsoneault would later criticize Walsh's decision to move to London, in a letter to the prefect of Propaganda Fide, on the premise that Walsh would cause discouragement on the part of the Catholics of the diocese, and would destroy the useful establishment of the Dominican friars who, in his words, had been well accepted in the diocese for their dedication and holy life. These, however, were not Pinsoneault's considerations when he made his move to Sandwich. See P.-A. Pinsoneault to Alessandro Cardinal Barnabò, 16 October 1868, APF, CAS, vol. 11, 122r–123v.

25 C.-F. Baillargeon to John Walsh, 14 January 1868, AAQ, 210 A, RL, XXIX:318.

26 See the notation made by Walsh's secretary, Ferdinand O.J. Ouellet, DLA, ROD II, 7.

27 Walsh to Barnabò, 29 December 1867.

28 Alessandro Cardinal Barnabò to John Walsh, 17 April 1868, DAL, ROD, 8; John Walsh to Alessandro Cardinal Barnabò, 6 June 1868, APF, CAS, vol. 11, 64r–65v; John Walsh to Alessandro Cardinal Barnabò, 5 March 1869, APF, Acta, vol. 235, 634v.

29 Dignan, *London Diocese*, 314.

30 APF, Acta, vol. 235, 582r–583v, 584v, 586v; Decree of Propaganda Fide changing the diocese of Sandwich to the diocese of London, 15 November 1869, DLA, ROD II, 37.

31 J.J. Lynch to John Walsh, 28 February 1870, DLA, HF 28/67–87.

32 John Walsh to Alessandro Cardinal Barnabò, 20 March 1870, APF, CAS, vol. 11, 597r–600v.

33 C.-F. Baillargeon to John Walsh, 17 May 1870, AAQ, 210 A, RL, XXIX:1232. On 18 March 1870, during a session of the First Vatican Council (1869–70), a new ecclesiastical province was created for Ontario, with Toronto as the metropolitan see. The bishop of Toronto was elevated to the rank of archbishop and the diocese to an archdiocese.

34 J.-M. Bruyère to I. Bourget, 21 December 1866, ACAM, 255.113, 866-6; J.-M. Bruyère to I. Bourget, 7 January 1867, ACAM, 255.113, 867-2.

35 Bruyère to Bourget, 21 December 1866.

36 Ibid.

37 Choquette, *L'église catholique*, 133.

38 It should be noted that the average wage for an unskilled labourer at that time would have been about $300 *per annum*, while a skilled labourer would have earned $600 *per annum*.

39 Bruyère to Bourget, 7 January 1867.

40 The actual amount of the pension to be paid to Pinsoneault was stated in Walsh's brief of nomination. It was reiterated at a later date, following the appeals made by the diocese; see Baillargeon to Walsh, 14 January 1868.

41 C.-F. Baillargeon to John Walsh, 21 February 1868, AAQ, 210 A, RL, XXIX:361.

42 Walsh to Horan, 7 October 1867.

43 Coffey had $40,000, *City and Diocese*, 31; Teefy had $35,000, *Jubilee Volume*, xv; Bruyère gave $30,000 in Bruyère to Bourget, 21 December 1866; and for the actual figures see Walsh to Barnabò, 20 March 1870.

44 Walsh to Barnabò, 6 June 1868.

45 C.-F. Baillargeon to John Walsh, 8 November 1868, AAQ, 210 A, RL, XXIX:620.

46 Power, "Walsh," in *DCB*, XII, 1084.

47 Flynn, *London Episcopacy*, 50–1. See also Dignan, *London Diocese*, 394.

48 Dignan, *London Diocese*, 358. William Flannery was an Irishman who came to Canada as a young ecclesiastic with a small group of Basilians in 1852, the same year Walsh arrived in Canada. Flannery was among the group that opened St Michael's College in Toronto. The following year, in 1853, he was ordained a priest by de Charbonnel, but when the Congregation of St Basil was reorganized by Pius IX in 1863, Flannery chose to become a priest of Toronto rather than bind himself by perpetual Religious vows. Following his fund-raising activity, Flannery accepted various appointments as pastor throughout the diocese of London.

49 C.-F. Baillargeon to Alessandro Cardinal Barnabò, 1 January 1868, APF, CAS, vol. 11, 3r–4v.

50 Baillargeon to Walsh, 14 January 1868. Baillargeon received a letter the next month from the prefect himself, complimenting Walsh on his efforts to relieve the diocese of debt; see Alessandro Cardinal Barnabò to C.-F. Baillargeon, 21 February 1868, AAQ, 10 CM, V:190.

51 Baillargeon to Walsh, 21 February 1868.

52 Ibid.

53 John Walsh to C.-F. Baillargeon, 2 March 1868, AAQ, 320 CN, Haut-Canada, V:51. There is no indication in any surviving correspondence what the "one exception" was to which Walsh referred in this letter.

54 Walsh to Barnabò, 20 March 1870.

55 J.J. Lynch to John Walsh, 13 June 1870, DLA, HF 28/67–87. Louis Amadeus Rappe was the first bishop of Cleveland, from 1847 to 1870.

56 Ibid.

57 Ibid., emphasis his. Jean-François Jamot was a vicar general of Toronto when he was nominated Vicar Apostolic of Northern Canada, 3 February 1874. He became the first bishop of Peterborough (1874–86) when the same vicariate apostolic was raised to the status of a diocese. The *cathedraticum* is the fee paid annually by parishes for the support of the bishop's office.

58 J.J. Lynch to Cardinal Barnabò, 10 July 1870, APF, CAS, vol. 11, 726r–727v.

59 Baillargeon to Barnabò, 1 January 1868.

60 Baillargeon to Walsh, 14 January 1868.

61 Walsh to Barnabò, 6 June 1868.

62 Ibid. In Walsh's mind, of course, would be the moral "ruins" as well as the literal "ruins" of the palace in Sandwich and of the barge on the bottom of the river.

63 Pinsoneault to Barnabò, 16 October 1868. John Joseph Conroy was a priest of the archdiocese of New York who became bishop of Albany (1865–77).

64 I. Bourget to John Walsh, 22 December 1868, ACAM, RLB 18, 271.

65 John Walsh to I. Bourget, 30 December 1868, APF, CAS, vol. 11, 152r–153v, emphasis his.

66 C.-F. Baillargeon to John Walsh, 2 January 1869, AAQ, 210 A, RL, XXIX:681.

67 The diocese paid him a total of $9,600 during the course of those years. See Coffey, *City and Diocese*, 73.

68 John Walsh to É.-C. Fabre, 11 January 1883, ACAM, 255.113, 883-1.

69 *Catholic Record*, 9 February 1893, wherein is found the news of his death and a summary of his life: "His Lordship had been for a long time in ill health, and looked forward himself with anxious desire to be released from this world of pain and sorrow. His demise, has, nevertheless, excited the very deepest feelings of regret throughout the country. In the diocese of London especially is the late prelate's loss generally and heartily regretted. His amiability of character, evenness of disposition, and especially his zeal for the glory of God endeared him to all who knew him ... We know that we speak the unanimous and heartfelt feeling of the Catholics of this diocese when we say that all regret his demise, and that his name and memory will ever be kept green in their hearts."

70 *Catholic Record*, 14 November 1879. See also Dignan, *London Diocese*, 395.

Chapter Three

1 See Coffey, *City and Diocese*, 61 and 70.

2 John Walsh to Propaganda Fide, *Relatio Reverendissimi et Illustrissimi Joannis Walsh, Episcopi Londinensis, in Ontario, in Dominione Canadiensi, de Statu Diœceseos Londinensis, juxta formam a Benedicto XIII praescriptam*, n.d. [received by Propaganda Fide early in 1877], APF, CAS, vol. 15, 11r–19v. See also *Catholic Record*, 2 May 1885; Coffey, *City and Diocese*, 61–2 and 70–1; and DLA, ROD II.

3 Westfall, *Two Worlds*, 10–11. See also *Catholic Record*, 2 May 1885, where the government's population statistics for the province appear as follows: in 1851 there were 167,695 Catholics out of a total population of 952,004; in 1881 there were 320,839 Catholics out of a population of 1,923,228. In the diocese of London, the number of Catholics increased by one-third from 44,122 persons to 62,677 persons during those years. Catholics would continue to be a minority in Ontario for another century, into the 1980s.

4 Coffey, *City and Diocese*, 33. This palace continued to be the residence of the bishop of London until 1912, when a new residence, called Blackfriars, was given to the fifth bishop of the diocese, Michael Fallon, OMI. The residence at the cathedral was demolished in 2004, and Blackfriars was sold in 2008.

5 *Catholic Record*, 29 October 1887.

6 *Catholic Record*, 17 January 1879.

7 *Catholic Record*, 16 May 1879.

8 *Catholic Record*, 29 October 1887.

9 The land for St Joseph's church had been purchased by Bishop Alexander Macdonell when the whole province of Ontario was part of the diocese of Kingston. Under the care of the Franciscan Friars, a new church was built for the parish in 1887 at a cost of $100,000. The famed architect Joseph Connolly, who had designed the Jesuit Church of Our Lady Immaculate in Guelph, St Patrick's Church in Kinkora, and London's own cathedral, oversaw the construction of the neo-Romanesque St Joseph's, with soaring towers that rose on the front to 55 metres. In the shape of a Roman cross, the church measures 23 metres wide and 59.5 metres long, with a transept of 34.5 metres in width. The interior has eleven stone columns on each side, topped by Corinthian capitals, separating the central nave from the side aisles, and two more decorated columns separating the nave from the sanctuary.

10 Teefy, *Jubilee Volume*, xxiii. Unfortunately, the full text of the sermon is no longer extant.

11 John Walsh to Messrs Cheff, Martin, Emery, and St Cartier, 27 May 1882, DLA, LB I, 58. All the dioceses in Ontario were given letters of civil incorporation by act of the legislative assembly of the Province of Ontario on 25 March 1845, making each bishop ordinary "Corporation Sole" and owner of all ecclesiastical property in the name of the Corporation. This applied specifically to the bishops of Toronto and Kingston and "to all other dioceses that would be created in the future." The law, though amended in 1883, remains in force.

12 John Walsh to J.A. Peck and others, 5 December 1882, DLA, LB I, 62. Today the town is known as Essex.

13 Ibid.

14 See John Walsh to J. O'Connor, n.d. [likely written between 10 January and 6 February 1887], DLA, LB I, 117; and John Walsh to J. O'Connor, 1 June 1887, DLA, LB I, 121.

15 John Walsh to P. O'Shea, n.d. [likely written between 15 June and 20 July 1880], DLA, LB I, 31.

16 J. Kennedy to J. Tierney, n.d. [likely written between 12 and 19 February 1885], DLA, LB I, 106.

17 John Walsh to M. Andrieux, 19 April 1880, DLA, LB I, 22.

18 John Walsh to Major Leyes, 5 March 1880, DLA, LB I, 17.

19 See John Walsh to W. Kiely, 31 January 1880, DLA, LB I, 5; John Walsh to A. Macadams, 2 December 1881, DLA, LB I, 52; and John Walsh to J. Ronan, 21 December 1882, DLA, LB I, 63.

20 Walsh to Kiely, 31 January 1880.

21 The term "African-Canadian" now sometimes used in Canada was unknown at the time. Here the more common term in Canada today will be used, that is "black," except where other terms are used in a direct quotation.

22 "[W]ithin the last six months, [Wagner] has, assisted by Fr. [Charles] McManus, taken steps toward bringing into the fold of the Church as many as possible of this interesting portion of humanity; and the united efforts of these two priests have so succeeded that it has become necessary to open a Catholic free school for colored [sic] children. Quite a number of adults have lately been received into thè Church and a class of twenty (20) juveniles are under instruction preparatory to baptism. Arrangements are being made to open the school immediately after the Christmas holidays. Temporarily it will be placed under the care of a lay teacher until next September, when the charge will be assumed by the Sisters of the Holy Names of Jesus and Mary. In the course of time, or as the work will grow in importance, the colored people will need a chapel of their own, and a priest will have to be detailed to attend to their spiritual wants. Meantime a number of pews are reserved at the 9 o'clock Mass so that they are enabled, as their white brethren, to fulfil their Christian obligations." See *Catholic Record*, 15 January 1887. The *Catholic Record* reported that the estimated black populations of Windsor and Chatham equalled 1,000 persons each, with sizeable communities in Amherstburg and Sandwich as well.

23 John Walsh, Decree of Erection for Catholic hospital, School for Negro children, and Orphanage for coloured orphans, 13 August 1888, DLA, ROD II, 228.

24 *Catholic Record*, 23 April 1887.

25 *Catholic Record*, 7 January 1888. See also John Walsh to Giovanni Cardinal Simeoni, n.d. [Propaganda Fide has noted "Reg. 2 Dic. 87," that is, registered 2 December 1887], APF, CAS, vol. 30, 522r–523v.

26 Walsh to Simeoni, n.d. [registered 2 December 1887], 520r–521v. See also John Walsh to Giovanni Cardinal Simeoni, 1 October 1886, APF, CAS, vol. 25, 623r–624v.

27 Pastoral Letter of Rt Rev. John Walsh relative to the annual diocesan collection for ecclesiastical education, n.d. [September 1888], *Catholic Record*, 29 September 1888.

28 Ibid.

29 DLA, ROD II, 236.

30 J.-M. Bruyère to I. Bourget, 7 January 1867, ACAM, 255.113, 867-1.

31 See John Walsh to the Catholics of West Williams, 8 April 1883, DLA, LB I, 69; John Walsh to P. Corcoran, 18 October 1884, DLA, LB I, 101; and John Walsh to D. McRae, 18 October 1884, DLA, LB I, 102.

32 See John Walsh to Messrs Smith and others at Zurich, 10 January 1884, DLA, LB I, 90. Walsh could not respond immediately to this request, as he needed to find a priest who could speak German, French, and English. He asked Augustus Schneider to visit. Also see the correspondence with the pastor of

the parish of St Agatha in South East Hope and Zora townships: John Walsh to E. Funken, CR, 19 February 1885, DLA, LB I, 107; and John Walsh to E. Funken, n.d. [likely written between 19 February and 27 April 1885], DLA, LB I, 108. While these letters dealt with the question of faculties for priests, they also concerned a parish with German-speaking Catholics; see Flynn, *London Episcopacy*, 90–1.

33 In 1880 there were 14,000 French-speaking Catholics in the diocese out of a total population of 62,677. See John Walsh to J.J. Lynch, 12 June 1880, DLA, LB I, 29. No figures are found for any other language group at that time.

34 See John Walsh to J.-S. Raymond, 29 August 1868, ASSH, ASE2 32 5; and John Walsh to J.-S. Raymond, 29 October 1868, ASSH, ASE2 32 4.

35 John Walsh to Messrs Reaume, Ouellette, and others, 16 October 1874, DLA, LB I, 9.

36 C.-F. Baillargeon to John Walsh, 22 May 1868, AAQ, 210 A, RL, XXIX:175.

37 John Walsh to É.-C. Fabre, 24 October 1881, ACAM, 255.113, 881-1; John Walsh to É.-C. Fabre, 27 January 1882, ACAM, 255.113, 882-1; John Walsh to É.-C. Fabre, 23 January 1884, ACAM, 255.113, 884-1; and DLA, ROD II, 143. A note in ROD states that Lorion stayed five years in the diocese, returning to Montreal in March 1887. Today, Ruscom River is known as St Joachim, and the parish has been amalgamated with Stoney Point and Comber.

38 John Walsh to É.-C. Fabre, 25 November 1885, ACAM, 255.113, 885-6.

39 John Walsh to É.-C. Fabre, 2 January 1886, ACAM, 255.113, 886-1, emphasis his.

40 John Walsh to É.-C. Fabre, 25 August 1886, ACAM, 255.113, 886-4. Lévesque himself wrote a note on the back of this letter: when he went to visit Archbishop Fabre, he did not find the archbishop at home, but he wanted to inform him that he had accepted the offer of the bishop of Sherbrooke. He apologized for writing on the letter from the bishop of London, but he did not have any other paper. See also É.-C. Fabre to John Walsh, 12 August 1886, DLA, ROD II, 201; É.-C. Fabre to John Walsh, 10 October 1887, DLA, ROD II, 219; and ROD II, 199.

41 See John Walsh to L.-Z. Moreau, 20 February 1885, AESH; and J.T. Wagner to L.-Z. Moreau, 20 February 1885, AESH. The parish came to be known as Our Lady of the Rosary; Walkerville was one of the border towns later annexed by the city of Windsor.

42 See L.-Z. Moreau to John Walsh, 21 February 1885, AESH; and L.-Z. Moreau to John Walsh, 10 March 1885, AESH. The "week of Quasimodo" is the week after Easter. An *exeat* is a letter from a bishop formally releasing one of his priests to the jurisdiction of another bishop. The process is also known as "excardination" and "incardination."

43 See L.-Z. Moreau to John Walsh, 28 March 1886, AESH; and John Walsh to L.-Z. Moreau, 31 March 1886, AESH.

44 See John Walsh to É.-C. Fabre, 20 August 1884, ACAM, 255.113.884-2; John Walsh to É.-C. Fabre, 11 April 1885, ACAM, 255.113.885-1; John Walsh to É.-C.

Fabre, 27 April 1885, ACAM, 255.113.885-2; and John Walsh to É.-C. Fabre, 26 August 1885, ACAM, 255.113.885-4.

45 For example, see the *Catholic Record*, 28 November 1879.

46 John Walsh to Giovanni Cardinal Simeoni, 15 March 1880, APF, CAS, vol. 21, 172rv, emphasis his.

47 John Walsh to J. Reaume, 3 December 1884 [sic, should read "1883"], DLA, LB I, 80.

48 Coffey, *City and Diocese*, 30.

49 Ibid., 35–6. See the complete account of the event, 34–8. An ostensorium is a monstrance.

50 Ibid., 39. For an account of the entire proceeding, see 38–42. The set of Migne is now in the collection of St Augustine's Seminary, Toronto.

51 Daniel O'Connell (1775–1847) was an Irish statesman who fought for the nationalist movement in his country. A descendent of Celtic chiefs who lost their lands to the English, and a Catholic, he experienced the fullest effect of the Penal Laws. He formed the idea of uniting Catholics under the leadership of their priests in the Catholic Association and, through this association, fought for reform in Parliament. Though some concessions were gained, he died before his dream of independence became a reality. O'Connell was known as "the Liberator" in honour of his efforts. His name was still held in high regard among many in Canada in the 1880s.

52 *Catholic Record*, 18 August 1882.

53 The *Catholic Record* on 22 September 1882 reported that the bishop had left Ireland on 17 September, and that he was expected to be home by the end of the month.

54 *Catholic Record*, 6 October 1882.

55 Ibid.

56 Ibid.

57 Teefy, *Jubilee Volume*, xxiii.

58 *Catholic Record*, 7 December 1889.

59 Coffey, *City and Diocese*, 35–6.

60 See, for example, John Walsh, Circular Letter to the Priests of the Diocese, 1 September 1884, DLA; and L.A. Dunphy, Secretary [to the Bishop], Circular Letter to the Priests of the Diocese, 27 August 1886, DLA.

61 See John Walsh to J.J. Lynch, 16 November 1882, ARCAT, L AD03.21; John Walsh to J.J. Lynch, 8 November 1883, ARCAT, L AD03.25; and John Walsh to J.J. Lynch, 5 September 1887, ARCAT, L AD03.51.

62 *Catholic Record*, 28 October 1878. The subjects included Sacred Scripture, Dogmatic Theology, and the History of the Church.

63 *Catholic Record*, 5 November 1887.

64 John Walsh, Circular Letter *Ad Clerum Diocesis Londinensis*, 26 February 1886, DLA.

65 Coffey, *City and Diocese*, 35.

66 *Catholic Record*, 7 December 1889.

67 John Walsh to J. Carlin, 27 April 1885, DLA, LB I, 109.

68 Grant, *Profusion of Spires*, 199. In Toronto, Lynch exacted a similar promise from priests with drinking problems.

69 See the *Catholic Record*, 1 November 1878, for coverage of a speech by a Fr Stafford, given at the cathedral.

70 Walsh to Baillargeon, 2 March 1868.

71 See John Walsh to J. Coffey, 26 April 1881, DLA, LB I, 46; and John Walsh to J. Coffey, 7 July 1881, DLA, LB I, 50.

72 John Walsh to J.-T. Duhamel, 13 April 1883, DLA, LB I, 71.

73 John Coffey became the editor of the *Catholic Record* under its second owner, Thomas Coffey, on 6 April 1883, and held this post until 5 November 1887. During that time he wrote *The City and Diocese of London* to commemorate the opening of the new cathedral in 1885.

There is no record of Coffey being in the London diocese after 1887; a note in the London archives says that by 1889 he was living in Quebec City. He then moved to the United States of America, living in various localities and working for various bishops, between 1892 and 1895. Coffey moved to Toronto sometime in the 1890s, after which he became a Baptist and, despite never having been dispensed from his priestly vows, attempted marriage.

74 John Walsh to W. Dillon, 1 February 1889, DLA, LB I, 128.

75 John Walsh to N. Gahan, 19 July 1882, DLA, LB I, 60.

76 John Walsh to Vicar General Laurent, 27 January 1883, DLA, LB I, 65, emphasis his. These Latin expressions refer to what were, and still are, considered among the most serious violations of priestly ministry: absolving an accomplice in sin and soliciting someone – in the confessional itself – to commit a sinful act. Laurent was originally from Brittany, France, and ordained a priest in Toronto in 1858. S. Best, archivist of the diocese of Peterborough, to J.P. Comiskey, 28 May 2010.

77 Walsh to Laurent, 27 January 1883.

78 John Walsh to M. Benedict, 17 May 1883, DLA, LB I, 74.

79 John Walsh to H. Japes, 20 May 1880, DLA, LB I, 27. Japes had been ordained by Pinsoneault in 1865.

80 C.H. Borgess to John Walsh, 1 October 1880, ADA, LB, vol, 10, 331. Casper Borgess, a priest of Cincinnati, Ohio, was named coadjutor bishop of Detroit in 1870. He succeeded to the see the following year (1871–87). He died in 1890.

81 John Walsh to P. Corcoran, 30 March 1881, DLA, LB I, 45. Corcoran was ordained by Walsh in 1872.

82 John Walsh to R. Beausang, 7 March 1874, DLA, LB I, 1.

83 John Walsh to J.J. Lynch, 7 April 1874, DLA, LB I, 2.

84 See B. Boubat to John Walsh, 10 December 1874, DLA, HF 16/71–87; and John Walsh to R. Beausang, 22 February 1880, DLA, LB I, 13.

85 John Walsh to R. Beausang, 22 November 1880, DLA, LB I, 39. See also John Walsh to R. Beausang, 22 February 1880, DLA, LB I, 13; John Walsh to R.

Beausang, 13 May 1880, DLA, LB I, 25; and John Walsh to R. Beausang, 13 September 1880, DLA, LB I, 33.

86 John Walsh to J.T. Egan, 30 April 1881, DLA, LB I, 47.

87 John Walsh to R. Beausang, 5 June 1882, DLA, LB I, 59.

88 John Walsh to R. Beausang, 16 August 1883, DLA, LB I, 77.

89 John Walsh to R. Beausang, 27 November 1883, DLA, LB I, 79, emphasis his.

90 See John Walsh to R. Beausang, 7 December 1883, DLA, LB I, 82; John Walsh to R. Beausang, 7 December 1883, DLA, LB I, 83; and John Walsh to R. Beausang, 20 December 1883, DLA, LB I, 83, emphasis his.

91 See John Walsh to Mr. Rousal [or "Rouscel"], n.d. [likely written between 28 December 1883 and 4 January 1884], DLA, LB I, 87; and John Walsh to Giovanni Cardinal Simeoni, n.d. [likely written 4 January 1884], DLA, LB I, 89.

92 John Walsh to R. Beausang, 11 September 1884, DLA, LB I, 97. See also John Walsh to R. Beausang, 20 July 1884, DLA, LB I, 96.

93 C.-F. Baillargeon to John Walsh, 26 March 1868, AAQ, 210 A, RL, XXIX:395.

94 Flynn, *London Episcopacy*, 90.

95 See Power, *Assumption College*, II, vii. This agreement is called a "concordat" on the original document, a term normally reserved for agreements between the Holy See and other sovereign countries.

96 DLA, ROD II; Flynn, *London Episcopacy*, 91. The Basilians now have only the charge of Assumption parish and Assumption University, both in Windsor.

97 John Walsh to J. Kilgenstein, OFM, 27 May 1886, DLA, LB I, 111. The Franciscans remained in charge of the parish until 21 September 1921, at which time they were forced to leave over a disagreement with the fifth bishop, Fallon, who wanted to establish a new parish in Chatham under the leadership of diocesan priests. When the Franciscans fought him on the issue, Fallon's will prevailed, and the Franciscans retired from the diocese.

98 Ibid.

99 Dignan, *London Diocese*, 457.

100 The Madams – now called Sisters – of the Sacred Heart eventually left the diocese, but at the request of Fallon who, in the 1910s, insisted girls and young women needed the opportunity to learn mathematics and sciences, just as boys and young men did, in order to compete in the world. The school closed June 1913, and the remaining Madams left in the spring of 1914. "This state of affairs was largely, if not entirely, due to the fact that the community failed to adopt the educational standard of the Province of Ontario, preferring to follow its own system of studies." Dignan, *London Diocese*, 458.

101 DLA, ROD II, n. 8.

102 St Paul (Mother), *From Desenzano to "The Pines,"* 195–6.

103 E.-A. Taschereau to John Walsh, 6 June 1871, DLA, HF 13/68–74.

104 J.T. Wagner to Giovanni Cardinal Simeoni, n.d. [Propaganda Fide has written "Giugno? 83" (June? 1883) on the document], APF, CAS, vol. 23, 303r–304v.

105 John Walsh to E.-A. Taschereau, 4 December 1877, AAQ, 320 CN, Haut-Canada, VI:163.

106 E.-A. Taschereau to John Walsh, 10 December 1877, AAQ, 210 A, RL, XXXII:385.

107 St Paul (Mother), *From Desenzano to "The Pines,"* 213–14. It is interesting to note that in her treatment of the matter of a mistress of novices, Mother St Paul made no reference to the bishop asking for help from Quebec. Having given up the post of superior after twenty-six years, Mother Xavier Le Bihan continued in several offices for the next seventeen years. She died 22 May 1896.

108 John Walsh to Mother Baptist, 6 January 1886, AUSCU.

109 John Walsh to Mother Baptist, 27 November 1886, AUSCU.

110 St Paul (Mother), *From Desenzano to "The Pines,"* 209–10.

111 See the *Catholic Record*, 11 July 1879; John Walsh to Mother Baptist, 27 June 1887, AUSCU; and John Walsh to Mother Baptist, 14 June 1888, AUSCU.

112 John Walsh to Mother Baptist, 1 March 1889.

113 *Catholic Record*, 26 October 1889.

114 Dignan, *London Diocese*, 474–6. A "select" school was a private school where tuition was normally charged.

115 John Walsh to Mother Superior, Community of the Sisters of the Holy Names at Hochelaga, 20 January 1881, DLA, LB I, 40.

116 Walsh to Mother Superior, 20 January 1881. See also John Thomas, 84. A few years after Walsh's departure from the diocese, in 1894, the Holy Names Sisters in Ontario and Detroit became an independent province by decree of Pope Leo XIII. The Holy Names Sisters gave the convent to the parish in the 1980s; it serves now as a community centre.

117 Dignan, *London Diocese*, 466. The Ladies of Loretto continued working in Stratford schools until June 1973, ANA-IBVM.

118 Dignan, *London Diocese*, 437–8. It would not have been a coincidence that the orphanage was opened on the feast of the Guardian Angels. Walsh often chose specific dates for such occasions, paying attention to religious and historical anniversaries.

119 J.J. Lynch to Sisters Mary Ignatia, Vincent, Ursula, Frances, Joseph, and Lucy, 10 December 1870, cited in Dignan, *London Diocese*, 439–40.

120 Dignan, *London Diocese*, 440.

121 Flynn, *London Episcopacy*, 68.

122 Chronicles of the House of Providence, ASSJ.

123 Dignan, *London Diocese*, 441. Dignan gives his list of dignitaries and erroneously names Macdonald as "Prime Minister." Macdonald resigned his first ministry on 5 November 1873 after an election defeat, and did not become prime minister again until 17 October 1878, after another successful election. Chronicles of the House of Providence, ASSJ.

124 *Catholic Record*, 20 October 1888. Michael Tiernan, a priest of London, dedicated the structure. The Sisters of St Joseph would further expand in the area of health care, establishing hospitals also in Sarnia and Chatham, while maintaining the orphanage and schools in several locales.

125 DLA, ROD II, 234; see also Decree of erection, 13 August 1888, DLA, ROD II, 229; and the "Verbal Process," the document of establishment, available in the archives RHSJ.
126 Notes from the archives RHSJ.
127 L.-Z. Moreau to John Walsh, 22 July 1888, AESH.
128 John Walsh to L.-Z. Moreau, 27 July 1888, AESH.
129 John Walsh to Mother Catherine-Aurélie, 13 August 1889, APBSH, emphasis his.

Chapter Four

1 The "Magisterium," from the Latin meaning "teacher," is the official teaching body of the Catholic Church. It includes the pope teaching in his own capacity or with all bishops working in concert, as well as bishops in their own dioceses, bishops in national conferences, and individual Roman Congregations.
2 Galley sheets, 94. DLA has a copy of a life of Walsh entitled *Most Rev. John Walsh, D.D.* It has no author's name, and appears to be a draft copy, or galley sheets of a manuscript for publication, based on the *Jubilee Volume*. What survives of the work is incomplete, beginning at page 76 and ending mid-sentence on page 105. It was written in 1942 for the centennial of the archdiocese of Toronto, as indicated on page 77.
3 See *Catholic Record*, 8 August 1879, 22 August 1885, and 20 October 1888; and J.J. Lynch to Monsignor Morais, 22 September 1887, ARCAT, L LB 05.186. Morais was the secretary to Cardinal Taschereau of Quebec.
4 *Catholic Record*, 20 October 1888.
5 Ibid.
6 *Catholic Record*, 28 May 1887. See also Teefy, *Jubilee Volume*, vi–vii.
7 *Catholic Record*, 16 May 1879.
8 *Catholic Record*, 29 October 1887.
9 *Catholic Record*, 18 May 1889.
10 C.H. Borgess to John Walsh, 10 December 1875, ADA, LB, 6, 676. There are no extant copies of the talks Walsh gave at retreats.
11 *Catholic Record*, 19 March 1887.
12 *Dei Filius* (or The Dogmatic Constitution on the Catholic Faith, its English title) instructed Catholics to read and meditate on the Scriptures, and emphasized fidelity to the Church and acquiescence to the Magisterium. Eleven years after Walsh's lecture, Pope Leo XIII would further emphasize these ideals, that is, more openness to the Scriptures and related sciences, in his encyclical *Providentissimus Deus* of 18 November 1898.
13 *Pastor Aeternus* (or The Eternal Pastor, in English) defined the jurisdictional primacy and infallibility of the pope in matters of faith and morals.
14 *Catholic Record*, 19 March 1887.
15 Ibid.

16 *Catholic Record*, 2 April 1887. The *Catholic Record* reported that the bishop developed these ideas on apostolicity in a later lecture in the series, given 27 March 1887.

17 For the lecture on divorce see *Catholic Record*, 5 December 1879. For the lecture on the coming of Christ see *Catholic Record*, 26 December 1879.

18 *Catholic Record*, 13 February 1880. The text of the pastoral letter is not extant.

19 Coffey, *City and Diocese*, 50.

20 *Catholic Record*, 14 November 1885.

21 John Walsh to J.J. Lynch, 20 January 1888, ARCAT, L AE06.98. Later, as archbishop of Toronto, in 1895, Walsh suggested an international convention be held to consider the important matter. See chapter 6.

22 Teefy, *Jubilee Volume*, xvi. Not all of the pastoral letters are extant. Copies of some are found in the London archives and in the archives of other dioceses. Some were recorded in the *Catholic Record*, while others were only reported to have been issued, as, for example, the pastoral letter on the Irish question.

23 Pastoral Letter of His Lordship the Right Reverend John Walsh, D.D., Bishop of London, Ontario, on Devotion to the Blessed Virgin and Her Appearance at Lourdes, France, 1 November 1876, DLA. Two years after the proclamation by Pius IX, Pinsoneault, as the new bishop of London, chose the Blessed Virgin under the title of the Immaculate Conception as the principal patron of the diocese.

24 Ibid. It should be kept in mind that the frequent reception of the Eucharist was not the usual practice among Catholics in the nineteenth century. This would only come about many years later following a decree from the Sacred Congregation for the Council, *On the Frequent and Daily Reception of Holy Communion*, given 20 December 1905. This new practice was plainly inspired by Pope Pius X (1903–14).

25 *Catholic Record*, 2 May 1885.

26 John Walsh, Pastoral Letter on the Commemoration of the Faithful Departed, 2 November 1878; *Catholic Record*, 8 November 1878.

27 See John Walsh, Lenten Pastoral Letter of the Rt. Rev. John Walsh, D.D., Bishop of London, to the Clergy and Laity of the Diocese, London, 24 February 1881, 2–21. ACAM, 255.113, 881-2.

28 Ibid.

29 Ibid. The "Easter duty" refers to the obligation that all Catholics who have received First Communion must go to the sacrament of Penance and receive the Eucharist at least once a year, sometime between the First Sunday of Lent and Trinity Sunday.

30 See "Lenten Regulations for the Diocese of London," *Catholic Record*, 24 February 1882; and John Walsh, Pastoral Letter on Lent, London, 21 February 1882, *Catholic Record*, 3 March 1882.

31 John Walsh, Lenten Pastoral Letter, London, 2 February 1885, *Catholic Record*, 14 February 1885.

32 Walsh, Lenten Pastoral Letter, 2 February 1885.

33 See John Walsh, Pastoral Letter for Lent 1887, London, 18 February 1887, in *Catholic Record*, 26 February 1887; and Walsh, Lenten Pastoral Letter, 14 February 1885, as cited in the *Catholic Record*, 9 March 1889.

34 Reprinted in the *Catholic Record*, 2 June 1882.

35 Rationalism grew out of the Enlightenment, promoting a reliance on reason as the only authority to determine one's actions or opinions. It eliminated any consideration of the transcendent or external revelation.

36 Walsh, *Thoughts on Devotion*, 14–22, DLA.

37 Ibid., 23.

38 Attacks on the pope were in fact a reflection of a broader question of the day, which was referred to as "the Roman Question." It concerned the independence of the pope and the Holy See within a united Italy. From the 1850s, the *Risorgimento* was a growing movement in the Italian peninsula to bring together all the small countries, provinces, and duchies – including the Papal States – into one unified country. The Kingdom of Italy, proclaimed in 1861 under Victor Emmanuel II (1860–78), included two territories of the Papal States which had been annexed, namely Romagna and the Marches. The pope, however, maintained temporal control of Rome and the immediate surrounding area with the help of France, and refused any negotiations that would lead to giving up his temporal power. When the Franco-Prussian War was at its height, France withdrew its troops in the summer of 1870 and left the pope defenceless, except for the Swiss Guards at the Vatican. Italian troops moved into the city of Rome on 20 September 1870 and Rome was joined to Italy, leaving the pope with only the area of the ancient walled city, roughly the equivalent of the area of Vatican City today. The pope declared himself to be a "prisoner of the Vatican."

39 Walsh, *Thoughts on Devotion*, 38.

40 Ibid., 40.

41 Henry Edward Cardinal Manning (1809–1892) was an Anglican minister who converted to the Catholic religion in 1851. He claimed it was the writing of St Thomas Aquinas that intellectually brought him into the Catholic Church, "but it was the Sacred Heart which drew my heart into it." Later, as archbishop of Westminster, Manning had great influence as a writer, preacher, and administrator in his diocese, promoting social teachings of the gospel and a vision of a strong papacy. He was partly responsible for guiding the First Vatican Council through the debates on papal infallibility and primacy. As such, Manning had an extensive audience for his thoughts and reflections on the Catholic faith. He was widely published in the journals of the day, including the *Catholic Record*. For his thoughts on devotion to the Sacred Heart, see Erb, "Henry Edward Manning," 14–17.

42 See Walsh's endorsement in the 30 May 1879 edition.

43 *Catholic Record*, 4 October 1878.

44 Thomas Coffey controlled the *Catholic Record* from 30 May 1879 until his death in 1913. The paper then passed to his daughter and her husband, Robert Burns. The last manager and proprietor was Francis Fallon, Thomas Coffey's great-grandson. Among the later editors of the paper were John Teefy, author of the *Jubilee Volume* and a priest of the archdiocese of Toronto, and Monsignor Francis Brennan, from London, who was its final editor. The *Catholic Record* ceased publication when it was purchased by the new Catholic weekly, the *Ensign*, in 1948.

45 *Catholic Record*, 14 November 1879.

46 Power, *Assumption College*, II, viii–ix.

47 *Catholic Record*, 8 September 1888.

48 *Catholic Record*, 19 September 1879. Princess Louise was one of the daughters of the reigning monarch, Queen Victoria, and her consort, Prince Albert.

49 St Paul (Mother), *From Desenzano to "The Pines,"* 207. Permission to teach the boys at the parochial school would not come until 1895, after Walsh was transferred to Toronto. The Ursulines, as indicated earlier, experienced continued growth in their community and field of influence – especially education – for a great many decades after Walsh left the diocese, expanding to such communities as Tilbury, Tecumseh, Wallaceburg, Dublin, McGregor, Stoney Point, and London, where they built Brescia College for women at Western University (today known as Brescia University College at the University of Western Ontario) with the assistance of Bishop Michael Fallon, and eventually to many places in western Canada. The Ursulines continued teaching at St Joseph's School in Chatham until 1988, and at the Ursuline Academy, or Ursuline College, as it was later called, until 1996, when the last Ursuline sister retired from teaching there. There are now only a few Ursulines involved in education in the diocese, including those at Brescia College, most at the level of the Board of Directors.

50 St John Thomas, *Rooted in Hope*, 77. See also *Catholic Record*, 21 May 1887.

51 *Catholic Record*, 21 May 1887.

52 St John Thomas, *Rooted in Hope*, 70–3. See also Coffey, *City and Diocese*, 72.

53 Westfall pointed out that Ryerson was not only anti-Catholic but anti-Anglican as well. When John Strachan, rector of the Anglican cathedral at York (later Toronto) in the 1820s, made an unflattering comparison between "the settled, well-educated, and sober-minded clergy of his own church and the Church of Scotland with the emotional, poorly trained Methodist preachers who wandered through the colony," the unknown and very young Egerton Ryerson "came forth from obscurity to do battle with the Anglican Goliath." In his response to Strachan, Ryerson "quoted with approval a passage from the Anglican book of homilies that branded Rome as the 'harlot, the most filthy of all harlots, the greatest that has ever been'. He also attempted to discredit Strachan and the Anglican Church by associating them with the Church of Rome, arguing that all establishments were essentially Romish." Ironically, through this outburst, Ryerson was later credited

with giving a ringing defence of religious freedom. See Westfall, *Two Worlds*, 24–5. Strachan later became the Anglican bishop of Toronto.

54 Westfall, *Two Worlds*, 6. See Grant, *Profusion of Spires*, 143–4, where this opinion was confirmed as widely held. See also Flynn, *London Episcopacy*, 116. I am indebted to Flynn's work on Walsh for much of the information in this section. Ryerson became the superintendent of Education in 1844, and held that position until 1876.

55 Flynn, *London Episcopacy*, 134–6. The provincial Liberal government of Oliver Mowat removed Ryerson from being superintendent in 1876 by eliminating the position. His responsibilities were taken over by an elected official, the minister of Public Instruction, later called the minister of Education. The Honourable Adam Crooks held that portfolio from 19 February 1878 to 23 November 1883. See Flynn, *London Episcopacy*, 136; and AO, MU 2175 F3, Mowat Scrapbook Re: Separate Schools, 145.

56 Power, "Walsh," in *DCB*, XII, 1085–6.

57 Walker, *Catholic Education*, II, 31. For further information on the issue, see the entire chapter, 30–59.

58 Circular Letter of His Lordship, the Bishop of London, to the Clergy of his Diocese, 2 December 1878, cited in Flynn, *London Episcopacy*, 127. See also Walker, *Catholic Education*, II, 60–81; and Power, *Promise Fulfilled*, 151–3.

59 Flynn, *London Episcopacy*, 127–9.

60 Ibid., 129–30.

61 Bell re-introduced his bill in March 1882, at which time the Ontario legislature had another debate on the issue. Bell attacked Archbishop Lynch and referred to earlier complaints about the handling of school properties. Fraser countered that this was a personal attack on the archbishop, prompted by "blind bigotry," adding that Catholic lay people did not need an Orangeman to defend them. The leader of the Conservative party in the legislature, W. Ralph Meredith, did not wish the party to be identified with opponents to the Catholic hierarchy and he called for a more neutral stance. He did not wish to force the ballot on Catholic school supporters if they themselves did not wish it. The premier agreed that there was no great support among Catholics for the ballot. The bill was defeated once again, receiving only thirteen favourable votes. See Flynn, *London Episcopacy*, 130–1.

62 John Walsh to R. Meredith, 15 January 1883, DLA, LB I, 64, emphasis his. In general, Catholics supported the Conservative party at this time.

63 Flynn, *London Episcopacy*, 128. Though Lynch had died by 1894, and Walsh had moved to Toronto, the issue was still being debated. In the end, Lynch had been greatly influential, with the help of Walsh and other colleagues in the episcopacy and in the legislature, in ensuring some freedom for Catholic trustees and Catholic education.

64 Flynn, *London Episcopacy*, 143.

65 Ibid., 144.

66 J.J. Lynch to John Walsh, 2 January 1885, ARCAT, L AO27.04.

67 J.J. Lynch to John Walsh, 13 January 1885, ARCAT, L AO27.08.

68 John Walsh to J.J. Lynch, 15 January 1885, DLA, LB I, 103.

69 Ibid.

70 J.V. Cleary to O. Mowat, 16 January 1885, DLA, LB I, 104.

71 J.J. Lynch to John Walsh, 19 January 1885, ARCAT, L AO27.11.

72 See J.V. Cleary to John Walsh, 29 January 1885, ARCAT, L AO27.17; and J.V. Cleary to John Walsh, 2 February 1885, ARCAT, L AO27.19.

73 J.J. Carberry to John Walsh, 6 February 1885, ARCAT, L AO27.20.

74 John Walsh to J.J. Lynch, 12 February 1885, DLA, LB I, 105. In 1985, the Conservative government of Premier William Davis signalled its intention to address the matter of inequitable funding for Catholic schools. It was left to a later Liberal government, under Premier David Peterson, to pass the legislation which gave extended but not equal funding to Catholic schools. Yet another government, under the New Democratic premier Bob Rae, passed legislation in the mid-1990s giving equal funding to Catholic schools, but with the provision that teachers of any religion had to be considered for hire, and students of any religion could attend Catholic secondary schools.

75 Pastoral Letter of the Right Reverend John Walsh, D.D., Bishop of Sandwich, publishing the Pope's Encyclical Letter of the 17th October, 1867, and Appointing a Triduum in Compliance with its Conditions, London, 1 February 1868, DLA.

76 Ibid.

77 Ibid.

78 Ibid.

79 See Aubert, *Le pontificat de Pie IX*, 311–59; and Aubert et al., *The Church in the Age of Liberalism*. The Council of Trent opened in 1545 and closed in 1563.

80 Pastoral Letter of the Rt. Rev. John Walsh, D.D., Bishop of Sandwich, to the Clergy and Laity of the Diocese, publishing the Bull of Indiction, "Aeterni Patris," by which our Holy Father Convokes a General Council, and Promulgating a Jubilee, London, 15 May 1869, as found in Walsh, *The Council of the Vatican*, DLA.

81 Ibid.

82 Ibid.

83 Ibid., emphasis his.

84 In England, Manning and William George Ward (1812–1882), editor of the *Tablet* and the *Dublin Review*, promoted a strong ultramontane Church. Both were converts from the Church of England to Catholicism. Ward, the more extreme of the two, held that the pope's every doctrinal statement was infallibly dictated by God. Although Manning was less in favour of this view, he himself at times had a curious tendency to identify his own ideas and statements with those of God. See Cwiekowski, *The English Bishops*; and Butler, *Bishop Ullathorne*.

85 See C.-F. Baillargeon to John Walsh, 8 November 1868, AAQ, 210 A, RLL, XXIX:620; and John Walsh to E.J. Horan, 10 May 1869, AAK.

86 J.J. Lynch to John Walsh, Rome, n.d. [likely written the end of December 1869 or early January 1870], DLA, HF 21/67-87.

87 Ibid. "Jesuitism" was a euphemism for papal support, or ultramontanism, as expressed in *La Civiltà Cattolica*.

88 Lynch to Walsh, 28 February 1870.

89 Ibid. Stephen Michael Vincent Ryan, born in Upper Canada, was ordained a priest of the Congregation of the Mission, the same community for which John Lynch was ordained. Ryan was appointed bishop of Buffalo, New York, and served in that see until his death (1868–96).

90 Power, "Walsh," in *DCB*, XII, 1085.

91 John Walsh, Pastoral Letter of His Lordship, Right Revd John Walsh, D.D., Bishop of Sandwich, to the Clergy and Laity of the Diocese, London, 2 February 1870, as found in Walsh, *The Council of the Vatican*.

92 Ibid.

93 Ibid.

94 Ibid.

95 Lynch to Walsh, 13 June 1870. During that session of the Council, the Vatican raised Toronto to a metropolitan see, consequently bestowing the title of "archbishop" on Lynch.

96 Circular Letter of His Lordship Right Rev. Dr. Walsh, Lord Bishop of London, to The Clergy of Said Diocese, London, 20 March 1871, DLA, emphasis his.

97 Walsh, Circular Letter, 20 March 1871. These prayers include the "Our Father," the "Hail Mary," and the short invocations "St Peter, pray for us" and "St Joseph, pray for us."

98 Walsh, *Papal Infallibility*, DLA.

99 Power, "Walsh," in *DCB*, XII, 1085.

100 Pastoral Letter of the Bishops and Archbishop of the Ecclesiastical Province of Toronto, relative to the Celebration of the Golden Jubilee of our Holy Father Pope Leo XIII, n.d. [September 1887], *Catholic Record*, 24 September 1887.

101 Ibid.

102 Ibid.

103 Ibid.

104 See "Address to the Holy Father Leo XIII from the Bishop and People of the Diocese of London," *Catholic Record*, 10 September and 5 November 1887.

105 See *Catholic Record*, 17 March, 24 March, 28 April, and 7 July 1888.

106 Pastoral Letter on the Visit of the Rt Rev. John Walsh, D.D., Bishop of London, to the Holy See and the Shrines of the Apostles, London, 28 August 1888, *Catholic Record*, 8 September 1888. So great was the number of gifts received by Pope Leo at his jubilee that it was announced in August 1888 he would send a gift to every cathedral in the world. See *Catholic Record*, 18 August 1888. Pope Leo sent a chalice and paten to St Peter's Cathedral, which are used there to this day.

Chapter Five

1 J.A. Macdonald to J.J. Lynch, 17 July 1869, ARCAT, L AE02.22. Macdonald had practised law and had been a municipal politician in Kingston prior to his election to the legislature of the United Province of Canada in 1844. Later, in concert with Georges-Étienne Cartier as co-premier, he worked to achieve the coalitions and agreements that led to Canada's Confederation in 1867. Cartier's support gained the French Canadians for the plan. In recognition of their work, Macdonald and Cartier were knighted by Queen Victoria. Macdonald remained active in federal politics until his death on 6 June 1891.

2 J.A. Macdonald to John Walsh, 11 July 1867, LAC, JAMLB, vol. 513, pt. III, 723–4.

3 In total, there are preserved in the National Archives copies of sixteen letters written by Macdonald to Walsh and thirty-four letters written by the bishop to the prime minister. Only one of the letters from Macdonald to Walsh survives in the London diocesan archives, along with a letter written to John Walsh when he was archbishop of Toronto. Interestingly, there are no records in Walsh's letter books of his letters to the prime minister. ARCAT has some of the Macdonald letters written during Walsh's London episcopacy.

4 J.A. Macdonald to John Walsh, 28 June 1872, LAC, JAMLB, vol. 521, pt. I, 18–19. See also John Walsh to J.A. Macdonald, 16 October 1878, LAC, JAMP, vol. 352, 162033–5; and J.A. Macdonald to John Walsh, 25 October 1878, LAC, JAMLB, vol. 524, pt. I, 31. A letter from Macdonald to Sir Alexander Campbell, the Postmaster General at Ottawa, indicates he relied on Campbell to get the support of Bishop Edward Horan in Kingston diocese in preparation for the next election. See J.A. Macdonald to Alexander Campbell, 23 December 1871, AO, MU469. In another letter, written six days later, Macdonald referred to the support he had from the Ontario Liberal Richard W. Scott, a Catholic, who was considered a federal Conservative. Macdonald added a postscript to this letter: "Scott had the approval of Bishops Lynch & Walsh – I don't know about Farrell." See J.A. Macdonald to Alexander Campbell, 29 December 1871, AO, MU469. Scott became a senator, and later served in the cabinet of the MacKenzie Liberal government as minister without portfolio from November 1873 to January 1874, then as secretary of state until October 1878.

5 J.A. Macdonald to John Walsh, 22 January 1887, DLA, HF 29/87, emphasis his.

6 J.A. Macdonald to John Walsh, 24 May 1882, LAC, JAMLB, vol. 524, pt. III, 734–5.

7 For example, while supporting Macdonald federally, Walsh willingly supported the Liberal party, the Conservatives' arch-rivals, at the provincial level for the benefit of Catholic schools during Oliver Mowat's premiership in Ontario. See chapter 4.

8 Walsh to Macdonald, 16 October 1878. Macdonald returned to power in that election and would be prime minister for the rest of his life. Walsh would back him for his remaining years in Parliament.

   MacKenzie, a stonemason and newspaper editor from Sarnia, was an elected member of the Legislative Assembly of the Province of Canada and a supporter of Confederation. In 1867 he was elected to the House of Commons and the Ontario Legislature, holding both seats until dual representation was abolished. He maintained his Commons seat as leader of the Liberals, and served as prime minister from 7 November 1873 until 8 October 1878. Two years after losing the general election of 1878, he retired from politics and became a writer. He refused several offers of knighthood from Queen Victoria. He died at Toronto, 17 April 1892.

9 John Walsh to J.A. Macdonald, 21 July 1872, LAC, JAMP, vol. 344, 157709–14. See also John Walsh to J.A. Macdonald, 27 February 1883, LAC, JAMP, vol. 391, 186378–9.

10 John Walsh to J.A. Macdonald, 27 May 1882, LAC, JAMP, vol. 384, pt. II, 180776–7. See also John Walsh to J.A. Macdonald, 5 July 1872, LAC, JAMP, vol. 344, 157659–62.

11 See Power, "Walsh," in DCB, XII, 1085; and J.C. Patterson to J.A. Macdonald, 3 October 1882, LAC, JAMP, vol. 388, 183538–40.

12 See John Walsh to Hon. R. Scott, M.P. [sic], Secretary of State, etc., 13 September 1877, DLA, LB I, 3; and John Walsh to J.T. Duhamel, 11 September 1878, AOA, emphasis his. Walsh had incorrectly identified Scott in the first of these letters as a member of Parliament when, in fact, he was a senator.

13 See John Walsh to F. Smith, Cabinet Minister, etc., 14 August 1883, DLA, LB I, 76; John Walsh to J.A. Macdonald, 21 April 1884, LAC, JAMP, vol. 402, 194198–201; John Walsh to J.A. Macdonald, 13 May 1884, LAC, JAMP, vol. 402, 194202–5; and John Walsh to J.A. Macdonald, 30 July 1884, LAC, JAMP, vol. 27, 10362–5.

14 Walsh to Smith, 14 August 1883.

15 Walsh to Macdonald, 13 May 1884. See also Walsh to Macdonald, 21 April 1884.

16 Walsh to Macdonald, 13 May 1884. Edward Blake was the second premier of Ontario (1871–72). In 1880, he became leader of the federal Liberal Party of Canada, serving as leader of the Opposition during Macdonald's time as prime minister. He resigned the leadership in 1887, and was followed in that position by Wilfrid Laurier.

17 See J.A. Macdonald to John Walsh, 15 August 1884, LAC, JAMLB, vol. 526, pt. I, 49–50; John Walsh to J.A. Macdonald, 20 August 1884, LAC, JAMP, vol. 27, 10366–9; and John Walsh to J.A. Macdonald, 6 July 1887, LAC, JAMP, vol. 27, 10370–2.

18 John Walsh to J.A. Macdonald, 1 October 1886, LAC, JAMP, vol. 39, 14553–5, emphasis his.

19 J.A. Macdonald to John Walsh, 2 October 1886, LAC, JAMLB, vol. 527, pt. I, 41–2.

20 See John Walsh to J.A. Macdonald, 2 June 1888, LAC, JAMP, vol. 39, 15539–42; John Walsh to J.A. Macdonald, 9 June 1888, LAC, JAMP, vol. 39, 15443–6; and J.A. Macdonald to John Walsh, 9 June 1888, LAC, JAMLB, vol. 528, pt. I, 26–7.

21 See John Walsh to J.A. Macdonald, 17 January 1887, LAC, JAMP, vol. 20, 7321–4; and Macdonald to Walsh, 22 January 1887. Coughlin lost in the election of 1891. Walsh, by then the archbishop of Toronto, received a personal letter from Macdonald dated 26 March 1891, informing him that he had met Coughlin and intended to carry out his 1887 promise of which Walsh was the guarantor. In an ironic note, Macdonald added, "I wish it were so easy for Patterson." See J.A. Macdonald to John Walsh, DLA, HF 29/91. Macdonald died in June that year, not living long enough to carry out his promise. Thomas Coughlin never served in the Senate.

22 John Walsh to J. O'Connor, Postmaster General, 14 May 1880, DLA, LB I, 26. In this letter, Walsh wrote to one Catholic who had received an appointment about another who wished to do so.

23 See J. Carling to J.A. Macdonald, 14 June 1979, LAC, JAMP, vol. 359, 165865–8; and J.A. Macdonald to John Walsh, 1 November 1873, LAC, JAMLB, vol. 523, pt. III, 876.

24 See John Walsh to J.A. Macdonald, 11 January 1881, LAC, JAMP, vol. 372, 173181–2; John Walsh to J.A. Macdonald, 10 May 1881, LAC, JAMP, vol. 375, 175109–11; and John Walsh to J.A. Macdonald, 19 May 1881, LAC, JAMP, vol. 375, 175241–2.

25 John Walsh to J.-E.-B. Guigues, 15 September 1871, AOA. See also, for example, John Walsh to C. LaRocque, 15 September 1871, AESH; John Walsh to E.-A. Taschereau, 15 September 1871, AAQ, 320 CN, Haut-Canada, VI:128; and John Walsh to I. Bourget, 15 September 1871, ACAM, 255.113, 871–2. In the letter sent to Taschereau, Walsh penned a note asking the archbishop to send him a copy of the Treaty of Paris of 1763.

26 Walsh to Guigues [et al], 15 September 1871.

27 John Walsh to J. O'Connor, 20 September 1871, AAQ, 320 CN, Haut-Canada, VI:130.

28 Ibid., emphasis his.

29 C. LaRocque to John Walsh, 20 September 1871. In actuality, Briand did not become bishop of Quebec until 1766, so LaRocque was mistaken in saying that he had exercised the right of dispensation from banns "the very next day after the signing of the Treaty of Paris." The see of Quebec was vacant from 1760 until Briand's appointment in 1766.

30 See John Walsh to E.-A. Taschereau, 7 October 1871, AAQ, 320 CN, Haut-Canada, VI:131.

31 John Walsh to J.A. Macdonald, 7 October 1871, LAC, JAMP, vol. 343, 157288–9. For the copy of the summons, see 157290.

32 J.A. Macdonald to John Walsh, 10 October 1871, LAC, JAMLB, vol. 519, pt. II, 299.

33 APF, Brevi e Bolle, vol. 6, 321r.

34 Walsh had visited Rome and was, at that time, in Ireland. He received a telegram from Michael Tiernan, chancellor of the diocese, announcing Bruyère's death. The pages of the *Catholic Record* recorded Bruyère's death five days later. The article spoke of the pious, zealous, and devoted priest: "His unfeigned piety, his devotion to duty, his never-failing presence at the altar or in the confessional, his singleness of purpose, his condescension and kindness ... commanded the respect and admiration, if not the affections of all classes ... The value of his services to the French Canadian missions in the county of Essex cannot be over estimated. Besides the parochial duties incumbent on him as pastor of Sandwich, from which he never relaxed, even to allow himself, at any time, one week's summer vacation, he was often deputed to fulfill difficult tasks of a diplomatic character, which he invariably accomplished without fear or favor and in the very best interests of all concerned." See *Catholic Record*, 18 February 1888. The next issue of the *Catholic Record* provided the details of the funeral services, conducted by Dean Murphy in the absence of the bishop.

35 John Walsh to M.J. Tiernan, as cited in the *Catholic Record*, 25 February 1888.

36 See Sanfilippo, "L'image du Canada," 9–24.

37 Ibid., 19. This declaration was made by Merry del Val while acting as apostolic delegate to Canada for the Manitoba Schools Question. See chapter 6. An apostolic delegate is a representative of the pope to the bishops of a country that does not enjoy full diplomatic relations with the Holy See. Where full diplomatic relations exist, the papal representative is called an apostolic nuncio and is the representative of the Holy See to the government of the country and to the Catholic bishops therein.

38 Lynch to Walsh, n.d. [December 1869 or early January 1870].

39 C.F. Cazeau to John Walsh, 17 February 1870, AAQ, 210 A, RL, XXIX:1129.

40 Lynch to Walsh, 28 February 1870.

41 Baillargeon to Walsh, 17 May 1870.

42 E.J. Horan to J.J. Lynch, 17 September 1870, as cited in Choquette, *L'église catholique*, 225.

43 John Walsh to J.J. Lynch, from New York, 24 March 1888, ARCAT, L AD03.55. See also John Walsh to J.J. Lynch, from New York, 26 March 1888, ARCAT, L AD03.56. Michael Augustine Corrigan was a priest of the diocese of Newark, New Jersey, when he was named coadjutor archbishop of New York in 1880. He became archbishop five years later, and died in 1902. Ronald MacDonald came from Antigonish. He served as bishop of Harbour Grace from 1881 to 1906 and died in 1917. The diocese of Harbour Grace is today known as Grand Falls.

44 John Walsh to E.-A. Taschereau, 7 September 1874, AAQ, 320 CN, Haut-Canada, VI:115.

45 *Catholic Record*, 26 January 1883.

46 John Walsh to J.-T. Duhamel, 13 August 1889, AOA. The correspondence, however, does not reveal what the ceremonies were, but likely they were connected to the silver jubilee of Duhamel's consecration as a bishop.

47 John Walsh to the Vicar General [of Quebec], 14 October 1870, AAQ, 31-15a, Papiers Mgr C.-F. Baillargeon, IX, 91.

48 E.-A. Taschereau to John Walsh, 21 March 1871, DLA, HF 13/68–74. There is no indication of what the gift was.

49 See the notation of letters sent by E.-A. Taschereau to the bishops of London, Toronto, Trois-Rivières, Saint-Hyacinthe, Montreal, Ottawa, Saint-Boniface, Kingston, Hamilton, Saint-Germain de Rimouski (now Rimouski), Chatham (now Bathurst), Saint-Jean de Nouveau Brunswick (now Saint John), Halifax, Arichat (now Antigonish), and Charlottetown, as well as to the retired bishop of Saint-Hyacinthe and the bishops of Burlington, Vermont, and Portland, Maine, 19 March 1871, AAQ, 12 A, Registre des insinuations ecclésiastiques, Q:240r–241r. This was a common practise of the Church in North America, especially in the early days when boundaries were not as clearly defined. Besides having a priest within the diocese with the powers of a vicar general, bishops of the neighbouring dioceses were asked to fulfill the role. With the passage of time, as boundaries and jurisdictions became better clarified, the office was granted solely *in titolare*. See F.G. Morrisey, OMI, to J.P. Comiskey, 7 February 1999.

50 See John Walsh to E.J. Horan, 22 November 1867, AAK; and C.H. Borgess to John Walsh, 27 December 1875, ADA, LB, vol. 6, 698.

51 See chapter 4.

52 C.H. Borgess to John Walsh, 30 December 1885, ADA, LB, vol. 12, 562.

53 DLA, ROD II, HF 21/67–87.

54 See ARCAT (Acta), 11 June 1877, L AA05.0437; 3 August 1881, L AA05.0613; 25 September 1884, L AA05.0817; and 10 November 1885, L AA05.0882.

55 See Walsh to Lynch, 8 November 1883; John Walsh to J.J. Lynch, 25 January 1887, ARCAT, L ADO3.41; and John Walsh to J.J. Lynch, 13 September 1887, ARCAT, L ADO3.52.

56 Walsh to Lynch, 16 November 1882, emphasis his.

57 See John Walsh to J.J. Lynch, 20 November 1885, ARCAT, L ADO3.29; John Walsh to J.J. Lynch, 21 December 1885, ARCAT, L ADO3.30; and John Walsh to J.J. Lynch, 4 April 1887, ARCAT, L ADO3.45.

58 See John Walsh to J.J. Lynch, from Rome, 17 December 1887, ARCAT, L ADO2.199; John Walsh to J.J. Lynch, from Paris, 20 January 1888, ARCAT, L AE06.98; and letters from New York including Walsh to Lynch, 24 March 1888; John Walsh to J.J. Lynch, 26 March 1888, ARCAT, L ADO3.56; and John Walsh to J.J. Lynch, 6 April 1888, ARCAT, L ADO3.57.

59 J.J. Lynch to Alessandro Cardinal Barnabò, 8 March 1876, APF, Acta, vol. 245, 164r–166r. Lynch's letter was incorrectly addressed, since Cardinal Barnabò had died on 24 February 1874.

60 George Conroy (1832–1878), born in Ireland, was ordained a priest in 1856. After teaching for fifteen years in seminaries, he was consecrated bishop of Ardagh in Clonmacnois in 1871 and, while serving as bishop of that diocese, he was in Canada by appointment of Pius IX from May 1877 to August 1878, to study some difficulties with the universities in Montreal and Quebec. He was the first of three apostolic delegates, the others being Bishop Henri Smeulders and Monsignor Rafaele Merry del Val. See APF, Registro dei Brevi e Bolle, vol. 6, 323v–325v; and Flynn, *London Episcopacy*, 39.

61 J.J. Lynch to Alessandro Cardinal Franchi, 17 September 1877, ARCAT, L RC60.09.

62 J.J. Lynch to G. Conroy, 25 June 1877, APF, Acta, vol. 245, 167v.

63 See G. Conroy to Alessandro Cardinal Franchi, 27 June 1877, APF, Acta, vol. 254, 166v–167v; and G. Conroy to Alessandro Cardinal Franchi, 12 July 1877, APF, Acta, vol. 254, 168r.

64 Lynch to Franchi, 17 September 1877.

65 General Congregation of 13 August 1877, APF, Acta, vol. 254, 163r.

66 G. Conroy to John Walsh, 16 September 1877, as cited in Teffy, *Jubilee Volume*, xviii.

67 See Lynch to Franchi, 17 September 1877. This letter would have followed the General Congregation and papal audience of 19 August, at which time the matter had been left unfinished.

68 Ibid.

69 Ibid.

70 Ibid.

71 Ibid.

72 G. Conroy to John Walsh, December 1877, as cited in Teffy, *Jubilee Volume*, xviii. Flynn, based on Coffey's report of the speech given by Walsh at the November celebration with his priests on his tenth anniversary of consecration, offered an insightful idea relating to the events of those months, that is, the bishop's words belied a sense of concern about leaving the diocese he loved so much: "The picture you draw of me is not mine, it is the ideal of what I ought to be, and indeed what I would wish to be, viz., the good shepherd who gives his time, health and life itself, for the spiritual welfare and sanctification of his people. God knows that to do this is my most earnest desire, and that my happiness here, and my hopes of happiness hereafter, are bound up with the spiritual weal and religious prosperity of the clergy and people amongst whom I have labored for the last ten years, and in whose midst I desire to toil on to the end." Coffey, *City and Diocese*, 37. See Flynn, *London Episcopacy*, 39.

73 Timothy O'Mahony was born 1 November 1825 in Cork, Ireland. He was ordained a priest on 24 March 1849 and consecrated bishop of Armidale, Australia, on 30 November 1869. He resigned that see in August 1877 and was named titular bishop of Eudocia and auxiliary to the archbishop of Toronto on 14 November 1879. He died at Toronto on 8 September 1892, hav-

ing served six years under Lynch and afterwards three years under Walsh as archbishop of Toronto. See ARCAT LAM 13.02.

74   Neither Dowd nor Fortune were ever chosen to be bishops but, as it turned out, Patrick Dowd's name would appear several times again, though never as *dignissimus*. Michael Joseph O'Farrell became instead the first bishop of Trenton, New Jersey (1881–94), and, as a friend of Walsh, he later preached at the dedication of London's new cathedral in 1885.

75   Teefy, *Jubilee Volume*, xviii.

76   See P. McIntyre to Giovanni Cardinal Simeoni, 19 July 1882, APF, SOCG, vol. 1016, 134rv; and J. Sweeney to Giovanni Cardinal Simeoni, 21 July 1882, APF, SOCG, vol. 1016, 136r. For the complete file, including the *terna*, see 120r–138v.

77   John Walsh to Giovanni Cardinal Simeoni, 17 October 1882, APF, CAS, vol. 22, 1064r–1067v.

78   John Walsh to J.J. Lynch, 10 January 1883, ARCAT, L AD03.23. O'Brien enjoyed nearly twenty-four years in Halifax. He died there, 9 March 1906.

79   See ARCAT subject report.

80   John Walsh, Pastoral Letter to the Clergy and People of the Diocese of London Promulgating the Decrees of the First Provincial Council of Toronto, 21 December 1883, *The Catholic Record*, 5 and 12 January 1883.

81   Coffey, *City and Diocese*, 52. This was the council that began promoting missions among aboriginals and blacks in the United States and gave birth to the long-standing *Baltimore Catechism*, a handbook for catechising youth in the beliefs and practices of the faith, widely used in Canada up to the 1960s.

82   John Walsh to J.J. Lynch, 20 June 1883, APF, SOCG, vol. 1019, 495r–498v. See also John Walsh to Giovanni Cardinal Simeoni, 5 October 1883, APF, SOCG, vol. 1019, 482r, in which Walsh assured Simeoni that he had not advised Gribbon to go over the head of Lynch to the Holy See; neither did he give a judgment on the case.

83   J.J. Shea to Giovanni Cardinal Simeoni, 29 October 1883, APF, CAS, vol, 23, 538r–546r; John Walsh to Giovanni Cardinal Simeoni, 5 November 1883, APF, CAS, vol, 23, 541rv.

84   J.J. Lynch to Giovanni Cardinal Simeoni, n.d. [ARCAT has written July 1886], ARCAT, L AC06.23.

85   John Walsh to Giovanni Cardinal Simeoni, 6 January 1884, APF, CAS, vol. 23, 821r–823v. See also 801r–826v for the entire case.

86   John Walsh to J.J. Brennan, 5 January 1889, DLA, LB I, 126.

87   See, for instance, a decree issued by Walsh on 27 November 1888, enacting certain directives from the Holy See for public exposition of the Blessed Sacrament, signed "+ John Walsh, Bishop of London and Administrator Apostolic of the Diocese of Hamilton," *Catholic Record*, 1 December 1888.

88   See Crinnon's appointment as vicar general, 2 December 1868, DLA, ROD II, 8; and the consecration of Crinnon as bishop of Hamilton, 19 April 1874, DLA, ROD II, 116.

89   Horan had become ill and Lynch intervened with his doctor, and eventually with the Holy See, to come to his aid. When Horan would not accept an

administrator to care for the diocese, Propaganda Fide asked him to offer his resignation. See Choquette, *L'église catholique*, 226.

90 J.J. Lynch to E.J. Horan, 13 May 1874, ARCAT, L ADO1.68.

91 See Alessandro Cardinal Franchi to J.J. Lynch, 9 September 1874, as cited in Choquette, *L'église catholique*, 228.

92 John O'Brien had been listed as *dignior* on the 1867 *terna* for Sandwich/London.

93 General Congregation of 16 August 1880, APF, ACTA, vol. 248, 400r–410v. None of the other three ever became bishops.

94 Walsh to Lynch, 10 January 1883.

95 Ibid.

96 Walsh to Lynch, 20 January 1888. Walsh had been in Rome for his *ad limina* visit and to participate in Leo XIII's jubilee celebration. He had stopped in Paris while *en route* to Canada.

97 General Congregation of 19 November 1888, APF, ACTA, vol. 258, 624r–630r. In all of the appointments, there was a concerted effort by the bishops of the ecclesiastical province of Toronto to have a common front when dealing with Rome. Interference from outside the province, as had previously occurred, sometimes led to compromise candidates being named who were not necessarily even nominated on the *ternae* submitted. Such interference almost always slowed the pace of the nomination process or circumvented it altogether.

98 Dominic of Saint-Denis, *Catholic Church*, 126.

99 Ibid.

100 John Walsh to J.J. Lynch, 12 June 1880, DLA, LB I, 29.

101 Ibid.

102 Ibid.

103 Pontiac later became the diocese of Pembroke in 1888. Much later, in 1938, the dioceses of Hearst and Timmins were erected and added as suffragan sees to the Ottawa archdiocese. The statement by Duhamel about the French character of Ottawa parallelled one made by Taschereau in a letter to Propaganda Fide: "The official statistics show that the French-Canadians are reproducing rapidly in the Ottawa region, whereas the Catholics of the English-language are diminishing. One can foresee the day when all the whole diocese will have become French-Canadian, even located in the province of Ontario." See Dominic of Saint-Denis, *Catholic Church*, 126.

When the diocese of Hull was created in 1963, the dismemberment of the archdiocese along the provincial borders occurred as the Ontario bishops had suggested in the 1870s. As well, since the 1970s, the number of French-speaking Catholics in Ottawa has steadily decreased, and Ottawa today is officially an English-speaking diocese with a bishop of Irish ancestry. Taschereau's prediction came to pass, but was short-lived.

104 General Congregation of 22 July 1889, APF, SOCG, vol. 1032, II a, 742r–743r, 745rv. The original diocese of Alexandria, erected on 21 January 1890, is today called Alexandria-Cornwall.

105 Miller, personal communication.

106 Miller, *The Donnellys*, 33–45.

107 Miller, personal communication. Miller pointed out that the Whiteboys took an oath similar to that of the Irish Republican Army members of the present day.

108 Miller, personal communication; and Miller, *The Donnellys*, 19–27.

109 DLA, ROD II, 113; and Miller, personal communication. Born in Ireland in 1824, Connolly studied at the major seminary of Quebec City and was ordained in the early 1850s by Charles-François Baillargeon, the coadjutor bishop of Quebec, where he served until 1879 until his appointment in London.

110 Miller, *The Donnellys*, 138.

111 Ibid., 142.

112 W.J. Donnelly to John Walsh, 11 October 1879, as found in Fazakas, *Donnelly Album*, 216; and R. Fazakas to J.P. Comiskey, 13 June 2010. Fazakas based his reconstruction of the letter on the report of the trial as given in the *Globe*, 3 March 1880.

113 See Fazakas, *Donnelly Album*, 216, where he reports an uncharacteristic response by Walsh, criticizing Donnelly for not using the right form of address for a bishop. Fazakas now thinks this may have been Connolly's insinuation, rather than the bishop's own words. Fazakas to Comiskey, 13 June 2010.

114 Miller, *The Donnellys*, 191–204; and Miller, personal communication. One of those who attempted to kill Will was the brother of his wife Nora. Ironically, the murders were committed one year to the day after Fr Connolly arrived in the parish as the bishop's peacemaker.

115 John Walsh to M. Stafford, P.P., Lindsay, Ontario, 16 March 1880, DLA, I, 18. Michael Stafford was born in Bathurst Township, Lanark County, Ontario in 1832 and died in 1882. Also see Miller, *The Donnellys*, 191–204.

116 Aemilius Irving represented the Crown, assisted by the Middlesex County Crown Attorney Charles Hutchinson. William R. Meredith acted for the defence. Hutchinson would later have an influence in the dismissal of the case. For transcripts of the inquests and trials and other related documents, see Reaney, *Donnelly Documents*.

117 Miller, *The Donnellys*, 205–20.

118 Miller, personal communication.

119 Power, "Walsh," in *DCB*, XII, 1086. In this view, Power also sees the appointment of Connolly as probably the only "blunder" which Walsh committed during his time as bishop of London. It was, in Power's mind, "an uncharacteristic mistake" by a man who usually showed a better judgment of character. Miller claims most men would have failed in Connolly's position.

Miller adds another important detail regarding Connolly's involvement. Miller had interviewed an old judge by the name of Collison who, as a boy, had been in the rectory at Lucan with his father, also a judge. The senior Collison inquired of Connolly if he had any papers, and then spent the afternoon burning them in a stove. Miller, personal communication.

120 Miller, personal communication. Only a few years before, Toronto had experienced what came to be called the Jubilee Riots, when Catholics were attempting to have outdoor processions in connection with the Holy (Jubilee) Year 1875. They came up against the mayor of Toronto and the Protestant press on the issue of being allowed to hold an outdoor procession, and met between six and eight thousand anti-Catholic rioters on the street when they did march. See Perin, *Rome in Canada*, 24.

121 John Walsh to É.-C. Fabre, 27 February 1889, ACAM, 255.133, 889-1. For other examples of the anti-Catholic hatred, see Walsh to Macdonald, 31 May 1884; and see also Perin. Reference to the "restitution" to the Jesuits was to the settling of the "Jesuits Estates" issue which had simmered for decades in Quebec.

122 The Irish settlers of the London area established, in 1877, an organization dedicated to assisting Irish immigrants when they landed in the New World, Catholics and Protestants alike. Officially incorporated as the Irish Benevolent Society, its presidency alternates each year between a Catholic and a Protestant, and it has chaplains of Catholic and Protestant faith. It continues its work today, promoting Irish culture and education, and fostering good relations among its members.

123 This is also why it is hard to accept the arguments of Power and Miller that Walsh was somehow protecting his career or his reputation. Besides, he had already shown he was not interested in moving from London when offered the coadjutorship in Toronto and later the archbishopric of Halifax. Even when the archbishopric of Toronto was offered him nine years later, he did not find it easy to accept the promotion. John Connolly remained pastor at Lucan until January 1895 when he was assigned to the parish of Sacred Heart in Ingersoll. He remained in that post until his retirement in 1907, and died in 1909.

124 See, for example, *Catholic Record*, 28 November 1879 and 4 June 1880.

125 John Walsh to J.J. Lynch, 22 October 1886, ARCAT, L AD03.37.

126 Walsh to Lynch, 16 November 1882.

127 John Walsh, Circular Letter to the Priests of the Diocese, 12 August 1883, DLA, HF 11/71–91.

128 DLA, ROD II, 161–2.

129 Walsh, Circular Letter, 1 September 1884. See also Walsh, Circular Letter, 27 August 1886. He usually requested these annual reports in the circular letters announcing the annual retreats for the priests.

130 Walsh to Horan, 10 May 1869.

131 See *Catholic Record*, 28 March 1879, 5 and 12 January 1883, and 31 December 1887.

132 Grant, *Profusion of Spires*, 174.

133 Pastoral Letter of the Rt. Rev. John Walsh, Bishop of London, to the Clergy and Laity of the Diocese of London, March 1881, *Catholic Record*, 25 March 1881.

134 John Walsh to J. Connolly, 16 March 1880, DLA, LB I, 19.

135 DLA, ROD II, 129 and 130. The cornerstone, opened in 1985 on the one hundredth anniversary of the dedication, was found to contain a zinc box holding a photo of Walsh and the clergy of the diocese, Canadian coins in use at the time, copies of the city's newspapers, and a document describing the cornerstone ceremony and listing all the bishops present at the dedication.

136 See J.T. Wagner to Pope Pius IX, n.d. [received by Propaganda Fide 21 November 1876], APF, CAS, vol. 14, 542r–543v; and J.T. Wagner to Alessandro Cardinal Franchi, n.d. [January? found in first part of the volume for 1878–79], APF, CAS, vol. 20, 58r–59v. Most probably, the cameo was a miniature portrait of the pope, mitigating any concern about simony.

137 Today the opera house is called The Grand Theatre.

138 *Catholic Record*, 10 January 1885. For examples of other fundraising activities see also 3 and 17 January 1885.

139 Flynn, *London Episcopacy*, 109. The towers were never finished according to the architect's original design. When John C. Cody, seventh bishop of London (1950–63), set out to finish the cathedral as planned, it was discovered that the foundations could not hold the desired additions. Modifications were made in the plans, and instead of the originally planned height of 70.3 metres, the towers stand at only 46.9 metres.

140 John Walsh to H. McMahon, 27 May 1882, DLA, LB I, 57.

141 John Walsh to J.A. Macdonald, 28 February 1882, LAC, JAMP, vol. 381, 178571–3; J.A. Macdonald to John Walsh, 10 February 1883, LAC, JAMLB, vol. 525, pt. I, 71–2.

142 E.B. Kilroy to J.C. Patterson, 18 May 1883, LAC, JAMP, vol. 393, pt. II, 187952–4.

143 The final tally of costs for the cathedral in 1885 reached $136,000, far above the intended $60,000, but still a manageable figure that did not financially cripple the diocese.

144 *Catholic Record*, 4 July 1885.

145 Coffey's history of the city and the diocese was written for this very event. It contains, as an appendix, the ceremony for the blessing of a church; see 74–7. Bernard John Joseph McQuaid was a priest of the diocese of New York who served as the first bishop of Rochester for over forty years (1868–1909). He was a personal friend of Walsh.

146 *Catholic Record*, 4 July 1885.

147 Ibid.

148 Ibid.

149 Walsh had supported O'Farrell's nomination for the coadjutorship in Toronto in 1876.

150 See *Catholic Record*, 14 November 1885 and 12 October 1889. These Stations of the Cross were donated by Bishop Michael Fallon to the Shrine of the Canadian Martyrs at Midland, Ontario, where they hang to this day.

151 John Walsh to J.A. Macdonald, 3 April 1889, LAC, JAMP, vol. 472, 234632–6.

152 J.C. Patterson to J.A. Macdonald, 12 July 1889, LAC, JAMP, vol. 475, 235449–51.

153 Address from the priests of the diocese, *Catholic Record*, 7 December 1889.

154 Flynn, *London Episcopacy*, 86.

155 *Catholic Record*, 7 December 1889.

Chapter Six

1 Information about Lynch's death and funeral is largely based on Anglin in Teefy, *Jubliee Volume*, 193–5. Merritton is now part of St Catharines. St John's Grove is now the Sherbourne-Wellesley area of Toronto.

2 F.P. Rooney & J.M. Laurent to Giovanni Cardinal Simeoni, 20 May 1888, APF, SOCG, vol. 1032, pt. II a, 756r–757v.

3 T. O'Mahony to Giovanni Cardinal Simeoni, 23 May 1888, APF, SOCG, vol. 1032, pt. IIa, 754r–755v.

4 McGowan, *Waning*, 8.

5 John Walsh to Giovanni Cardinal Simeoni, 21 May 1888, APF, SOCG, vol. 1032, pt. IIa, 752r–753v.

6 J.A. Macdonald to Lord Lansdowne, 21 May 1888, LAC, JAMLB, vol. 528, pt. I, 10–11. Macdonald's hesitations about Cleary were no doubt a reflection of Cleary's overt political opinions. He was strong-willed and opinionated, and did not hesitate to use ecclesiastical censure nor to express his thoughts when he felt it necessary. Many might have thought such a personality would not be successful in the see of Toronto. One can only imagine Cleary's resignation to the idea that he would not have been a popular choice. See Price, "Cleary," in *DCB*, XII.

7 Duke of Norfolk to D. Jacobini, 15 June 1888, APF, SOCG, vol. 1032, pt. IIa, 759rv.

8 J.A. Macdonald to John Walsh, 9 June 1888, LAC, JAMLB, vol. 528, pt. I, 26–7.

9 APF, SOCG, vol. 1032, pt. IIa, 743v–744r. See also John Walsh to Giovanni Cardinal Simeoni, 12 September 1888, APF, SOCG, vol. 1032, pt. IIa, 761r–763r. Neither Rooney nor Doherty was ever named a bishop in Canada.

10 See C. Tupper to J.A. Macdonald, 18 September 1888, LAC, JAMP, vol. 284, 130524–7; and J.A. Macdonald to C. Tupper, 2 October 1888, LAC, JAMLB, vol. 528, pt. I, 161.

11 APF, SOCG, vol. 1032, pt. IIa, 745rv; and APF, Brevi e Bolle, vol. 7, 123v.

12 The pope held the audience on 28 July 1889.

13 *Catholic Record*, 3 August 1889.

14 J.A. Macdonald to John Walsh, 2 July 1889, LAC, JAMLB, vol. 528, pt. I, 493–4.

15 John Walsh to J.-T. Duhamel, 5 August 1889, AOA.

16 Giovanni Cardinal Simeoni to John Walsh, 27 August 1889, as found in the *Catholic Record*, 21 September 1889. A consistory is a meeting of cardinals with the pope. At such meetings, on occasion, new cardinals are welcomed and given their "red hats."

17 APF, CAS, vol. 31, 466r–468v and 710rv.

18 John Walsh to D. O'Connor, [14] October 1889, ARCAT, W AA10.03 and W AA10.02.

19 John Walsh, Pastoral Letter, 1 November 1889, *Catholic Record*, 16 November 1889.

20 Ibid.

21 Ibid.

22 Teefy, *Jubilee Volume*, xxv. See also the *Catholic Record*, 6 August 1898.

23 A circular was sent throughout the archdiocese by the administrators Rooney and Laurent, to form the committee, inviting prominent gentlemen to assist in the planning. They also announced the appointment when the papal Brief was received, along with the upcoming reception. See ARCAT, W AB04.05 and W AB05.01.

24 *Catholic Record*, 7 December 1889 and 6 August 1898.

25 The account of Walsh's arrival in Toronto and his installation is taken largely from the *Catholic Record*, 7 December 1889.

26 Ibid.

27 Teefy, *Jubilee Volume*, xxv.

28 *Catholic Record*, 7 December 1889. The archbishop also received several letters from concerned lay people. See John Walsh to Mrs J. Sadlier, 3 December 1889, ARCAT, LB06.02; E.A. Ashman to John Walsh, 23 December 1889, ARCAT, W AB04.08; and M.F. Howley to John Walsh, 26 December 1889, ARCAT, W AB04.09.

29 See APF, SOCG, vol. 1032, pt. IIa, 764r–749v; and McGowan, *Waning*, 19.

30 Power, "Walsh," in *DCB*, XII, 1087. There were many cornerstone stories in the *Catholic Record*. Examples are the St Basil's novitiate (14 May 1892), St Gregory's church, Oshawa (1 September 1894), a new church in Richmond Hill (1 December 1894), the Good Shepherd convent (21 May 1898), and St Patrick's church in Merritton (25 June 1898).

31 See *Catholic Record*, 10 May 1890; Power, "Walsh," in *DCB*, XII, 1086.

32 Power, "Walsh," in *DCB*, XII, 1086. See also Power, *A History of Mount Hope Cemetery*.

33 John Walsh to the Clergy of Toronto, Easter Monday [30 March] 1891, ARCAT, W AA07.05.

34 P.T. Conway to John Walsh, 3 December 1893, ARCAT, W AA09.03.

35 A. Leonard, RSHJ, to J.P. Comiskey, 19 November 2009, with information from ARSHJ (Montreal). "Lay Sisters" were distinct from the "Choir Sisters" who taught in the schools. The former carried out domestic work in the community to support the latter.

36 "Little Mary, R.H.S." to John Walsh, 31 March 1890, ARCAT, W AA08.04. See also W AA08.06, W AA08.09, W AA08.10, and W AA08.12.

37 "Little Mary, R.H.S." to John Walsh, 3 May, 20 May, and 21 May 1891, ARCAT, W AA08.10.

38 I. Campbell [CSJ] to John Walsh, 21 April 1893, ARCAT, W AB04.19. The Sisters of St Joseph had left the diocese of London under Pinsoneault and

returned under Walsh. Since Mother Ignatia was the superior at the time of the second founding, she is considered the founding superior. Her portrait and some of her artifacts can be found in the current residence of the Sisters in London.

39 For example, see Lynch's announcement regarding a priests' conference, ARCAT, W AA07.03; and Walsh's announcement of a retreat, ARCAT, W AA07.04.

40 John Walsh to Giovanni Cardinal Simeoni, February 1890, ARCAT, LB06.19, 19.

41 John Walsh to P. McCabe, 10 January 1891, ARCAT, LB06.36, 39; and ARCAT, LB06.37, 40.

42 J. Moore to John Walsh, 25 February 1896, ARCAT, W AB04.29; and J. de Lavigne to John Walsh, 10 May 1896, ARCAT, W AB04.30. Several letters also indicate that Walsh discontinued his support for certain candidates.

43 John Walsh, Pastoral Letter for the Annual Collection for the Ecclesiastical Educational Fund, 30 August 1890, ARCAT, W AA06.07. See also, for example, John Walsh to P. Kellett, 29 July 1890, ARCAT, LB06.28, p. 27.

44 APF, NS, vol. 81, 335r–444v. Propaganda Fide declared its definitive approbation of the institute and its constitution on 6 July 1896. The Sisters would maintain a monastery in the Toronto archdiocese until 2004, when decreasing membership forced them to amalgamate their monasteries and move to Hamilton.

45 Such visits were often reported in the *Catholic Record*. See for example 5 and 19 July 1890 and 29 November 1890.

46 McGowan, *Waning*, 107–8.

47 Ibid. The shame and distress of having a member of one's family marry a Protestant cannot be emphasized enough; it led many Catholics to leave the Church altogether. It was widely considered reason enough to disown a family member. Even when the dispensation was granted, there could be no nuptial Mass, and the Marriage ceremony had to take place in the priest's house or the sacristy. Sometimes, vindictive pastors would not bother to heat the sacristy in the winter for these weddings.

48 These had begun sometime around 1540 in northern Italy. This annual time in each parish was dedicated to adoration of the Blessed Sacrament, with emphasis on catechesis in sermons, and opportunities to go to Confession. The focal points for these devotions were a monstrance containing a large consecrated Host and the altar resplendent with flowers and candles. With special eucharistic hymns and prayers and incense billowing in clouds throughout the church, each day of the Forty Hours would end with solemn Benediction of the Blessed Sacrament.

49 See, for example, *Catholic Record*, 8 March 1890 and 7 May 1892.

50 *Catholic Record*, 8 March 1890. See also 14 April 1894 at Our Lady of Lourdes parish at St John's Grove, and 29 January 1898 at St Joseph's parish in Leslieville.

51 The *Baltimore Catechism* was produced in 1884 for catechizing youth. See chapter 5. In time, it took on even greater importance than the Scriptures as a guide for Catholic spiritual life.

In response to the problem, the Church found it necessary to make as one of the laws of the Church, the requirement that all Catholics "make their Easter duty"; that is, to go to Confession and receive Communion at least once in the time between the first Sunday of Lent and Trinity Sunday. Failure to do so, as the catechisms stated, would leave one in a state of mortal sin.

The organization of many of the devotions fell to parochial and diocesan associations and confraternities, which abounded at the time and which led to new levels of activity. "Devotional practices and religious confraternities also had far-reaching appeal because they stir the emotions of men and women, cultivate religious sentimentality, and transform laypersons into active participants in the life of the Church." This was due to the emphasis given to corporal and spiritual works of mercy in catechisms. See McGowan, *Waning*, 92.

52 McGowan, *Waning*, 165. See also *Catholic Record*, 14 May 1892.

53 Very similar to those of the Knights of Columbus, the aims of the CMBA "were both spiritual and financial: to bring Catholic men together for the purposes of strengthening their faith; to disseminate and encourage the reading of Catholic literature; and to extend charity and life-insurance benefits to association members." See McGowan, *Waning*, 165–6. Bishop Ryan was a personal friend and colleague of Archbishop Lynch, since both were members of the Congregation of the Mission. Walsh would have met Bishop Ryan through Lynch. See chapter 4.

54 *Catholic Record*, 1 March 1890.

55 *Catholic Record*, 20 March 1890.

56 *Catholic Record*, 30 January 1892.

57 Many had heard the oft-repeated words – entirely out of context – of Pope Boniface VIII, "outside the Church there is no salvation," from his famous encyclical, *Unam Sanctam*, issued in 1302.

58 *Catholic Record*, 30 January 1892. The lecture was repeated by Walsh on various occasions. It was later printed in booklet form after one of those speaking engagements, and sold throughout the archdiocese under the title *Some Things Which Catholics Do Not Believe – or – Protestant Fictions and Catholic Facts*, Toronto: Catholic Register Press, 1897 (ARCAT, W AA04.07).

59 *Catholic Record*, 29 November 1890.

60 *Catholic Record*, 22 December 1894. The official state funeral for Thompson took place in Halifax on 3 January 1895.

61 See John Walsh, *Devotion to the Blessed Virgin*, 25 April 1891, ARCAT, W AA06.05; *Lenten Pastoral Letter*, 25 February 1892, ARCAT, W AA06.08; *Lenten Pastoral Letter*, 15 February 1898, ARCAT, W AA06.04; and *Pastoral Letter [on financial support of the Holy Father]*, 21 September 1896, ARCAT, W AA06.06. The above were all printed in booklet form by the Catholic Register Print, Toronto.

62 John Walsh to Giovanni Cardinal Simeoni, 1 December 1890, ARCAT, W AA10.05. This letter was marked "draft."

63 The Council opened in 1869 but was adjourned *sine die* in 1870 when Garibaldi invaded Rome.

64 John Walsh, *Pastoral Letter [on financial support of the Holy Father]*, 21 September 1896. See also *Catholic Record*, 17 October 1896. "Peter's Pence," as it was called, was an ancient Catholic custom to support the work of the pope, which Pius IX revived in his encyclical letter *Saepa Venerabilis*, on 5 August 1871.

65 McGowan, *Waning*, 190–3. Over the years, many changes have taken place in its editorial leadership and style, but the *Catholic Register* continues publishing weekly to this day.

66 *Catholic Record*, 8 March 1890. See also 2 July 1892 and 4 July 1896 regarding visits to schools.

67 McGowan, *Waning*, 130.

68 Catholic education at the university level was available at that time in Toronto at St Michael's College, and at the University of Ottawa.

69 *Catholic Record*, 26 July 1890. See also McGowan, *Waning*, 132.

70 Power, "Walsh," in *DCB*, XII, 1087.

71 Ibid.

72 The issue was a source of serious national stress, especially after Quebec and Ontario entered the fray. The matter would not be resolved to the satisfaction of Catholics until well into the twentieth century, and remains an issue of concern in the few remaining provinces that have Catholic separate schools. The definitive work on the Manitoba Schools Question is that of Crunican, *Priests and Politicians*.

73 See R.W. Scott, "Synopsis of the Manitoba School Case," Ottawa, 18 February 1896, ARCAT W AB03.04. Scott had been a senator since 1874 and served in various federal cabinet posts under Alexander McKenzie, and later would serve under Wilfred Laurier.

74 "To His Excellency the Governor General of Canada in Council," 31 December 1892, ARCAT W AB03.09.

75 Power, "Walsh," in *DCB*, XII, 1086.

76 Perin, *Rome in Canada*, 129 and 156. See also Crunican, *Priests and Politicians*, 179–80; and the draft of a letter in Walsh's handwriting, 15 December 1894, ARCAT W AB03.01.

77 I. Aberdeen to John Walsh, 15 December 1894, ARCAT, W AB03.02.

78 Ibid.

79 L.-P.-A. Langevin to John Walsh, 6 April 1895, ARCAT, W AB03.14; and L.-P.-A. Langevin to John Walsh, 22 February 1896, ARCAT, W AB03.03.

80 Scott, "Synopsis."

81 Merry del Val (1865–1930) was born in London, England. He was ordained a priest in 1888 and served in various Vatican posts, including as apostolic delegate to Canada. In 1903, he was made a cardinal and appointed secretary

in the Secretariate of State. That same year, having resigned that post, he was named secretary to the Holy Office, a post he held until his death.

82 Leo XIII, *Affari Vos*, Rome, 18 December 1897, as found in John Walsh et al., *Pastoral Letter of the Archbishop and Bishops of the Ecclesiastical Province of Toronto publishing the Pope's Encyclical Letter "Affari Vos" on the Manitoba School Question*, Toronto: Catholic Register Print, 1898, 14, ARCAT, W AA06.09. The encyclical was also printed in its entirety in the *Catholic Record*, 15 January 1898. The next week, on 22 January, the *Catholic Record* printed the bishops' pastoral letter.

83 Leo XIII, *Affari Vos*, 15.

84 John Walsh et al., *Pastoral Letter ... on the Manitoba School Question*, 2.

85 John Walsh to L.-P.-A. Langevin, 7 February 1898, ARCAT, W AB03.06.

86 Oddly, with regard to this issue, it has been suggested that archbishops Walsh and C.-H. Gauthier "confessed ignorance of an issue which should have riveted [sic] their attention." It is clear that Walsh was not ignorant of the issue but was well-informed, based on his possession of Scott's report along with all the relevant correspondence. Gauthier was not even named a bishop at the time the question was debated. See Perin, *Rome in Canada*, 156; Aberdeen to Walsh, 15 December 1894; and Langevin to Walsh, 22 February 1896.

87 McGowan, *Waning*, 59–60.

88 John Walsh to J.A. Macdonald, 8 July 1890, LAC, JAMP, vol. 487, 243254–7. Also see McGowan, *Waning*, 213.

89 The volume of correspondence between them stands as evidence of this.

90 McGowan, *Waning*, 213.

91 See John Walsh to J.A. Macdonald, 25 September 1889, LAC, JAMP, vol. 477, 237583–6; J.A. Macdonald to John Walsh, 3 January 1890, LAC, JAMLB, vol. 530/2, LB 27, 365–6; John Walsh to J.A. Macdonald, 2 March 1891, LAC, JAMP, vol. 498, 249732–5; John Walsh to J.A. Macdonald, 19 July 1890, LAC, JAMP, vol. 136, 56313–6; and John Walsh to J.A. Macdonald, 12 September 1890, LAC, JAMP, vol. 488, 244080–3.

92 See Macdonald to Walsh, 3 January 1890; and J.A. Macdonald to John Walsh, 28 April 1891, LAC, JAMLB, vol. 534, LB 28-1, 37–8.

93 See J.A. Macdonald to John Walsh, 26 November 1890, LAC, JAMLB, vol. 320/2, LB 27, 261–3; and J.C. Patterson to J.A. Macdonald, 7 December 1890, LAC, JAMP, vol. 491, 245787–90.

94 See Walsh to Macdonald, 8 July 1890; and Macdonald to Walsh, 3 January 1890.

95 McGowan, *Waning*, 56.

96 Ibid., 213. One might also note the dearth of correspondence between Walsh and Macdonald's successors.

97 It should be kept in mind, regarding Walsh's support for the Conservative party, that the attitude of the Catholic Church in Canada, especially in Quebec, was that the Liberals came directly from the devil. Even the common expression, in French, of speaking of heaven as blue (therefore, Conserva-

tive) and hell as red (therefore, Liberal), would permeate political discussions well into the twentieth century. The almost unflinching support of Canadian Catholics for the Liberal party only began with Laurier and blossomed after the First World War. It exists still in some places throughout the country, though less and less as time goes on.

98 L.-N. Bégin to John Walsh, 10 September 1894, ARCAT, W AB04.23. Langevin was named archbishop 8 January 1895, in the midst of the Manitoba schools controversy.

99 See Dossier [for the Appointment of the New Archbishop of Montreal], APF, NS, vol. 121, 34r–48r. Bruchési was named archbishop by Leo XIII on 22 June 1897. Lorrain became the bishop of the new diocese of Pembroke when it was established in May 1898. LaRocque remained bishop of Sherbrooke until his death. Racicot became an auxiliary bishop of Montreal in 1905.

100 Dossier [to Name a new Archbishop of Kingston], APF, NS, vol. 170, 2r–80r.

101 Ibid.; also see *Catholic Record*, 2 April 1898.

102 Alexandria was established as a diocese in January 1890, being severed from the diocese of Kingston, soon after Kingston was elevated to the status of an archdiocese in 1889.

103 J.-T. Duhamel to Mieczysław Cardinal Ledóchowski, 8 February 1897, APF, NS, vol. 120, 349r–350v. For the whole dossier, see 323r–405v.

104 Ibid.

105 John Walsh to Propaganda Fide, 364rv.

106 Memorial of J.-T. Duhamel to Mieczysław Cardinal Ledóchowski, 24 February 1897, 352r–375v.

107 Duhamel expressed thanks to Ledóchowski, the prefect of Propaganda Fide, in a letter dated April 1889, as found in the dossier.

108 Petition of the Priests of London Diocese to Mieczysław Cardinal Ledóchowski, 19 February 1898, APF, NS, vol. 127, 359r–365v.

109 See Mieczysław Cardinal Ledóchowski to John Walsh, 7 April 1898, APF, NS, vol. 127, 370r–371v; John Walsh to Mieczysław Cardinal Ledóchowski, APF, NS, vol. 127, 372r–376v; Mieczysław Cardinal Ledóchowski to D. O'Connor, 12 July 1898, APF, NS, vol. 127, 377r–378v; D. O'Connor to Mieczysław Cardinal Ledóchowski, 15 August 1898, APF, NS, vol. 127, 379r–381v.

110 John Walsh to D. O'Connor, 26 May 1896, ARCAT, W AA10.09.

111 See W. Laurier to Secretary of State [Mariano Rampolla del Tindaro], 30 October 1897, ARCAT, W AB05.21; and F. Marchand to Secretary of State [Mariano Rampolla del Tindaro], 19 November 1897, ARCAT, W AB05.22.

112 While the permanent Apostolic Delegation to Canada was erected in 1899, full diplomatic relations between the government of Canada and the Holy See were not officially established until 1969 under Prime Minister Pierre Trudeau, at which point the Delegation became a Nunciature and the government of Canada appointed an ambassador to the Holy See. The first Canadian ambassador was a Protestant, Dr John E. Robbins. See APF, Registro dei Brevi e Bolle, vol. 6, 323v–325v; and Flynn, *London Episcopacy*, 39.

113 See, for example, *Catholic Record*, 30 July 1892 and 10 February 1894.

114 *Catholic Record*, 26 September 1896.

115 Ibid.

116 *Catholic Register*, 22 June 1893. See also Power, "Walsh," in *DCB*, XII, 1087.

117 See *Catholic Record*, 12 April 1890, 5 March 1892, and 21 November 1896 respectively.

118 *Catholic Record*, 23 January 1892.

119 Manning had the largest funeral in Victorian England, next to the Queen's own funeral, of course. The Queen was represented at Manning's funeral by Lord and Lady Dufferin, who occupied faldstools near the altar during the Requiem Mass. Frederick Hamilton-Temple-Blackwood, styled Lord Dufferin, had been the governor general of Canada and later the viceroy of India. His presence at the funeral Mass marked "a decided change in the spirit of the rulers in England toward the Catholic Church." *Catholic Record*, 11 June 1892.

120 The "Month's Mind Mass" was said on the one-month anniversary of a death. It was the custom for family and friends to gather for the occasion.

121 *Catholic Record*, 10 May, 17 and 24 September 1892.

122 Details of Walsh's death are drawn largely from the *Catholic Record*, 6 and 13 August 1898, and from the *Globe*, 1, 5, and 8 August 1898. See also the bill for services from F. Rosar Sr, Undertaker, Toronto, September 1898, ARCAT, W AA11.02.

123 By this time, the archbishop's nephew, James Walsh, was pastor of Our Lady of Lourdes parish, situated in St John's Grove, next to the archbishop's residence.

124 Power, "Walsh," in *DCB*, XII, 1087.

125 *Catholic Record*, 13 August 1898.

126 For mainly Protestant and Orange Toronto, this was a remarkable gesture.

127 It was a rare tribute for those days to have dignitaries from other churches and religions present at a Catholic bishop's funeral.

128 *Catholic Record*, 13 August 1898.

129 As found in *Catholic Record*, 13 August 1898.

130 Ibid. Stephen V. Ryan was the bishop of Buffalo, New York, and died in 1896.

131 Ibid.

132 1891 Census of Canada, Province of Ontario, District 119, East Toronto, St Thomas Ward, 6 May 1891, 17. At that time, Walsh's household included his nephew James Walsh (age 33), Agnes Morris listed as "house maid" (age 27), Mary Culliton listed as "housekeeper" (age 32), and John Fitzpatrick, listed as "church sexton" (age 18).

133 Page 2 of notes respective to the estate of John Walsh, [May 1899,] ARCAT, W AA11.07.

BIBLIOGRAPHY

Archives

Archdiocese of Detroit Archives, Detroit, Michigan, United States of America

Archdiocese of Ottawa Archives, Ottawa, Ontario

Archives of the Archdiocese of Kingston, Kingston, Ontario

Archives of the Archdiocese of Lyons (Archives de l'Archidiocèse de Lyon), Lyons, France

Archives of the Archdiocese of Quebec (Archives de l'Archidiocèse de Québec), Quebec City, Quebec

Archives of the Bishopric of Saint-Hyacinthe (Archives Évêché de Saint-Hyacinthe), Saint-Hyacinthe, Quebec

Archives of the Chancery of the Archbishopric of Montreal (Archives de la Chancellerie de l'Archevêché de Montréal), Montreal, Quebec

Archives of the Congregation of the Sisters Adorers of the Most Precious Blood, London, Ontario

Archives of the Congregation of the Sisters Adorers of the Most Precious Blood, Saint-Hyacinthe, Quebec

Archives of the Congregation of Sisters of St Joseph, London, Ontario

Archives of the Diocese of Peterborough, Peterborough, Ontario

Archives of the Law Society of Upper Canada, Toronto, Ontario

Archives North America – Institute of the Blessed Virgin Mary, Loretto Abbey, Toronto, Ontario

Archives of Ontario, Toronto, Ontario

Archives of the Ontario Medical Association, Toronto, Ontario

Archives of the Priests of St Sulpice (Archives des Prêtres de Saint-Sulpice), Montreal, Quebec

Archives of the Religious of the Sacred Heart of Jesus, Montreal, Quebec

Archives of the Roman Catholic Archdiocese of Toronto, Toronto, Ontario

Archives of the Sacred Congregation for the Evangelization of Peoples (Propaganda Fide), Rome

Archives of the Seminary of Saint-Hyacinthe (Archives du Séminaire de Saint-Hyacinthe), Saint-Hyacinthe, Quebec
Archives of the Society of Jesus for Upper Canada, Toronto, Ontario
Archives of the Ursuline Sisters of the Chatham Union, Chatham, Ontario
Diocese of London Archives, London, Ontario
Library and Archives Canada, Ottawa, Ontario

Newspapers

Catholic Record (London)
Catholic Register (Toronto)
Globe (Toronto)

Secondary Sources

Aubert, Roger, Johannes Bachmann, Patrick J. Cornish, and Rudolf Lill. *Le pontificat de Pie IX (1846–1878)*. Vol. 21 of *Histoire de l'église*. Edited by Augustin Fliche and Victor Martin. Translated by Peter Becker. Saint-Dizier, France: Bloud & Gay, 1952.

Aubert, Roger, Johannes Bachmann, Patrick J. Cornish, and Rudolf Lill. *The Church in the Age of Liberalism*. Vol. VIII of *History of the Church*. Edited by Hubert Jedin and John Dolan. London, England: Burns & Oates, 1981.

Butler, Cuthbert. *The Life and Times of Bishop Ullathorne, 1806–1889*. London, England: Burns, Oates & Washbourne, 1926.

Chapeau, André, OSB, Louis-Philippe Normand, OMI, and Lucienne Plante, CND. *Canadian R.C. Bishops, 1658–1979*. Ottawa: St Paul University, 1980.

Cheney, David M. *The Hierarchy of the Catholic Church*. http://www.catholic-hierarchy.org. Accessed November 2011.

Choquette, Robert. "English-French Relations." In *Creed and Culture: The Place of English-Speaking Catholics in Canadian Society, 1750–1930*, edited by Terrence Murphy and Gerald Stortz. Montreal & Kingston: McGill-Queen's University Press, 1993.

– *L'église catholique dans l'Ontario français du dix-neuvième siècle*. Ottawa: Éditions de l'Université d'Ottawa, 1984.

Codignola, Luca. *Guide to Documents Relating to French and British North America in the Archives of the Sacred Congregation "de Propaganda Fide" in Rome, 1622–1799*. Ottawa: National Archives of Canada [Library and Archives Canada], 1991.

Coffey, John F. *The City and Diocese of London, Ontario, Canada, An Historical Sketch*. London: Thomas Coffey, 1885.

Comiskey, John P. *The Foundation of the Diocese of London in Canada, 1760–1856*. Unpublished license thesis. Pontifical Gregorian University, Rome, 1997.

– *John Walsh, Second Bishop of London in Ontario, 1867–1889*. Doctoral thesis. Pontifical Gregorian University, Rome, 1999.

Creighton, Donald. *John A. Macdonald, The Young Politician*. 2 vols. Toronto: Macmillan and Company, 1974.

Crunican, Paul. *Priests and Politicians: Manitoba Schools and the Election of 1896*. Toronto: University of Toronto Press, [1974].

Cwiekowski, Frederick J. *The English Bishops and the First Vatican Council*. Louvain, France: Publications Universitaires de Louvain, 1971.

Dignan, Ralph H. *History of the London Diocese*. Unpublished manuscript, n.d. Joseph P. Finn began preparations for publication and produced an updated manuscript, to which this work refers. The manuscript was never published. (DLA)

Dominic of Saint-Denis, OFM, CAP. *The Catholic Church in Canada, Historical and Statistical Summary*. Montreal: Editions Thau, 1956.

Erb, Peter C. "Henry Edward Manning, the Sacred Heart, and the Reality of the Incarnation." In the *Canadian Catholic Review* 15 (June 1997): 14–17.

Farrell, John K.A. *The History of the Roman Catholic Church in London, Ontario, 1826–1931*. Unpublished MA thesis. London: The University of Western Ontario, 1949.

Fazakas, Ray. *The Donnelly Album*. Willowdale, Ontario: Firefly Books, 1998.

Fenning, Hugh. "The Three Kingdoms: England, Ireland and Scotland." In *Sacrae Congregationis de Propaganda Fide Memori Rerum: 350 Ans au Service des Missions, 1622–1972*, vol. 2, 604–29. Edited by J. Metzler. Freiburger, Germany: Herder, 1975.

Flynn, Jerome Terence. *The London Episcopacy, 1867–1889, of the Most Reverend John Walsh, D.D., Second Bishop of London, Ontario*. Unpublished MA thesis. Washington: Catholic University of Washington, 1967.

Flynn, Louis J. *Built on a Rock: The Story of the Roman Catholic Church in Kingston, 1826–1976*. Kingston: Roman Catholic Archdiocese of Kingston, 1976.

Government of Canada. *Guide to Canadian Ministries since Confederation, July 1, 1867–February 1, 1982*. Ottawa: Canadian Government Publishing Centre, 1982.

Grant, John Webster. *A Profusion of Spires: Religion in Nineteenth-Century Ontario*. Toronto: University of Toronto Press, 1988.

Halpenny, Francess G., ed. *Dictionary of Canadian Biography*. 24 vols. Toronto: University of Toronto Press, 1966.

Kennedy, Sister M. Teresita, CSJ. "History of the Diocese of London." In *The Newsletter of the Diocese of London*, 1985.

Kennedy, W.P.M., ed. *Documents of the Canadian Constitution, 1759–1915*. Toronto: Oxford University Press, 1918.

Kowalsky, N., OMI, and J. Metzler, OMI. *Inventory of the Historical Archives of the Congregation for the Evangelization of Peoples or "de Propaganda Fide"*. Rome: Urbaniana University Press, 1988.

Lajeunesse, Ernest J., CSB, ed. *The Windsor Border Region. Canada's Southernmost Frontier*. Toronto: The Champlain Society, 1960.

Lemieux, Lucien, and Alexander Baran. "Provision pour l'Église Canadienne." In *Sacrae Congregationis de Propaganda Fide Memoria Rerum: 350 Ans au Service des Missions, 1622–1972*, edited by J. Metzler, vol. III, 729–57. Freiburger, Germany: Herder, 1975.

Marsh, James H., ed. *The Canadian Encyclopedia*. 3 vols. Edmonton: Hurtig, 1985.

McGowan, Mark G. *Michael Power: The Struggle to Build the Catholic Church on the Canadian Frontier*. Montreal & Kingston: McGill-Queen's University Press, 2005.

– *The Waning of the Green: Catholics, the Irish, and Identity in Toronto, 1887–1922*. Montreal & Kingston: McGill-Queen's University Press, 1999.

McMahon, John R. *The Episcopate of Pierre-Adolphe Pinsoneault: First Bishop of London, Upper Canada, 1856–1866*. Unpublished MA thesis. London: University of Western Ontario, 1982.

Miller, Orlo. *The Donnellys Must Die*. Toronto: Macmillan, 1962.

Perin, Roberto. *Rome in Canada: The Vatican and Canadian Affairs in the Late Victorian Age*. Toronto: University of Toronto Press, 1990.

Perkins Bull, William. *From Macdonell to McGuigan: The History of the Growth of the Roman Catholic Church in Upper Canada*. Toronto: The Perkins Bull Foundation, 1940.

Point, Pierre, SJ. *Histoire de Sandwich (1843–1860)*. Translated by F.J. Nelligan, SJ. Unpublished manuscript, n.d.

Power, Michael, ed. *Assumption College, A Documentary History of Assumption College*. 5 vols. Windsor, Ontario: Assumption University, 1986–2000.

– *A History of Mount Hope Cemetery, Toronto, Ontario, 1898 to 1998*. Toronto: Catholic Cemeteries, 1998.

– *A Promise Fulfilled: Highlights in the Political History of Catholic Separate Schools in Ontario*. Toronto: Ontario Catholic Schools Trustees Association, 2002.

Power, Michael, Daniel J. Brock, et al. *Gather up the Fragments: A History of the Diocese of London*. London, Ontario: Diocese of London, 2008.

Propaganda Fide. *Bullarum Diplomatum et Privilegiorum*. Rome: Taurinensis Editio, VI, 1860.

Reaney, James C. *The Donnelly Documents: An Ontario Vendetta*. Toronto: The Champlain Society, 2004.

Sanfilippo, Matteo. "L'image du Canada dans les rapports du Saint-Siège, 1608–1908" in *Revue internationale d'études canadiennes* 5 (Spring 1992): 9–24.

St John Thomas (Helen Batte), Sister, SNJM. *Rooted in Hope: A History of the Sisters of the Holy Names of Jesus and Mary of the Ontario Province*. Windsor, Ontario: Sisters of the Holy Names of Jesus and Mary, 1983.

St Paul, Mother M., OSU. *From Desenzano to "The Pines."* Toronto: Macmillan Company, 1941.

Stortz, Gerald J. "Archbishop John Joseph Lynch of Toronto: Twenty-Eight Years of Commitment." In *Canadian Catholic Historical Association, Study Sessions* 49 (1982): 5–23.

Teefy, J.R., CSB, ed. *Jubilee Volume, The Archdiocese of Toronto and Archbishop Walsh*. Toronto: George T. Dixon, 1892.

Têtu, Henri. *Les Évêques de Québec*. Quebec: Narcisse-S. Hardy, 1889.

Thériault, Michel. *The Institutes of Consecrated Life in Canada From the Beginning of New France Up to the Present*. Ottawa: National Library of Canada [Library and Archives Canada], 1980.

[UNKNOWN] Galley Sheets, *Most Rev. John Walsh, D.D.*, unpublished manuscript [Toronto, 1942].

Urquhart, M.C., and K.A.H. Buckley, eds. *Historical Statistics of Canada*. Toronto: Macmillan and Company, 1965.

Walsh, John. *The Council of the Vatican and the Doctrines it Suggests and Illustrates*. London: Prototype, 1870.

– *The Doctrine of Papal Infallibility Stated and Vindicated; with an Appendix on Civil Allegiance, and Certain Historical Difficulties*. London: The Free Press Printing and Publishing Company, 1875.

– *Thoughts on Devotion to the Sacred Heart, and Also on the Life and Work of our Blessed Lord*. New York: P. O'Shea, 1884.

Walker, Franklin A. *Catholic Education and Politics in Ontario*. 3 vols. Toronto: Federation of Catholic Education Associations of Ontario, 1976.

Westfall, William. *Two Worlds: The Protestant Culture of Nineteenth-Century Ontario*. Montreal & Kingston: McGill-Queen's University Press, 1989.

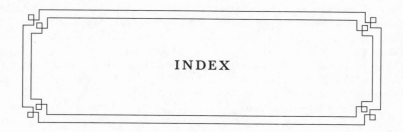

INDEX